THE UNIQUE CHILDHOOD OF A
HUMMER

By Lewis N. Rinko

For Susan and Ron,
long admired friends.

Lew Rinko

6/8/13

MUSINGS
PRESS

THE UNIQUE CHILDHOOD OF A
H U M M E R
*Hummer — what fatherless boys called each other
growing up near Center City Philadelphia
in America's most extraordinary orphanage*

© 2012 Lewis N. Rinko

Published by Musings Press
Box 424
Olde Sproul Village,
1138 Baltimore Pike, Springfield, Pennsylvania 19064

www.MusingsPress.com

First Edition 2012

First Printing July 2012

The author received oral approval from Girard graduates
for the use of their names in this memoir.
A number of fictitious names have also been used
and any resemblance to actual persons is entirely coincidental.

All photography courtesy of Girard College.
Author photograph by Kay Rinko.

Printed in the United States of America

Library of Congress Cataloging-in-Publication Data

L.C.C. No. 2012906463

ISBN 978-0-578-10432-4

Acknowledgments

Appreciative thanks to my wife, Kay, for her support and creative suggestions, and my son-in-law, Dave Finnegan, for his vital computer knowledge. To my classmate brothers, the many Hummers I interviewed and the 1952 alums who meet monthly for lunch at Otto's Restaurant. To Mhairi Shepherd and my daughter, Nicole Rinko Finnegan, for their invaluable editing and comments, and for the photography and research services of Gil Bunker, Volunteer Archivist, Girard College, and Elizabeth Laurent, Girard's Director of Historic Resources.

Dedication

This book is dedicated to my mother, Dorothy Lewis Rinko, who loved me so much she was willing to give me up and send me far from home for a better education, and to Stephen Girard, my generous and compassionate stepfather, who provided me, and many thousands of Hummers, with the opportunity to get that education.

Preface

I did not set out to write this book. While eating lunch at my desk years ago, I amused myself by writing down entertaining incidents from my life growing up at Girard College. It didn't happen every day, but often enough to eventually cram a file drawer.

Then I recalled how our daughters, Sonia and Nicole, and their friends enjoyed hearing stories about Girard, the rules, the escapades and punishments, asking me to tell them more. Our adult friends clearly enjoyed tales of "life at Girard" and when I spoke before community groups, the audience's interested questioning continued long past the deadline. Realizing our life at Girard really was unusual, I wondered how I could use my material to inform readers in a colorful way about the school and its founder, Stephen Girard.

Hummer began when I created Nick, the main character, to be a combination of myself and dozens of other Hummers, drawing on my experiences and those of the Hummers I've known and questioned. Every few chapters I've also inserted personal vignettes about my life and some aspects of our world at Girard.

There is no adversary to defeat in *Hummer;* the challenge was to grow up in this controlling world. As a youngster, you were fearful of the demands and resented the power strangers had over you. Years later, approaching graduation, you'd learned to acknowledge personal responsibility and live by your decisions. In your last few months, you realized how secure you were at home behind Girard's stone wall.

I believe most Hummers look back fondly on those years; daily life was so busy we never had time to consider whether we were happy or not. I have tried to picture life at Girard as faithfully as possible. I hope you enjoy *Hummer*, my remembrance of a unique school.

Lewis N. Rinko

Swarthmore, Pennsylvania

THE CAMPUS

A: West End. **B**: Mechanical School. **C**: Armory.
D: Junior School. **E**: Good Friends and Lafayette.
F: Chapel. **G**:Infirmary, Banker and Merchant Halls.
H: High School. **I**: Founder's Hall. **J**: Library.
K: Bordeaux and Allen Halls.

ONE

It was Nick's fourth day in this prison and it would be his last — he was about to die. Why would these boys who didn't know him, that he didn't do anything to — want to kill him? He clawed at the cord around his throat as he suffocated, gasping for air. Childish faces of eight, nine and 10-year olds, witnessing his death, some smiling, some curious, some frightened, some sympathetic, swirled away in a stream of tears. Lightheaded, swaying, he began falling forward, but arms grabbed and held him up. Nick struggled, but they were too strong and too many. His head rocked back and forth. He closed his wet eyes. Why did my mother bring me here and leave me? If I call her, she'll hear me and save me. He could only make a gurgling sound and knew she could not hear him. Maybe she didn't want to hear him? The thought weakened him and he dropped his hands to his side seeming to surrender to his fate. Suddenly the tightness around his neck was gone. Arms let go of him. He staggered, but stood. Convulsively sucking in air, he wheezed, drawing in his breath in a hoarse growl.

"Stand back, you guys," someone shouted, "we got ourselves a grizzly bear!"

"Naw, Brannigan," another voice called out, "he ain't no grizzly bear, he's a Pooh Bear." The room echoed with derisive laughter.

Nick rubbed his eyes with his knuckles, flinching forward at a sharp pain in his back. Someone punched him. "Don't worry, newbie," the assailant yelled in his ear, "you'll live — at least for today!"

Before the crowd could respond, a bell rang and the tormentors and onlookers abandoned Nick, noisily swarming through the doorway and up the stairs to the dining room.

◆

Alone, Nick felt for the cord around his throat. It was his tie. Broad stripes of brown and blue he'd been given with the other new clothes when he arrived.

1

As he gently pulled it loose from around his aching throat, he noticed a man standing by the doorway. He must have been watching. *How could he stand there and let them do this to me?* Anger tightened Nick's mouth. *I hate this place. Everyone's nasty, these boys and even the grownups. I'll never ever stay here!*

Hurrying out of the room, he felt a hand touch his shoulder.

"New boys are a great source of entertainment until they become Hummers. Even then," the man's voice rose as Nick started up the stairs, "life at Girard can be rough and it's not always fair. It's 1944 and you're just starting out."

Nick's eyes widened and his body shivered with fear when he heard the man's last words. "Depend on yourself. It's the only way you'll live through the next eight or nine years."

TWO

Nick kept to himself for the rest of the day, following at the back of the crowd. During classes he either looked at the teacher or the book, not turning to watch kids who were called on. He gave the right answer in a one word monotone when Miss Bishop called on him. At dinner he ate quietly, looking down at his meat loaf and mashed potatoes; shaking his head when seconds were offered. At free time, back in the section, while others played loud games of checkers or Parcheesi or just chatted with each other, he sat, hands folded on his desk.

Inside, Nick was agitated, confused. He wanted to be angry at his mother, but he couldn't. She never did anything mean to him, even when she punished him. But why did she bring him here? Why did she leave without telling him what was happening? Will she ever come back?

As he leaned forward to put his face in his hands, he heard, "Hey, newbie, how's your neck?" Nick looked up as an older boy approached between the desk aisles. "You'll be okay." He smiled. "Just don't let them see they scare you."

As he passed, Miss Saunders, Section Eleven's Governess, stood up at her desk. "Time to put the games away in the closet. Everyone line up in the hall, quietly. If I hear any noise going up to the dormitory, the lights will go out immediately after showers and there'll be no time for reading."

But there was too much talking and as soon as everyone got in bed, the lights went out. On his back in the hard, narrow bed, Nick stared up into darkness, slowly rubbing his sore neck. He could hear boys in their beds tossing and turning, an occasional cough, some mumbled words and something that seemed like sniffling.

Then he heard "Psst, Psst! Hey, are ya awake?" Sitting up he looked around. It was too dark to even see nearby sleepers.

3

"Hey, newbie!" The voice was a little louder and closer.

"Shaddup!" an angry voice hissed and the room was silent again. Nick began to lie back when a shape loomed up next to him. "Hey!" Nick said angrily.

"It's just me, Vic Tunila. I wanted to see if you'd wet your bed."

Bob Hennessey later told Nick that Tunila was already ten years old, that he'd been at Girard, in West End and Junior School, since he was six and was going to another building this week.

"Sorry, sorry," Tunila whispered with a hint of sarcasm, "Just want to know what happened. Some guys said you got strangled today." He kneeled, turned his face and leaned close to Nick.

Nick spoke softly, describing how the incident came about.

◆

Nick's first lesson in self-reliance had begun the previous Tuesday morning, after his first, gently tearful night. The lights suddenly went on and Miss Saunders said, "Good morning, Girardians. It's 6:30, time to get up and get ready for another day."

The dormitory was suddenly alive with boys pulling on white tee-shirts, tugging up pants. Shoes on, they made their beds and put their folded nightshirts under the pillows. Some were silent, others talked quietly. One or two, still sleepy, sat on the edge of their beds staring into space or sullenly watching the activity. With his shirt, tie, vest and coat over his arm, Nick joined others as they walked rapidly — no running allowed — to the stairway where they then broke into a noisy race down three floors.

Reaching the basement, they quieted down, making their way through a throng of other boys to Section Eleven's lavatory.

The lavatory with its black and white tile floor and white tiled walls was below ground with windows up near the ceiling along one wall. A long bench at the end of the room had wooden boxes beneath jammed with polish cans, daubers and brushes. Along the other wall and running down the center of the room were rows of small-scale

4

washbasins. Above each was a mirror and a shelf that held a hairbrush, a comb, a white china mug, a toothbrush and a can of Pepsodent tooth powder. Along the base of the washbasins was a thin railing where each boy hung his washcloth and towel.

Nick hung his clothes on the long hook rack that covered the wall below the windows, washed his face, neck, and underarms. He wasn't small for this age, but he wasn't as tall as he wished he was. And he wasn't chubby like Charlie Hughes and Rich James at home. He hadn't seen any fat kids here so far.

He ran the comb through his dark brown hair, parting it neatly on the side and making a wave on top. It got curly when it rained and got him teased by the girls at home. All these other kids, he noticed, had short hair.

Boys, alone and in groups, were leaving for the section room when Nick, just buttoning his shirt, felt a sudden fear. Turning quickly, he held his tie up to a boy passing by.

"Hey, could ya help me?" The boy pushed Nick against his washbasin, took the tie and tied it, letting it hang loosely around Nick's neck. Before Nick could say, "Thanks," the boy was gone.

The next morning, Nick dressed quickly, washed and brushed his hair, polished his shoes and waited nervously by his washbasin. He didn't have to say anything. The boy, talking with two others, saw Nick, stopped abruptly behind his buddies and hurriedly began to tie Nick's tie. His buddies came back and looked at Nick with disdain.

"Let's go, Bill. He's just a newbie. We're gonna be late for breakfast." Bill finished, turned and joined them.

On the third morning, Nick waited nervously, hoping Bill would stop again. And he did. But his buddies stopped too and were curiously silent.

This time Bill very slowly tied the tie, then looked Nick in the eyes and said emphatically, "Ya better learn how to do it yourself, newbie."

Then he pulled the knot up tight — very tight! Nick's face got red. He couldn't breathe. Bill's buddies, anticipating it, burst into scornful laughter, surrounding Nick as he struggled to breathe. Heads suddenly appeared over washbasin shelves, mouths foaming white with toothpowder. Hairbrushes stopped mid-air. Boys passing paused to observe. Some laughed with the banter while others watched uneasily. Then the breakfast bell rang.

◆

"His buddies held me so I couldn't pull my tie down. When I finally caught my breath," Nick said to the dark shape beside him, "everybody was gone, so I washed my face at the hallway fountain, dried it in my handkerchief and just got to the dining room in time for grace."

Nick went silent when Miss Saunders' door suddenly opened and a shaft of light flashed across the ceiling. Nick dropped back on the bed, motionless. She must have heard me whispering, he thought. After a few seconds, she closed her door and the dormitory went black.

Then, out of the darkness came Nick's tie, just visible by the dim red exit light over the dormitory door. Nick sat up. A hand touched his shoulder turning him sideways. Then the tie was looped around Nick's bare neck. Very slowly two hands crossed it over itself several times. One hand then held up three fingers in front of Nick's face. Nick nodded.

Then the tie was slipped off Nick's neck and handed to him. Nick put it over his neck and looped it twice. The hands then slowly brought one end up, around once and tucked it through, pulling it down to form a loose knot. This time Nick undid it, took it off his neck, then put it back on, looped it, inserted it, created a loose knot and finally pulled it up gently to his throat. When he turned with a satisfied grin, no one was there. At the far end of the dormitory there was the sound of someone getting into bed. It had to be Vic.

I've got a friend, a real friend, he said to himself. I'll be his friend forever — no matter how bad it is in here.

He untied the knot, hung the tie over his shirt on the back of the chair, lay back and fell asleep, his new-found camaraderie slowly carving a faint smile on his face.

JUNIOR SCHOOL
Grades 2, 3 and 4 – Ages 8, 9 and 10
1944-1945

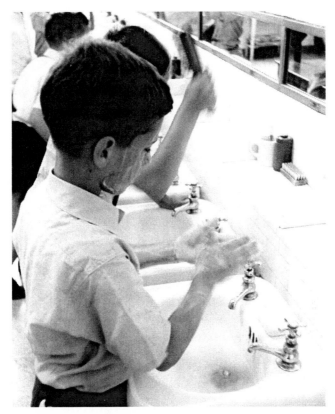

Lavatory and Junior School Playground

THREE

Hundreds of unbridled eight, nine and 10 year olds stormed the playground chasing each other, wrestling under the sand tent, pumping legs to swing higher and higher, seesawing, roller skating and stilt walking up the curved marble steps to Junior School's second floor entrance. Four baseball games were underway with outfielders standing in adjacent games warily watching all batters. There was constant shouting, cheering, arguing and laughter, but Nick, surrounded by the chaotic clamor, didn't hear it. He shook his head when some newbies in his section, atop the monkey bars, waved for him to join them. At the far end of the playground he found an empty bench and sat down, leaning forward on his knees, staring glumly at his strange brown brogues.

It was just Monday, five days ago when his mother put her hand on his face and wakened him in his own bed. How could his room, his mom and his sister have suddenly disappeared? It was cold upstairs, but the kitchen was warm and he had his favorite breakfast, a thick slice of Mom's bread toasted over the stove coals and covered with melted cheese. Welsh Rabbit his grandfather called it. They walked down the steep hill to the railroad station at the bottom of Wilkes-Barre's Heights when it was still dark.

He remembered how his father used to bring him here to watch the trains. Today they were getting on the train and going to a big city. He thought it odd that the other people had bags and suitcases and they didn't. The train jolted to start, but it wasn't long after, as it raced along in the dark, that he'd fallen asleep, waking when his mother said, "Nick, luv, we're here." Looking out he saw a sign that said: Welcome to Philadelphia — City of Brotherly Love.

The taxi drove them through big iron gates and stopped by the biggest building he'd ever seen. His mother said it looked like a Greek temple. They were told to walk down the Main Road to the long white building on the right, the Junior School. As they walked, they saw boys everywhere — going in and out of buildings, sweeping steps and sidewalks, calling to each other. All of them were older. Probably in high school, his mother said.

At the Junior School, they were directed down a long hall to Section Eleven. Looking in, they saw an older woman at a desk and about 30 boys at small desks, reading, writing or talking to others. Some boys were sitting on the carpet playing board games. Miss Saunders, in her fifties, was the Governess. She introduced herself to Nick's mother as a number of boys silently observed.

"Robert," she called out. "Robert Hennessy, will you take our new boy to the seamstress?" An athletic looking boy with curly, blond hair folded his book.

"Why don't you give your mother a kiss before you go?" she said to Nick. His mother hugged him tightly and kissed him several times. As he left the room he looked back to see her wiping her eyes. Miss Saunders had a hand on her shoulder.

Nick stayed just a little to one side and behind Hennessy. Some boys were making a lot of noise coming down the long, broad hall that connected both wings of the building. "Have you been here long?" Nick ventured.

"Almost four years," was the reply. "I went to the West End first 'cause I was just six when my mother brought me here. Ya hafta be six to get in and if you're ten, they won't let you in. Then, when I was almost eight they moved me from West End up here to the Junior School. Now I'm ten and when I pass Fifth Grade 'bout Christmas, I'll go over to Good Friends Hall. It's right across the Main Road."

"Hey, Hennessey!" a short, wiry kid called out as he passed. "Can't wait to see you babies crying on Saturday when we kill you guys!" His two buddies looked over and sneered. One thumbed his nose at Hennessey who suddenly rushed towards them. They banged into each other, scrambled around the corner, and yelled something

9

back at him. After a few steps Hennessey stopped short and turned back.

"Guys from Seckie Nine. We're playing them for the West Wing Soccer Championship. I'll get some of our guys and we'll find them — after we win," he said with confident anticipation, "and make them cry for real." Nick's eyes widened. He wanted to ask, "Does everyone fight all the time?" But didn't.

They went into a room where a pleasant older woman said, "Welcome, new boy. Take off your clothes and we'll make you look like a Girardian."

Nick felt embarrassed, but Hennessy and the seamstress didn't seem to notice that he was nude. He quickly pulled on the new, white briefs Hennessey handed him. She tossed his underwear in a large cardboard barrel. And his new socks. What would his mother say! He slipped on a white tee-shirt without arms. The sleeves of a stiff, white shirt dangled over his hands so he was given another to try on. It fit and next was a tan vest he buttoned up as Hennessy tied a knot in his striped tie. He sat down to pull on the blue and brown argyle socks but they were so long they fell in a crumpled circle around his thin ankles when he stood up. Before he could speak, the woman said, "Would you like blue or brown knickers?"

"Blue, please," he replied. She handed him the strangest pants he'd ever seen. They weren't long trousers but they weren't shorts like he wore in the summer. Balancing on one leg, he stepped into them. When he pulled them up they had round bottoms and just covered his knees. Not thinking what else he could say, Nick said politely, "I don't think they fit."

His Welsh Baptist family was always polite to each other, even when they were angry. And he certainly didn't want to say how ugly they were.

"No, they fit." Hennessey and the woman seemed amused when she said, "These are called knickers. Pull your stockings up to your knees. With your other hand, pull the pant leg down to cover the top of them."

Hennessy reached into a shoebox on the counter, took out two black things and handed one to Nick. "These are called garters." They were elastic circles about an inch wide. "Pull them up and put them over the bottoms of your pants with the tops of your stockings underneath — like mine." Nick saw the little puffed-out area of pants just below Hennessey's knees. He realized all the boys he'd seen had strange pants like these; he'd been too anxious to notice. "They're great for killing flies in the summer," Hennessey advised. Pulling the second garter back with his thumb, Hennessy shot it at Nick, who caught it and, smiling back, put it on. "But don't get caught with your socks hangin' down, sloppy like, 'cus your garter's off, or you'll catch it from the guvvies or Old Hick."

The blue coat the seamstress passed over was the same prickly material as the knickers and seemed tight. After he raised his arms for her, waved them and stretched over his head, she decided the coat was fine. Carrying a heavy blue and brown plaid overcoat and wearing a blue cap with a peak, he hurried as they left, eager to show his mother his new clothes. "We're not finished yet, newbie. We have to go to the Shoey."

At the Shoe Shop, the man told Nick to take a seat. He took Nick's shoes off and casually threw them in a big cardboard box. Mom didn't want me to come here in my old shoes so she bought me brand new ones. I wonder if she'll notice? The man put dark brown shoes with high sides on Nick's feet and laced them. "Those brogues feel okay? Stand up and walk around." They felt okay but seemed really heavy. He wouldn't run very fast in these.

"You," he pointed at Hennessy, "can carry his second pair. You," he pointed at Nick, "wear these brogues for everyday. These," he held up brown oxfords, "are for Sunday Chapel and special occasions, and these," he held up a pair of rubber galoshes, "are to keep the others clean in bad weather. If the heels come off or you get holes in the soles, take them to your section's shoe monitor. And keep them polished and shined."

From there they ran up two flights of stairs and down a hall to a large room with four rows of beds, one along each wall and two, head to head, down the center.

"This is our dormitory," Hennessy said. "That's Miss Saunders' apartment. We'll put your stuff on the chair by her door 'til she assigns you a bed. Now we can go back to the seckie." Nick stayed with him as they ran back, stopping at the door to walk in properly. As Hennessey went to his desk, Nick looked for his mother. She wasn't there. He felt disappointed but only for a moment. Miss Saunders probably told her to take a walk and look around until I got back, he thought. But everyone seemed to be frozen. They were watching two boys standing by Miss Saunders, crying.

"I know it's hard for new boys," she announced firmly, "but it's best this way. In a day or two, you'll have new friends here and you'll be busy with school and playing on the playground. It won't be long before you'll see your mother again." One boy leaned over a checkerboard and whispered to his opponent, just loud enough to be heard, "Yeah, it's only September — Christmas vacation is coming." Some chuckles were heard. Miss Saunders scowled and said angrily, "Some of you smart mouths did your share of crying, I remember! Everyone line up in the hall. It's almost time for dinner, and I don't want to hear one sound out there!" Kids rushed by Nick, some bumping against him, but he didn't notice.

Well, my mother must be here somewhere, Nick thought. Hennessey was watching him. The look on his face filled Nick with dread — he knows, he knows she's not coming back. When I kissed her it was the last time. She's gone, gone for good.

He covered his face with his hands; he could feel tears coming. Turning away from the room, he saw through his fingers boys in the hall, crowded together. Faces stared at him, waiting for him to cry. It made him mad, made him hold back the tears. Lowering his hand, he did the only thing he could think of — he made a face and stuck his tongue out at them. The hall resounded with laughter. There were even some whistles and cheers. Now he smiled at them.

"I told you all to be quiet!" Miss Saunders shouted. "Now, get into a column right now and if I hear one more word, there'll be no radio tonight." Nick, at the end of the line, saw Hennessy, at the front look back with an approving smile. But Nick couldn't smile back and thought, why didn't they just let me say goodbye to my mom one more time?

Nick sat quietly at the dinner table, ignored by the others as they animatedly chatted, teased and argued their way through the meal. Now, at the little desk Miss Saunders assigned to him, he stared down at his clasped hands, oblivious of the others in Section Eleven playing games or reading.

He felt empty inside, too sad to cry. Everything he knew was gone and there was nothing he could do about it. Over a year ago his dad died. His mother said there was a fire in the mine. She said his dad escaped but went back in to help his buddies; then there was an explosion. Nick remembered his dad lying in the hospital bed, leaning over to hug him, seeing his smile twisted with pain. And then his dad was lying in a coffin and people were hugging Nick.

He missed talking with his dad as they walked down Stegmaier's Hill, hearing the beer bottles clinking through the open brewery windows and the funny smell of hops. Seated at the railroad station, across from Stegmaier's, they watched the trains come and go. On Saturdays they went to a place with wide open doors. Looking in, he could see big sheets of paper whirling up and down through clanking machines. Men came out to say hello. One always folded a bright sailor's hat out of the comics and put it on Nick's head.

When they left their house on Fulton Street and went out to the shops on busy Market Street, everybody knew his dad. He liked to walk in and talk to the owners, the Lasmans, at their drug store; at the seafood store, where they bought a hundred littleneck clams and the man gave his dad a free pound of butter. At Shurfine Market he'd watch to open the door for customers. It was because, his mom said, he was always looking to help out. He found what customers wanted at Walter's Hardware Store. He straightened rows of produce while talking to Mr. Fireverker. Leo, the barber, always waved him in and the men in front of the Stankey's Corner Beer Garden never let him pass by without stopping to chat.

His dad loved to dance, especially the Polka. He liked to say it was in his Russian blood, teasing Nick's mom. At parties and weddings, single women sought him out as a dancing partner. Nick's mother, as a Welsh Baptist, was not allowed to dance and really didn't know how, but she always said yes to their requests. He called her his "great big beautiful doll" after the popular song.

His dad was gone — and now, so was his mother. Would he ever go home again? How could he possibly get out of here? He didn't know where he was or where to go. If he could get over the wall somehow, what then? He would be lost, as he was on this side of the wall. How did they force his mom to bring him here? Why didn't she tell him what was going to happen? He sighed, deciding the only thing he could do was to stay here for now. He forced himself to get up and stand by a nearby table to watch some boys playing Parcheesi.

FOUR

Sitting in bed, his back against the pillow, Nick was enjoying a story about a toad and a hedgehog living near a pond in the English countryside. A boy in the bed across the aisle had lent it to him, saying he had just finished it and didn't have to take it back to the library until Friday.

"Five minutes 'til bedtime," Miss Saunders called from her room. Nick immediately closed the book, set it on his chair and reached into his coat hanging on the back of the chair. It was the letter from his mother. It had arrived two days ago and each night, just before lights out, he reread it.

> *Dear Nicholas, I'm sorry about leaving you without saying goodbye. They said it was time to take you away and it was best if I just gave you a kiss and a hug and then went. It made me cry on the train. You know how much I love you. Nothing can ever make me stop loving you. That's why I'm sending you away from home because I know you'll get a better education there than here in Wilkes-Barre. You'll never have to work like Daddy. Before the accident, he said he was going to get out of the mines soon. I will write to you every week. Please write back to me even if it's just a little. Tell me what you are doing, how you are being treated, what you are learning. I'm sure you'll find some nice boys who will be friends with you.*

Nick noticed that some of the words were blurry, but he could still read them.

> *Some people in the family are mad at me. Uncle Jack, Daddy's brother wanted me to send you to the Hershey School*

15

out in the country but I didn't think you'd want to become a farmer. I prayed for what I think is best for you and the Girard school seems best, though it is so far away. But you'll be home for Christmas and we'll be together. I know you'll be a brave and good boy. Eat everything they serve you.

I'll close now. I have to leave for the mill. Nannie will be home from the mill soon and take care of baby Janet until I come home again. Say your prayers every night and if you listen you'll hear me saying mine too and asking God and your Dad to watch over you. I know they will. Remember how much we love you even far away.

Mother XXXOOO   XXXOOO from Janet

Before he folded the letter and put it back in the envelope, he read his name and the address, Girard College, 21st Street and Corinthian Avenue, Philadelphia, Pa., and ran his finger over 27 S. Fulton Street, Wilkes-Barre, Pa. He returned it to his pocket just as Miss Saunders came out for prayers.

Pulling up their white nightshirts, everyone knelt on the floor with elbows on the bed, hands together. Miss Saunders started everyone saying the Lord's Prayer. With the Amen she said, "Now it's time to say a silent prayer for your mother and your sisters and brothers and your family and that you'll be a good Girardian and study hard and make your mothers proud of you." After a quiet minute she announced, "Okay, everyone under the covers. Goodnight." The lights went out.

Staring into the darkness, Nick thought about the letter and what his mom said. Then he mouthed quietly to himself. If Mom wants me to stay here, I'll stay here.

FIVE

"Okay, you newbies, stand over there against that wall. And no talkin.' Distract me and I'm liable to cut somebody's ear off. You, the first kid, when'd you get a haircut, last Christmas? Get in the chair and don't move. When I take this sheet off you, you run right back to your section."

Nick watched as the line moved forward. It didn't take long to get a haircut. The man was rough; lots of the kids flinched and a few even cried "Ouch!" but he ignored them. He started on one side of the head and went over to the other side. He got mad when a kid had lots of long hair. Had to get out scissors, clip off big clumps and brush them off the sheet. Finally, he put down his electric trimmer and whipped the sheet off the kid. As the kid hopped down and headed for the door, rubbing his neck gingerly, the barber barked, "Next!"

He stopped every so often, grabbed a push broom and swept the hair into a growing pile in the corner. It was brown, black, blond with bits of red. Some kid in line pointed at it and asked, "Mister Barber, can I have some a that hair to save for Halloween so's I kin be a Jungle Man?" Everyone's laughter was cut short by the nasty look the man gave him.

The next morning, as Nick raised his toothbrush to his mouth, a strange kid looked back at him. When he opened his mouth to begin brushing, so did the kid. The kid's hair was so short; then he reached up to touch his head just when Nick did. It was his head!

"Goin' bald already?" Jock McKnight said from his washbasin opposite Nick's. This was the first time Nick had a chance to look at himself. He'd felt his head and knew his wave was gone, but so short — like his grandmother's hairbrush — and his ears stuck out like Olive Oyl's!

"He got mowed down yesterday, Jock," Dack Popdan, next to him, said. Mowed down is right, Nick thought, staring at his image. "Yeah, now he looks just like the rest of us indentured orphans!"

◆

Nick was learning names in the section and in the dining room. He'd look up from his plate and then around the table, but not so often someone could yell, "Whatta you starin' at newbie?"

"Where's Chink?" someone asked McKnight. Everyone was seated for lunch but Cernicki's chair, on Nick's right, was empty.

"He's at the Infirmary," Don Barr answered, "got sick in last class. Told me I could have his dessert." That drew a laugh from everyone including Barr, the smallest guy at the table.

Nick leaned across the empty chair toward McKnight on his right. "Do you know Vic Tunila? I haven't seen him in the section or anywhere?"

"You won't see Vic anymore. They sent him over to Good Friends, across the Main Road. We can't go over there." First saddened by the news, then angry, Nick jabbed at the pineapple covered ham slice with his fork, then looked up to see Mr. Newhardt, a housemaster, standing by the table, looking suspiciously at him. He pointed at the chair next to Nick.

"I want this new boy to sit in that empty chair for now." The boy standing next to him pulled out the chair and sat down. He was skinny and small with white hair and a pale, pinkish face.

As soon as grace was said, Dom Lazarra, a loud Italian asked, "Where you from, newbie?"

"Pennsylvania," the boy replied softly.

"No kidding, you dopey little rabbit. Practically everybody here's from Pennsylvania — what town?" The boy looked at him and said, "Shickshinny."

"What?"

"Shickshinny," he replied a little louder.

18

"Shickshinny?" Smokey Stover cried from his end of the table. Then he grabbed up his brass napkin ring, put it to his mouth and sang through it. "Shickshinny, Shickshinny, we got us a ninny," he thought for a second, "a Rin Tin Tinny from that hick town, Shickshinny!" Nick had to laugh out loud when Stover flopped his white linen napkin over his head and eyes so you could only see the napkin ring and started to sing again in a squeaky voice.

But a loud ringing sound stopped his performance. The ringing sound of a glass being tapped by a knife signaled there was too much talking, and it was too loud. Quiet down was the message.

Then Nick heard a scraping sound and turned to see the newbie start to tilt backwards. Down he went, arms out, crashing to the floor. The entire dining room started buzzing. Heads craned in their direction. Nick looked down. The kid wasn't crying. He lay back in the chair, looking straight up, mouth open, astonished. His hand rubbed the back of his head.

"Boy," Mr. Newhardt, appeared above him. "Because you're new, you can get up and finish your meal. But nobody's allowed to lean back in his chair. If that happens again you'll leave the dining room without your meal and stand in the grudge line at 4 o'clock. Now, get back in that chair and sit up straight.

"Well, don't sit there the rest of you, someone help him up!" Nick leaned over, as did McKnight, on the other side, and they righted the chair with the kid still in it. You could barely hear the "Thanks." He sat frozen, staring at his pear half, hands below the table.

I wonder if he knows his fig newton is gone, too, Nick thought. Looking around the table, he saw some amused faces; then he saw Lazarra's smirk and knew — he'd put his feet under the rungs of that chair and pulled it. Someday, Nick swore, I'd like to do that to him.

A bell rang and everyone began getting up. Nick leaned over to the boy and said, "From now on we gotta keep our feet right in front of the chair, so nobody can do that again, okay?" Lazarra was staring at him, wondering what was said. The boy nodded yes, turned and disappeared in the crowd.

At the next meal, Cernicki, back from the Infirmary, sat in his old chair next to Nick. Barr told him what happened.

"So, where's the kid now?" Cernicki asked.

"I ain't seen him anywhere," Lazarra said. "Maybe he cried for his mama, and she came and put him in his little crib. A little twerp like that could never be a Hummer." Lazarra pointed at Nick. "Whadda ya think about that newbie, think he'll make it?" No one answered. Nick stopped buttering his toast and looked over at Lazarra with an emotionless face, purposely not an angry one, but didn't say anything. Lazarra was suddenly flustered. "Aw, he'll prob'ly be okay. He'll learn to be a Hummer someday."

"Hey," McKnight said, "Don't take so long with the milk, willya, Smokey?"

"Did you guys hear about weird Bob Engelhardt down at the sand tent?" Barr asked. Nick listened intently, his feet planted in the front of his chair.

Junior School Dining

SIX

Miss Saunders assigned guides to help newbies for a few days, staying with them, leading them to the dining room, to the right classroom, lavatory and dormitory, to the seamstress, the infirmary or dentist, if necessary. Dan Seroka, a tall, muscular 10 year old, was assigned to Nick.

He made it clear he didn't want to guide newbies. He rarely spoke to Nick, giving him a bored look and a toss of his head to say, "Let's get going." He went as fast as he could, never looking back to see if Nick was there. Often he'd say to Nick, when he saw some of his friends, "Stay here, I'll be back," and when he did return, glared resentfully at Nick. Nick decided never to speak to him, not one word, but that didn't bother Seroka.

Once, left alone, Nick thought he recognized a boy from Section Eleven and decided to catch up and talk to him. He trailed the boy out of the Junior School where he turned left and started up the Main Road. Nick was a good distance behind him when the boy turned up a walk leading to a building Nick didn't know. Nick turned to start back to the Junior School when he heard a loud voice. He knew something was wrong.

"Hey, you, boy!" Nick saw a man walking on the other side of Main Road. "Come here." Nick crossed over to him.

"Where do you think you're going? Where's your pass?" Nick was about to say he was new and lost and was going to go back to his section when the man said, "You're out here on the Main Road without a pass?" Nick nodded yes.

"Get back in that building," the man said, scowling. Nick turned and started toward the Junior School East Wing entrance. "I don't ever want to come across you again without a pass."

Then Nick felt a sharp pain as his head rocked forward. The man had hit him! Nick felt tears coming. He wanted to rub his head but he didn't. And he didn't look back. He kept his head down, went up the steps quickly and into the building, where he looked out and saw the man in the distance heading up the road. What a mean place when any grownup can hit you, he thought, rubbing the sore spot.

One morning Seroka didn't turn up and Nick figured he was on his own. For the next few days Nick spent most of his time hurrying about, often not knowing where he was going, just keeping up with some kids whose faces he'd been studying in the section room; now he even recognized the backs of their heads.

When Miss Saunders would say, "Okay, Section Eleven, off to the lavatory…and take off your shirts to wash up for dinner," everyone would jump up from their desks, speed-walk to the door and then begin racing down the halls. A governess or housemaster at the other end of a hall might yell, "Stop that running…and be quiet!" And it would quiet down for a while. But the pushing and shoving game to get ahead continued.

Racing really increased when it came to stairways, metal steps and railings. One flight from the section rooms down to the lavatories and auditorium, one flight up to the classrooms, and two flights up to the dormitories. Nick followed the crowd, trying not to be the last, just wanting to keep up.

A kid in front of Nick wasn't going very fast. He was holding onto the railing and taking every step one at a time, instead of at least jumping down two at a time. Nick moved into the left lane to get around him and felt a sharp pain as someone punched him in the back.

"C'mon, newbie, get outta the way. You'll get knocked on your ass stayin' out here." Nick lurched to the right and crashed into another boy who yelled, "Ow!" and tried to push Nick back out. Nick elbowed him so he could get back in the slow lane, said "Sorry," and then jumped out into the fast lane but got shoved from behind and swerved to the right as Vince Bernardi, the biggest kid in the section, flew by. I guess, Nick thought, going up stairways is safer. Just go as fast as your legs will go in either lane.

When class was out one afternoon, Nick was shoved to the right by some kid in the "fast lane" with a call to "move over, you goddamned slowpoke!" He was pushed into two others and all three tumbled down the last few steps to a landing. The crowd rushing by saw them, but no one said a word.

Sitting on the floor, Nick rubbed his elbow. The other two, unknown to him, sat, knickers pulled up, looking at scraped legs. They got to their feet and started down the stairs.

"Guess we better stay in the slow lane for a while," said one, holding his handkerchief to his bleeding knee, as he hopped down one step at a time.

Later, Sam Thomas, came up to him on the playground. "Hey, kid, saw you get it on the stairs. I got knocked down, too, 'til my brother, he's a Biggie, told me what to do."

So Nick let the crowd rush down and then began practicing on the empty steps or racing past a few stragglers. When he got four steps from a landing, he'd jump and reach for the metal newel post and try to swing around and land on the first or second step going down. After some bruised knees and knuckles and several twisted ankles, he felt confident enough to join the "fast lane" gang. More than that, though, Nick felt he was becoming a Hummer.

SEVEN

Nick dried himself as he walked down the hall from the shower room. Tossing his damp towel in the big laundry bag as he entered the dormitory, he heard laughter.

"Ha, gotcha newbie!"

Nick didn't see what had happened but knew something was up. He slowed his walk, then stopped and sat on the metal railing of an empty bed. As he glanced toward the door as though waiting for someone, he remembered something his grandfather told him just before he died last summer.

Pop always sat in his high-backed chair, next to the little box on legs that Nick liked to look in when Pop wasn't there. It held his tobacco in a round tin and three pipes and had shiny copper walls. And the smell was Pop. Next to his chair was a tall radio with a tiny orange dial. On Saturday afternoons he sat quietly, his eyes closed and listened to music that sounded strange to Nick. Opera, he called it — not at all like the music sung at church or at home when Uncle Bill played the piano and his mother, Nannie and Aunt Arlene sang.

Pop sang at the church too, but said he really liked to sing at the Orpheus Club. Nick could see Pop's clean, sharp chin, his pale blue eyes; the light covering of white hair and his hands that looked rough, with all the scars from the mines, but almost seemed delicate when he moved them. "Nicholas, my luv, he said, "I tried hard not to seem fearful when I left my home back in Wales. I was not as young as you, but it was hard to say goodbye to my family and friends. To feel I would probably never see my parents again. But, I felt this was what I had to do. I would learn how to do things in America that I would never learn in the old country and I hoped to be able to help my family back home. I was frightened of the unknown, but excited by it, too, and my future was filled with promise, like yours is now." He reached over and touched Nick's hand with his. Nick had learned it didn't mean you had to accept what he was about to say; it meant, to Pop, an important thing for him to say to you.

He was proud of being Welsh. And Grandma's real name was Jennie Jenkins, just like the song. On the wall above the radio was a saying, framed:

> *To be born Welsh is to be born privileged,*
> *Not with a silver spoon in your mouth,*
> *But with music in your blood*
> *and poetry in your soul.*

"You're going to a strange place this Fall. Far away from your mom, from your baby sister and from me. But I think it will be good for you. You'll be much smarter than growing up here; you'll get a better education, and maybe even be wiser. There's just one thing, I'll ask of you." He leaned down closer to Nick's head. "Most people speak first, instead of observing. An observation can take just a second or two, but it will prepare you in case you have to speak or answer. Look first, Nicholas. Observe — then speak or take action. It has saved some of my friends in the mines." Pop looked upward at the ceiling. "And I've lost some friends who didn't."

"Yow!" Nick jumped up from the bed railing, startled. Another newbie named Surgeoner stood in front of him with a curious look on his face. "Sorry, wrong bed," Nick said, starting down the aisle.

"Ha, here comes another newbie, now," someone said as Nick approached his bed.

Pop's advice leapt into his head. Rubbing his face with his hand, he looked through his fingers as he walked. Another newbie in the next aisle over was struggling to get into bed amid muffled laughter. Nick knew he was being watched as he got to his bed. Sitting next to his pillow, he carefully rearranged his clothes on the chair. Then he inspected his shoes and put them under his chair. Then he straightened the chair. Finally, he sat up, let his feet hang over the side of the bed and didn't move. He just sat there. It seemed like forever.

26

He could hear whispering. As soon as he heard Miss Saunders' door open, and knowing everyone would turn to see what she was going to say, he swung his legs under the covers, lay back, head on his pillow, looked up at the ceiling and grinned. "Yo, he cheated!" someone yelled. Some kids sat up in bed to get a better look.

"How'd he do that?"

"Wise ass!" he heard just as the lights went out and Miss Saunders announced gruffly, "Quiet! No more talking. Good night."

Nick had been short-sheeted, a trick he had learned about from guys at his table. The sheet was folded so that he would jam his feet up against it and not be able to straighten out his legs. But he had tucked his legs tightly under his body as he slid under the covers and lay scrunched into the upper end of the bed.

After a few minutes, when the room was quiet except for some adenoidal snoring, Nick got out of bed and quickly fixed the sheet. As he got into bed and stretched out his legs, he heard, "Good for you, newbie, you got em!"

Nick, head again on his pillow, smiled at his success, silently mouthed, "Thanks, Pop," and was soon asleep.

◆

Nick knew the Junior School was shaped like an E. The East Wing was at one end with Sections One to Six. At the other end was the West Wing with Sections Seven to Twelve, including his Section Eleven. Halfway down the long, broad main hall connecting them was the dining room. Nick had never been down to the East Wing. There were probably kids in his class in some of the East Wing sections, so, coming up from the lavatory after washing up, he decided to go down and look around.

When he got down the long, broad corridor and reached the East Wing hallway, three kids standing by a water fountain, stepped in front of him. Three big kids he never saw before. One grabbed his belt and yanked it loose from the buckle. Nick pulled it out of his hand. "Hey, watch it, newbie," one of them said.

"Yeah," said the other, "Don't cut corners so sharp, you'll bump inta the boogey man."

"Why don't we protect this newbie," the biggest guy said with a nasty smile. "Let's walk him to his section, he ain't in ours."

"Right, Pete, do our Scout's deed for the day!"

When a hand touched Nick's shoulder, he turned and ran.

"He's a Westie! Get him!" The long, empty hallway reverberated with the thudding of brogues. If I can just get to the West Wing hall, Nick thought. Head down, legs churning, he was running faster than he ever had. But they were gaining on him. He could hear their heavy breathing.

"We'll get you!" a grunting voice said. "Let's skin the sonofabitch."

Suddenly the two dining room doors opened. Out stepped the dietitian in her white coat, about to announce dinner. "Stop running!" she barked. "I said slow down!" Everyone slowed…to a fast walk. "Stop now!"

Nick was nearing the West Wing hallway. She can't see my face, he thought. I'm gonna run for it! Bolting forward, he turned the corner into the West Wing and leaned against the wall to get his breath. Getting down on his knees, he slowly peered around the corner. Down the hall, the gang was headed back to the East Wing, arms waving, talking animatedly. One looked back and saw Nick's head. The others turned and, as their mouths opened to yell, Nick leaned out and waved a broad, fake-friendly goodbye and a big smile. Pulling back, he sat with his back against the wall.

"What are you smiling about?" Miss Saunders stood above him. "Get back to your desk, you should be there waiting for dinner. I hope you have a big appetite."

"Yes, Miss Saunders, I do now."

Grace over, there was a loud scraping as three hundred boys pulled their chairs out and sat down. Linen napkins were pulled from brass rings and spread on laps, as waiters in white coats burst through the swinging kitchen doors with platters of food. Conversations began immediately.

"Geez, that was a tough test today about the Egyptians, Mac. Do you know if Pharaohs wives were put to death with them, too?"

"They put their dogs to death — if she was a dog, they probably did."

"Thanks, smart-ass."

"I heard from Frank Sabol, that kid from Seckie Nine that runs the movie projector, we're gonna see Abbott and Costello Saturday night."

"I wish they'd show that pirate movie again," Dick Conradi said, snapping his napkin at Jim Landry, who ignored him, "I heard they're kicking Larry Carswell out."

"Nah, his mom's getting married and they're moving to Florida."

"Great, there goes one of our best goalies."

"Lucky guy, I wish someone would get me outta here."

"Just keep giving dumb answers in class, you jerk, and you'll be back in South Philly before Easter vacation, right guys?"

"Screw you, Tobin. You guys can laugh all you want. Jed and me's the only ones at this table who'll make it to graduation."

"In the meantime, pass the milk."

"Say it like a gentleman, please."

"Pass the fuckin' milk, you big turd. That's being polite to you."

"Grab the waiter. We want more bread. An' white this time, none of that brown stuff."

"Tell him if we don't get it, we'll butter the plates and turn 'em upside down. He'll have such a tough time getting them up, by the time he gets to the waiter's table to eat after lunch, there won't be any food left."

"What the matter with you, Nick? You wanna sit at somebody else's table?"

Dom Lazarra said, "Are we boring you?"

"I was just looking to see if I could see those East Wing guys who chased me." No one stopped eating, but Nick had everyone's attention.

"What happened?" Jock McKnight and Don Loder asked in unison. Nick finished his last mouthful of gravy-soaked bread, then described what happened. Everyone laughed when he told them how he waved goodbye.

"You should be safe down there if you're not a newbie. They'll figure you got friends in some of their seckies and probably won't bother you."

"But, how did they know I was a newbie?" He saw knowing smiles.

Then Smokey Stover said, "That's easy."

"Pull out the end of your belt, Nick," Barr interrupted, "and look at the back of it."

Nick did. It wasn't black, like the front side. "So…it's white."

"Look at mine," said McKnight, leaning back in his chair. It was brown, with a few traces of white.

"So?"

"So, only newbies have white on the inside of their belts. 'Cus they're new — like their belts," Barr added.

"Geez," Nick said disgustedly, "How long do I have to be a newbie around here. I've been here for weeks already. When do I get to be a Hummer, like you guys?"

"Old Hick says everybody's just a newbie until the next gang a orphans come in."

"Jock, tell him how to fix his belt so guys in other seckies can't tell he's a newbie."

McKnight always made Nick laugh. He was funny to watch. Shook his head back and forth sideways a little right before he spoke. He laughed a lot and always at himself and what he said. He never seemed to get mad when he was ribbed and everyone liked to tease him. He was a popular kid.

"Look in the trash cans on the playground and find a soda bottle. Then go way out to the end of the playground, by the sand tent. Don't let a housemaster see you when you break the bottle. Take your belt off," he flipped open the end of his belt, "and rub it hard with an edge of glass 'till you scrape the white stuff off maybe eight or ten inches. That way, no one can prove you're a newbie." Nick nodded his head in understanding and thanks.

"Where'd the word Hummer come from?" he asked McKnight. "Miss Saunders never calls anybody a Hummer. She calls us Girardians, and so do housemasters. But I hear guys saying make sure you're with some Hummers when you leave the Hum in case you come across some town kids. And you know everybody calls this place the Hum."

"You need an education, newbie," Jed Timmons, at the end of the table, said quietly. He was a skinny, sort of tall kid. Black hair stuck out behind large pink ears. He had a long, freckled face with a pinched mouth and wore thin round glasses like Ben Franklin's. Hennessy said he got picked on a lot. Someone found out he lived near the Pocono Mountains, so now he's a hick. And having the name Jed didn't help. Or when Mr. Sparks laughed at him in front of everybody and said, "Stop loping, just walk." No wonder, Nick thought, he never smiles. Living with all these wise guys, you have to answer back. I already learned being sarcastic is a game, especially at the table. Some kids can't learn to be insensitive to it, I guess.

"Jed, please tell us, does it hurt 'cus you gotta wear shoes?"

31

"Hey, do hicks take showers, or just wait 'til it rains?" He never says anything, Nick thought. Sometimes doesn't even scowl. Just ignores it. Maybe, he feels it's better not making a reply — and showing them they didn't get to him.

"This is what I read in a reference book in the library." Timmons broke the silence, looking at Nick. "It was a history of the Hum — Girard — and it said no one knew for sure why it was called the Hum. They think it happened awhile after the school opened in 1848. That was because they were indentured orphans, like we are. But then they not only had to go to class, they were sent to places outside school where they had to work, like Oliver Twist when he was sent to Mr. Sowerbury's, the undertaker."

"Whatta brain, and in a hillbilly, too!"

Timmons paused and then went on. "The book said they didn't want everybody outside to know they were in a Home, that's what orphanages were called then. It made them seem like the lowest kinda person, so they changed it to Hum. That's the only explanation…and that's why, if you can live in this abusive place," he waved his hand deprecatingly, — everyone watched, mute, — "you'll be called a Hummer. And don't forget, all Hummers are indentured orphans."

"But, there's another theory," Norm Cohen added. "Y'know the gingies, the big ginger cookies that we get for dessert?"

"He means Hum Muds, Nick," Barr said.

"Miss Taylor told us in second grade that back during the Civil War, the man baking them was Charles Hummel. He had a book with recipes and in it was one for ginger cookies. She thinks he called them mud-pies, and they were called Hummel's mud-pies. So, eventually they were called Hum's Mud-pies."

Tiny Ronnie Davis had a thin little voice that fit him. "And," he screeched, "then they became Hum Muds. And that fits perfect with us being Hummers."

"I don't care what anyone says," Conradi declared, "I know I wouldn't wanna be pointed at as someone from a Home. I go with their callin' the place the Hum."

Suddenly there was the clanking of a knife handle on a china plate and the room was quiet. Dinnertime was almost over.

Toogie Groome leaned over the table and gestured to Nick. "If you see the East Wing bastards that chased you, point them out to the big guys in our seckie like Guida or Heffner. The next time we play them in soccer, they'll shin them real good."

Section Room and Classroom

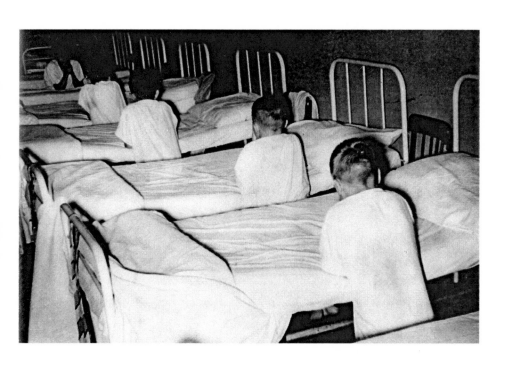

Prayers and Bed Making

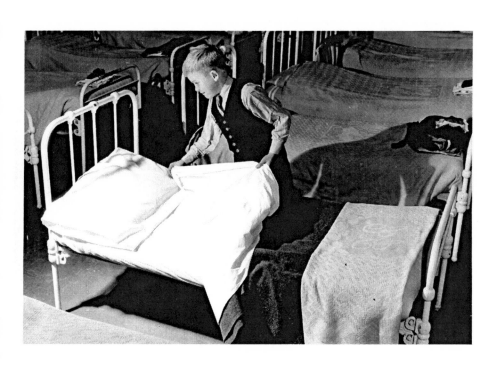

EIGHT

Dear Mom,

Miss Saunders - she spelled her name for us - put paper on our desks and told us to write to our mothers. We should tell you what we do every day so you know and can see us in your mind. She said this would make you feel better. So this is the letter. At 6:30 she puts the lights on. Then we get up and get dressed, except for our shirts. Everyone makes their beds and folds their nightshirts and puts them under the pillow. Then we go downstairs to wash up. I counted 32 boys in our section eleven. We wash our hands and face and arms and chest and brush our teeth and comb our hair. Then we put on our shirt and tie and our vest and coat. We polish our shoes if we have to. We walk behind her up to the dining room and stand behind our chairs. Every day a different boy reads from a grace book and we all sit down. The table has bread and big pitchers of milk that we pass around. Some kids take more and get yelled at by others. I always get my share. We have a bowl of cereal, either white, creamy stuff or brown stuff with sugar on top. Sometimes it has raisins in it. We get toast and sometimes an orange half. Sometimes two figs that I don't really like. It gets between my teeth. When the housemaster hits his spoon on a glass, we have to stop talking. That's near the end of breakfast. At lunch and supper too. We go to the section and get our books and run up to school on the second floor. It starts at 8:15 and the bell rings for lunch at 11:45. One teacher teaches us everything. And we have music class and art class and they're fun. We go down to the section and leave our books, wash up again and go to the dining room. Then we get our books and go back to school. School is harder than home. We can't talk or look at anybody. Boys who don't know the answer have to come in after school. A bell rings at 3:15 and we take our books to our desk in the section room and go out to play. I had to stay after class on Monday because I didn't know some answers. I studied and Miss Rank tested me and I passed but it was too late for playing. I promise to study hard. Sometimes I play on the jungle gym and swings and sometimes I get in a game of baseball or kickball. When the Housemaster blows a whistle we all stop and run and stand in section lines then we go wash up and go to dinner. After dinner we go to the section and sit at our desks and do our homework if we have it. No talking or games. Miss Saunders seems mean then. When she says its 7 a clock, we go upstairs to the dormitory. We put our clothes on the chair and go down the hall to the shower room. We take a towel to dry off and throw it in a big thing called a hampur. We put on nightshirts and get into bed. We can sit up in bed and read. No talking is allowed, but some kids do it. Sometimes on Friday and Saturdays she brings out her radio and we listen to the FBI in Peace and War or Inner Sanktum. Sometimes a kid who saw a movie will stand on his bed and tell us about it. After 8 o'clock she comes out and we all get out of bed and kneel down to say prayers and then a silent one. I always pray for you and Janet and everybody at home. Then we get into bed and the lights go out. Some kids cry, but not too long. Miss Saunders is taking all the letters. She said she'd mail them.

I will write to you again next week. Please write to me.

Love, Nicholas
XXXXX and OOOO for you and Janet.

NINE

Three times Nick called softly from his desk, "Hey, Fug," but got no response. Hunched over, Bob Furmanski was concentrating on writing something. Nick furtively dropped a folded up message by his shoe intending to slide it across the floor to his new friend.

Section Eleven was in quiet time — no games or chatter. Until dinner, in half an hour, everyone was supposed to sit at their desk and do something productive. So, everyone heard the loud "crack" as a pencil point snapped.

"Darn it!" Furmanski said and threw the pencil down hard at his feet. Bouncing on the eraser, it hopped under Ed Rosen's desk and landed out of sight, generating an undecipherable curse and some nearby snickers.

"That will be two demerits, Robert. One for losing your temper and throwing the pencil as though it was its fault and another for your language." Miss Saunders returned to reading the newspaper on her desk.

◆

"What's a demerit, Jock? Nick asked." Bill Heisler looked up, shook his head side to side in wonder and resumed attacking his Salisbury steak.

Nick noticed amused faces. "Let the newbie have it, Jock!" someone said. McKnight took a long drink of milk, put his glass down and leaned forward on his elbows. "The demerit system is one a the ways they control us. They make us do what they want or we get punished."

"Yeah, but it's for every freakin' thing," Heisler griped.

"Like what?" Nick asked.

"Like talking when we're supposed to be quiet. Like bein' slow getting in line outside when Mr. Hickerson blows his whistle."

"And running in the halls, Jock, and on the stairs, too," Cernicki contributed, "an' not stayin' in line, an' talking or runnin' around after lights out." Now, everyone began educating Nick. Not having your brogues polished. Stragglin' instead of keepin' up. Not getting a rip in your shirt or knickers fixed, even having your knickers hang down.

"I got two demerits for pulling some kid off the swings the other day," Conradi grumbled. "He pulled me off first but Mr. Dunkel didn't see that."

"What's a demerit do? What do you do with them?"

"You don't do with them, dummy, they do with you!"

"Shut up," Flanagan said. "He's a newbie. Each demerit," he went on, "means a half hour on the grudge line. You know what the grudgy is, don't cha?"

"Is that when guys stand in a line near Miss Saunders' desk, looking away from everybody?" Nick asked. Seeing nods of approval, he went on, "I've seen guys walking around two trees on the playground, while everybody's playing."

"That's if you're lucky," Flanagan said. "It's worse if you hafta stand in front of the Hum wall. You look straight ahead at the stones. No talking. Stand up straight, heels together and no slouchin'."

"I looked down once and got whacked on the back of my head. I didn't know the housie was watchin' us," Heisler recounted, "Then he says, 'That's another fifteen minutes for you, smart guy.' What I hate is you can get demerits from anybody!"

"I threw a fig at Swartz when we came outta the dining room, just in fun and a guvvie from Seckie Four . . ." Cernicki complained.

"Butch Irving," Heisler noted.

"She sees me, grabs me by the ear and pulls me over to Mr. Wileman. She didn't even tell him what I did, just says I deserve demerits, so I get three demerits and he gives me another one for bothering her!" That brought grins around the entire table.

"Do they write them down?" Nick wondered.

39

"They don't write them down," McKnight said with reverence, "but somehow guvvies remember about kids in their seckie and when housemasters see you on the playground they know if you owe them hours."

"That's right, Mr. McKnight," a deep, male voice said. Mr. Newhardt had edged over to the table, unnoticed. "You need to teach these new boys what to expect; and it's a shame," he looked at Nick, "when those who know the rules ignore them and get in trouble themselves."

Everyone watched as Mr. Newhardt gently patted McKnight on his shoulder. "One demerit for you, professor. You should know better than to keep your elbows on the table."

TEN

A teenager opened Section Eleven's door and approached Miss Saunders' desk. "My brother's Jimmy Fitzgerald. May I take a walk up the Main Road with him?"

"Yes, Mister Fitzgerald, you may, but bring him back in time to wash up for dinner." Just as they got to the door, Miss Saunders spoke again. "Would you mind very much taking one or two new boys along and showing them what the buildings are?" Although clearly surprised, he answered, "Sure."

"You and you," she pointed at Nick and a new kid he didn't know sitting at the desk nearby. The boy looked up and began coughing.

"Oh, you'd better stay in. Just take one boy, then…and thank you."

In the hall, Jimmy said, as they trailed along, "Matt's fifteen, he's in Mariner Hall."

Outside, the older boy turned and asked, "What's your name, kid?" Before Nick could answer, Jimmy told him. "And he's pretty good for a newbie, Matt. They don't get him with all the tricks."

As they walked out of the West Wing of Junior School, Matt said, "Do you know Good Friends?" He pointed to the stone building directly across the Main Road from Junior School.

"Yes, it was Stephen Girard's favorite ship. That's where we go when we go to fifth grade. We learned that already," Nick said. "Miss Saunders told us about how he was the captain of a ship when he was real young and then owned lots of ships that sailed around the world."

"And that's Lafayette Hall next to it," Jimmy boasted to his brother. "Why's it called Lafayette?"

"Lafayette was a good friend of Stephen Girard, though Girard was much older than Lafayette. He was Marquis de Lafayette, a Frenchman like Girard, and a General. He was on our side, helping us fight the British during the Revolutionary War. He's probably the most famous Frenchman in American history."

"These buildings look like they belong together," Nick ventured.

"They do," Matt replied. "When I was little, the Junior School felt safe to me and those buildings, sitting next to each other, looked scary even during the day. They looked like ugly twins with their stone ledges and protrusions that stuck out like they're trying to escape something awful inside."

Matt had what Nick's mother would call a mischievous look about him. "The tall skinny windows are sunk in like horrified eyes and make it dark inside even during the day. And when you look way up to the third floor, with those black fire escapes gripping the sidewalls, what a great place to murder someone and then drag them slowly down the steps...*thump, thump, thump*..."

"Stop, Matt! He's always trying to scare me," he cried to Nick.

Matt looked at Nick, grinned and nodded toward the buildings. "They're not as bad as they look and you get used to them." Matt looked down at his watch. "We'd better get moving, I want to be back at Merchant Hall by five."

Instead of going up the Main Road, they turned down, passing the empty Junior School playground on the right and the Middle School playground, next to Good Friends, on the left.

"I know that's called the Armory," Nick said, pointing at an enormous concrete building at the end of the Middle School playground. "I never saw a building with a road running uphill to the doorway like that."

"The curved drive let's them take trucks up to the second floor, which is really the main entrance. They can unload equipment for indoor practice — like hurdles for the track team and seats for basketball games. The ground floor, underneath, is kinda dark but it has a lot of basketball courts, though you can't shoot the ball too high;

it hits the ceiling. The main floor is wood and has basketball courts too, and the balcony running around it is good for the track team. There are a lot of other rooms. Some for the 'Batty,' our military battalion. When you get to be Biggies you have to join that; and there are other rooms for band and orchestra lessons if you take music. It's a busy building."

Over to their right Nick saw a two-story, L-shaped building with ivy growing all over the bricks. "That's the Mechanical School, right, Matt?"

"Right. That's where I spend half of my school day."

"Half?" Nick questioned.

"I'm taking Drafting, it's my vocation. When you become a Biggie you have to choose. Then you go to class, y'know, English, French, Math, Public Speaking, History and such, half a day and the other half at your trade here in the Mechanical School."

"I don't know what I wanna do," said Jimmy, apprehensively.

"I wouldn't worry about that now. You just better stop getting Ds or you'll never get the chance." Turning to Nick, he said, "There are probably 360 kids in Junior School, maybe 400 with the four West End Houses. But only about fifty or so Hummers make it to graduation day. You really have to study to get through and you don't have anybody reminding you or nagging you about your homework. It's all on your shoulders."

"Over there's the West End," Jimmy told Nick, "for the six and seven year olds, but I was never there."

"Neither was I," replied Nick, "They put me right in Junior School. Did you stay there, Matt?"

"Yeah, and it was scary. Everybody was away from home for the first time. Deserted by your mom, at least that's what you thought. Nobody knew anybody, at least for the first month or so. And everybody crying, especially after lights out. Once you start to get used to not seeing your mom, you might be sad at night thinking about her, but you didn't cry. And when the new kids did, it made you mad. And we were mean to them. Some guys are mean to newbies whether they start at the West End or the Junior School."

"Oh, look!" Jimmy exclaimed, "There's a big door, I mean a gate. I didn't know the Main Road went out down here, too."

"Yeah, this is how they bring in supplies and stuff and some teachers and seamstresses and nurses and kitchen people and watchmen go in and out and park here."

"Where does it go to?" Nick asked.

"To Girard Avenue. Girard Ave is a really long street. It starts way down by the river and runs up, crosses Broad Street, goes along the front of the Hum and jogs a little bit around the end of the Hum and then runs all the way out through some of Fairmount Park, even passing the Zoo, and ends way out in West Philly in what they call Overbrook. It's about 60 or 70 city blocks long. If you go out this gate and around the corner, you come to Girard Ave where it turns in front of the Big F."

"What's the Big F?" Nick asked.

"It's the Fairmount, the movie. With a Big F above it, all lit up. That's where the Biggies take the Wall Rats."

"Rats?" Jimmy, poised to run, eyed the base of the stone wall for any menacing movement.

With a quiet laugh, Matt said, "They're girls who live around here and go with some a the guys. The housemasters call them Wall Rats because some of them stand next to the wall on Girard Ave up by the high school at night when we're studying and yell out to the guys."

"Like, Nick, Nick," Matt spoke in a high voice, "I'll see you at the Big F on Saturday at 2."

Nick felt his face burning. Matt smiled. "Just kidding, Nick. But guys get yelled at by the housies and razzed by everyone else. Now, we'd better start back."

When they passed the Junior School, Jimmy ran ahead and pointed at a three story building, all stone, with steps from three sides going up to the doorway.

"That's the Infirmary, but Nick already knows that. And back there," he pointed to a wing that ran off to the left, "up those first floor steps are the dentists."

Matt waved him back. "We'll have to stop here. It's getting late and I want to get back to my hall."

"Aw, Matt, c'mon, just a little further!"

"No, Jim. And if you're late going back to your section, Miss Saunders won't let me take you out again."

"Aw, phooey. Nice brother you are," he said, and ran toward the West Wing entrance.

Matt looked sad, not angry, Nick thought. "If he doesn't get better grades," Matt said, looking after him, "they're gonna kick him out and our mom doesn't have enough money to take care of us. If you can talk to him, Nick, I'd really appreciate it."

"I'll try," said Nick, who paused, not knowing what he might do about Jimmy, then said, "thanks for telling us about the Hum."

"You're welcome. I'll come back next week. See ya then."

"Matt, if I can go with you, can we see the great big building I saw when I came with my mother? The one with tall poles around it and lots of steps?"

"Sure, I forget you Lower School kids only get to go past it when you go to the Library. I'll take you inside Founder's Hall next week." Then he turned and started walking away fast. Nick watched him go and wished he had an older brother.

The Chapel

Religious Torture

As I recall Sunday mornings, when the service was over in the Chapel, we Junior Schoolers walked in ragged columns back to our section rooms for a Sunday School Lesson. Rather than sitting formally at our desks, all 30-some eight, nine and 10-year-olds sat cross-legged in a group on the floor in front of the governess. No leaning back against anything. No lying down in any position that might be considered 'lolling about.' She'd bring her chair around from her desk, sit before us and open a big, thick book, Hurlburt's Story of the Bible.

Each week brought a different chapter — one week about the walls of Jericho, the next week about David and Goliath or the burning bush. She would pause and make comments or ask questions. Did we know the meaning of begat? From our classroom studies, who can tell us anything about the Egyptians? What is an idol? What did we learn from what happened to Lot's wife? The lesson usually took about 40 minutes, after which she would close the book, look at us solemnly, and say, "I hope you all paid attention. Section Eleven better not embarrass me this afternoon at Vespers"

"This afternoon at Vespers" — that phrase struck fear in the hearts of over 300 boys every Sunday. At about 2:45, each of the twelve sections made its way down to the auditorium in the basement of the Junior School building. On Saturday nights, the wide hallway with its tiled floor and walls resounded with excited voices anticipating the night's cartoons. But Sunday afternoon's procession was quiet, orderly, reflecting the apprehensive atmosphere. Everyone sat up soberly in the semi-circle of miniature theater seats. On the bare stage were two men. One was Mr. Hickerson. He was in charge of the Junior School — governesses, other housemasters, kitchen help, seamstresses, everyone, including the boys. He was a big man with little eyes set in a round face, a small mouth and above it a tiny, two-part black moustache. Crazy Bill Creighton said they were little caterpillars trying to escape from his face, but Old Hick's sniffing for troublemakers kept pulling them back. Old Hick had broad, powerful shoulders and a short temper he

47

didn't try to hide. He would grab a boy by his shoulders and, lifting him, would shake him back and forth violently. Or grab his tie and shake that back and forth. It even hurt to watch. You felt sorry for the kid even if he deserved to be punished.

What you did learn was to disappear from Mr. Hickerson's presence as soon as he came into yours, if that was possible. But do it quietly, slowly, as though there was something you suddenly remembered you had to do. Too obvious and he might notice you and call you over. "Where are you going, boy?" With a credible answer you might not get a "shaking," but he might put his arm around your neck and rub his knuckles on your head — hard, a brush burn on your scalp. It hurt. Then he'd let you loose and off you would go, not daring to look back. When I watched him do it to others, with a smile on his face, I wondered if, somehow, it was his strange way of showing affection.

The other person on the Sunday afternoon stage might be Mr. Small, who was in charge of outdoor activities, overseeing games and directing chores like sweeping the building steps and walks or picking up trash. He was a short, pleasant man liked by the kids. He smiled and joked around a lot. Mr. Small alternated with Mr. Davis. Joe Davis as we called him was a tall, thin, stern man, feared even more than Old Hick. He didn't wander around like Hickerson looking for kids doing something wrong. You were sent to Mr. Davis and severe punishment was sure. You knocked at the door and waited for him to say "Enter." Then, hat in hand, you approached his broad desk. He would look up from something that probably defined your crime and say, "So, boy, I haven't seen you before. I'm sorry you're here. But you should know better than to . . ." and he described your transgression. Then, picking up a large wooden paddle, he rose from his desk.

Punishment ranged from having the palm of your hand smacked a number of times until it was pink and stinging to bending over and holding onto the edge of the desk and getting a series of hard whacks on your butt. Because you were insulated with underwear and knickers, I think he struck even harder. He was the disciplinarian, although we didn't even know the word.

Mr. Hickerson started the Sunday service program with a prayer. Then Mr. Small or Mr. Davis would point at the audience. "That boy back there in Section Nine. Yes, you, whispering to your friend. Tell him and all of us what you learned from today's Bible story?"

Oh, how you squirmed in your seat, hoping not to be called. The boy would stammer out some reply, enough for Mr. Davis to describe it in greater detail. Then he might ask: "Who can tell me how David got into trouble?" If no one answered, which was normal, he would simply point at a boy or at a section. "Someone in Section Three. Can you tell me?"

Usually the governess would hiss a name, one of the smart kids she trusted to have the answer. And sometimes Old Hick would call out the name of a boy. "Where's that boy Sterling in Section Two?"

It was really bad if they knew your name; that happened because you got caught in trouble a lot. It was best to be unknown, anonymous. For that entire hour, most kids, known and unknown, sat up in their seats, moving as little as possible, barely glancing at their neighbors. When Mr. Hickerson finally stood up to signal the end of the program, the auditorium itself seemed to breathe a sigh of relief. A brief prayer was said and we quietly and happily filed out of the room.

Usually, among all those boys, some would know the answers. But there were times when a boy didn't, or wouldn't even offer a lame one, just stood silently, shoulders drooping, looking down. This drew a sharp remark from the man on stage. "Were you at the Infirmary this morning, boy, and missed the lesson?" The response was barely audible. "No, sir."

"Next week maybe you ought to sit at Mrs. Gardner's feet." There was no expression on Mrs. Gardner's face. The heavyset governess of Section Ten had a Southern accent and a right hand that clenched a thick, oversized, jangling ring of keys, a weapon that drew surprised cries of pain, and sometimes blood, when it struck the back of a miscreant's head.

But that hour could be entertaining as well as educational. One time Mr. Davis called on a kid from Section Twelve, asking him why baby Moses had been put in a basket in the bulrushes. As the boy rose, he put his hand to his mouth, furtively asking for help, clear to all he didn't have the answer. Someone must have whispered something to him for he dropped his hand, looked out up at Mr. Davis and, smiling with confidence, announced loudly, "Because he couldn't swim."

The room erupted into gales of laughter. Kids jumped up from their seats, turning around to delight in the gleeful cries of others. Some waved to friends in sections across the room and they waved back, sharing the moment. Still others poked the backs of those sitting in front of them in joyful celebration. It was a slapstick scene from Saturday night's cartoons — not Sunday School afternoons. Every governess, except one, tried to suppress smiles. Even Mr. Davis and Old Hick were holding their noses to hide their response.

Finally, Old Hick slapped his hands together. With a last few ripples of laughter ebbing across the room, silence was restored. Mr. Davis then rather quickly explained why Moses was in a basket in the bulrushes and brought the meeting to a close.

We left Sunday School enjoyably poking each other. But one poor kid awaited quick punishment when he returned to his section room, and he faced torment when he ventured outside that room. "Hey, guys, look — Moses finally got outta the bulrushes!" "Hey, Moses, did you learn the Jewish or Egyptian crawl?" And an occasional chorus of "Go Down, Moses, Go down to Sunday School. Tell old Joe Davis — let our Moses go!"

Fortunately, after a few weeks they tired of it and he became just another kid in the crowd.

Thus were young orphans — Protestants, Catholics, Jews, and future agnostics and atheists — exposed to Christianity.

ELEVEN

"Darn, it must be an hour now and I'm still walking in circles."

"Rectangles, you mean," a passing voice said.

"Hey," Nick said to Carl Reisinger, "do you see Netherman anywhere? My hour must be up and I wanna go free."

"Nah, I don't see him anywheres. Maybe he went in to take a leak."

"I hate walking around trees when everybody's playing."

"Yeah, well it's better than standing over there with those guys facing the wall and not seeing anything but stones."

Reisinger was walking in front of Nick. As one turned to start back toward the distant tree and passed by the other, they put their hands to their mouth, rubbing their noses when they spoke.

"Stop that talking, you two." Mr. Dunkel was the other housemaster on the playground this afternoon. "You in the back, stop and let him get further away from you and any more talking and you'll be here all afternoon."

Nick stopped until Carl circled the tree and started back toward the other one, about thirty feet away. Passing Nick he rolled his eyes and pushed his lip out in a dramatic pout. Nick laughed and looked to see if Mr. Dunkel was watching. He was on the other side of the playground in a circle of boys; probably settling a penalty kick in that soccer game.

Nick told Reisinger, just before Mr. Dunkel separated them, that it was Norm Cohen's fault — he should be here.

At breakfast, Nick was so thirsty, he poured a glassful of milk as the room was filling up, and drank it standing up before grace was said. Others at the table watched him askance, at the risk he was taking. Sitting down, he decided to refill his glass from one of the two aluminum pitchers. He reached for it when Cohen, across the table, suddenly grabbed the handle. Nick, hands on the base, pulled it back; then Norm pulled it toward himself. "C'mon, Norm, I got it first."

"No, I saw what you did. Let me have the next glass"

"No, no matter, I didn't get caught. That's what counts. And now I grabbed it first. There's more than enough for you and other guys, too." With each retort, the pitcher was tugged, milk sloshing wildly.

Nick ignored the onlookers' snickers when he tried a sincere-toned "Please, Norm, you can have it as soon as I take just a little, okay?"

"Okay, nice guy, you can have it," he said and let go of the handle. Norm's sly smile was the last thing Nick saw before the wave of white hit him. Everyone roared, watching milk run off his eyebrows, nose and mouth. He wrapped his face in his napkin and began dabbing at his soaked tie and shirt when he heard Mr. Newhardt.

"If you're so greedy, Mister, that you have to grab like that, try grabbing the door handle over there and get yourself out of the dining room right now. Get a clean shirt from the seamstress and stay in your section room. Lunch is over for you."

"Sir, Cohen did it too, he let go…" Mr. Newhardt turned to Cohen who returned a blank expression. Turning back, he pointed at Nick, "You — find me on the playground after school," then walked away.

"That's when Cohen smiled so nice at me I kicked him hard on the shin under the table," Nick said to Reisinger. "He yelled and Mr. Newhardt looked back for a second but didn't stop." Reisinger snorted when he heard Nick say, "And I'll shin 'im again, too."

"Shh, here comes Netherman," Reisinger said, with an approving smile at Nick's tale.

◆

Nick walked away from the grudge line unhappy. All the soccer games had started and he couldn't get in one now. So he went over to the game where Section Eleven was playing Section Nine to cheer the guys on. Funny how he never heard of soccer before and here everyone played it. He really liked it and tried to play every day. Wandering along, scuffing his brogues on the concrete walk, he finally sat on one of the benches, long wood slats bolted to concrete blocks.

"Kin I sit here?"

Nick didn't know the kid. Never saw him. "Are you in Seckie Nine?" Nick thought maybe he was here to root for them.

"Naw, I'm in Seckie Four. But we're losin' so bad to Seckie Six, I don't wanna watch." He looked at Nick intently. "Why aren't you playing? Hurt?"

"No. Just got off grudge line and the housemaster won't let me in the game now." Nick told the kid what happened that morning. "The grudgy's a rotten punishment, you waste your time when you could be having fun."

"Are you kidding" the kid said, "that's not being punished."

"Huh?"

"That's 'cus you probably haven't been paddled yet. I got it on my hands so many times. Housemasters hate me and it really stings when they swing down hard and hit my hand. Now I start dropping my hand at the last second so's I don't get the whole hit. It still stings a helluva lot, though," he said, rubbing his thumb in the palm of one hand."

"I never got caught yet and paddled," Nick said nervously.

"Getting it hard on your butt, that's when it really hurts," the kid continued. After about ten of them it stings so much ya can't sit down without its hurting again."

"You must get into a lot of trouble."

"Yeah," he nodded, "but the way they treat us in here, I just get so mad. Ya gotta do everything they say from when you get up 'til when you go to bed. And you get in trouble even when you didn't do it, like the guy and the milk you told me about. And ya can't even talk

53

to your mother about it, or anybody to make it right. One of my buddies calls this place Girard Cruelege!"

"What'd you say, Brisbane? They turned to see Mr. Dunkel seated at the far end of the long bench. Now we're in for it, Nick thought. Mr. Dunkel rose and came to sit down next to them. Some boys, smelling trouble, sauntered over to watch.

"You think it's tough here now, he said, but it's really not that bad. Not as bad as it used to be."

"Then what was the worst they could do to you, Mr. Dunkel?" some kid asked. Nick sensed that the one housemaster kids liked the most was Mr. Dunkel. He noticed they just walked up and talked to him. How there always seemed to be some kids either talking to him or waiting to talk to him. He was the quietest housemaster, too. Never seemed to yell. Just blew his whistle, called the troublemaker over and talked to him. Lots of older Hummers talked to him when they saw him on the Main Road. They said he was the fairest housemaster around because he was a Hummer himself, graduated a long time ago and knew how it felt.

He leaned forward on the bench, his hands crossed between his knees. "The worst time," he said, "was a long time ago, about 1865, when the Civil War was underway. The Battalion, our military training program, started then."

"With four companies, like now?"

"Yes. We had sixty students in each company getting ready to go to war if they had to. They had to put on their uniforms and drill every day, not like now when it's just on Friday nights and some Saturday mornings."

"Yow, I wouldn't like that, but that's not really bad," said Heffner.

"Bad," Mr. Dunkel smiled in anticipation, "was when Major Smith, the new president, ran the school like a reformatory. You didn't get paddled then, you got flogged with a whip. Just like in the English

Navy movies you've seen." The three innocents sat with open mouths. "And they might throw you in the Lockup. It was a room on the third floor of Bordeaux Hall. Had no furniture in it, just a mattress on the floor. It was hot in the summer and there was no heat, so it was really cold in the winter."

More kids, seeing Mr. Dunkel talking, joined them and, the bench was soon filled, a small crowd standing behind them. Mr. Dunkel stood up and faced everyone, like an outdoor class they sometimes had, which brought even more kids over. "Whatcha' talkin' about Mr. Dunkel?" someone asked.

Heffner stood up and announced, "He's talking about what it was like in the Hum a long time ago if you got caught doin' something wrong and got put in a special room they locked you in."

"Yeah," Nick added, "it was cold, 'cause it wasn't heated and only had a mattress on the floor, that's all."

"Sure," someone in the crowd said suspiciously, "and how'd ya go to the bathroom?" Everyone laughed when another voice piped up, "Are you just tryna scare us, Mr. Dunkel?"

"Shuddup! Quiet, you guys." Talkers were sneered at. "Go ahead, Mr. Dunkel."

"I'm not making this up. It's from the archives in Founder's Hall, not the Library. It's about the history of the school." He looked at his watch and resumed speaking. "So-called bad kids were put in the Lockup room for a couple hours or for a couple days. Some even stayed there for longer than that. It didn't say so, but I'll bet there was more than one Lockup." The ever-growing audience was stunned.

"Wow! Geez!" was heard softly. Others sat spellbound. "What'd they eat?"

"They could have my liver and lima beans!" someone yelled.

Everyone laughed until Mr. Dunkel said," They would have liked that. They got bread and water twice a day, as long as they were in there, and...oh, someone asked about a bathroom. In a corner of the room was a large bowl. It was their toilet." He paused, enjoying the effect before he continued. "One boy who was left in the Lockup for three months during the winter had to have parts of his toes removed because his foot froze." The little crowd was also frozen.

Mr. Dunkel looked at his watch again. "The Civil War was going on then, and several boys ran away and joined a regiment nearby that was going to fight in the war. They were caught, brought back and severely flogged. The Girard president, Major Smith, even required boys in the Infirmary to get out of bed to attend chapel services in Founder's Hall. One had been in the Infirmary for several weeks and was too weak to walk, but was forced to go. The boy died the next day."

With another glance at his watch, he raised his whistle to his mouth, faced the playground and made a long, shrill blast. All play came to a stop. Balls were gathered up, coats grabbed off fence railings and pulled on. The horde rushed toward the Junior School entrance, forming twelve columns of boys, one for each section. Mr. Dunkel approached them, followed by the small, still shocked listeners.

◆

For the next few days, the Junior School was obsessed with the tales of the floggings and the Lockup. At meals, between classes, on the playground, even after lights were out, it was the topic of heated discussion. There were even sides — those who believed and those who said it was just made up to scare everybody into behaving. Governesses and housemasters said they never heard of it.

During lunch about a week later, Frank Newman leaned over to Nick. "Hey, Dunkel just came in with Newhardt. Get him over here so's we know whether you're telling the truth or all that coal crackin's cracked your brain, too."

"I'll get him," said McKnight and he began waving his arm and looking at Mr. Dunkel.

"Yea, here he comes," said Barr.

"Here they both come." Bill Parsons cautioned, "Don't anybody do anything stupid."

As the housemasters approached the table, Mr. Dunkel gave Nick a questioning look. "Mr. Dunkel," Nick said, "Some of the guys don't believe what you told us. Could you just tell them it really happened and there was flogging and a Lockup?" Everyone stopped eating and turned to hear the housemaster.

"Everything I told you happened. I didn't make it up. Some boys did ask me yesterday how these things were stopped. They stopped, and the president was fired when mothers noticed the whip marks and scars when their boys came home on vacation. And I didn't even tell you everything. One other thing that sticks in my mind is that one time the president discharged several boys…"

"You mean kicked them out?" Jim Swahl asked.

"Yes, but more than that, he had them put in the House of Refuge — a prison for juveniles. When they were asked, they said many times they'd rather be in the House of Refuge than back at Girard College."

No one spoke. Mr. Dunkel looked at Mr. Newhardt with a slight smile. "Everyone seems to be keeping his own counsel," he said to Mr. Newhardt. As they turned away, Mr. Newhardt looked at Nick for a second.

So, Nick thought, maybe the grudge line's not so bad after all.

The central entrance to the Junior School, with
Lafayette Hall and the Chapel on the right,
and farther up the Main Road, Founder's Hall

TWELVE

When Matt Fitzgerald stopped in on Sunday afternoon to see his brother, Miss Saunders told him Jimmy had a cold and she wanted him to stay inside, though the others were going outside to play. Nick, watching from his desk, was overjoyed when Matt said, "I'm dropping a book off at the Library and stopping back at Mariner Hall to meet some friends. We'll come down this way going out the back gate to the park. I can take a boy up the Main Road and bring him back when we go by." He turned and eyed Nick.

Several boys, listening, jumped up and waved their arms. "Kin I go, kin I go, too? Please, Miss Saunders?" Nick, already pulling on his coat, got the approving nod and responded correctly with "Thank you" and a smile.

When they got past the East end of Junior School, Matt said, "I know you've been in these two buildings. That one, the Infirmary," he said, pointing, "is for your physical health, and this big one, the Chapel," his arm swept to the right, "is, they hope, for your spiritual health."

Nick smiled. "I really like the Chapel. I've never been in such a big building. The ceiling's all gold and the organ music is so loud it seems like the whole building's growling. I wish my grandfather could've heard it." Matt had already moved ahead so Nick ran to catch up to him.

"When you're in Sixth and Seventh Grades you'll live in Good Friends and Lafayette Halls and go to the Middle School, behind the Chapel, for classes. Then, when you turn fourteen, you'll become a Biggie in Ninth Grade, move to Banker or Merchant Hall, and get long pants."

"Yeah, and never wear these knickers again. But, where are we in Eighth Grade?"

"Girard doesn't have an Eighth Grade. That's why most Hummers graduate when they're seventeen. If you get to Tenth Grade, without getting thrown out, you'll notice your classes getting smaller every year and some of your friends will disappear. And you'll be in Mariner Hall, where I'll go next semester. Then you go to Bordeaux Hall on the other side of Founder's Hall. It's named for the city in France where Stephen Girard was born." Pausing, he took a deep breath. "Finally, if you make it, you'll be a Senior, and for that last half year you'll live in Allen Hall, named for a past school president."

They stopped and Nick looked at the buildings; two sat opposite the Chapel, the third a little farther up the Main Road. They were like triplets; three story hulks of gray stone with a three-sided tier of steps up to a broad landing and another set up to a smaller landing at a narrow doorway.

"That's Banker Hall, that's Merchant Hall and next is Mariner Hall. They're named for Stephen Girard's three careers."

He started forward and then realized Nick wasn't with him. Nick stood mesmerized by the sounds and activity, his eyes moving back and forth from one building to the other. Biggies were everywhere. Dozens were standing or sitting on different levels and all sides of the stone steps. Some were racing up steps and plunging into the doorway; others pushing their way out through the narrow double doors and jumping around, sometimes tripping over the seated ones. Some were walking alone, even reading as they walked, slowly circling their building. Others, in small groups, were talking and gesturing. A few were chasing others or wrestling on the grass and still others were calling out from benches by one building to Biggies on benches by the other building. Nick could see kids in upper story windows, heads bobbing, arms waving, shouting out messages.

"They're like giant beehives," Nick thought, and then said it.

Matt chuckled. "I never thought of it that way, but you're right. And all the hall buildings, these three and Bordeaux and Allen, are exactly alike. After you spend some time in one, you can find your way in all the others in the dark."

After passing Mariner Hall, they heard, "Hey, Matt, we're leavin' at five, be back then."

Another voice added, "Yo, Matt. Who's your date? Cradle robber!" followed by boisterous laughter. Nick saw Matt grin, but he didn't look over at them. "The only time it's quiet around here is when everyone's in class, the last few minutes of meals, when there's a prayer being said in the chapel or when everyone's in bed. And even then it's not totally quiet, some guys are snoring and some guys stay up causing trouble."

"Oh, and that," Matt pointed back at a three-story modern looking building across from Mariner Hall. "That's the High School," Nick finished the sentence. Matt looked puzzled. "I heard a kid who has a Biggie brother point it out one time. Our teacher brings us up to the Library every two weeks. We're always in a column and she's up front, yelling for everyone to catch up, stay in line and quiet down. So, we don't know anything about some of the buildings, but everyone knows that's Founder's Hall in front of the circle."

"Right," Matt continued, "that's the first thing everybody sees when they come on campus — Founder's Hall with the Circle in front of it. They divided the Circle into two large arcs with a broad walk leading up through it to Founder's Hall. Everything planted on one side of the Circle was planted exactly the same on the other side, like a mirror. The tall trees are magnolias with huge pink blooms in the spring. And there are white birch trees and azaleas, rhododendron and other evergreen shrubs, all grown in that thick green grass.

"The Circle with Founder's Hall is the Hum's most spectacular place on campus," Matt said, as he led them up the walk, "perfect for proms and graduation pictures, except, of course," he arched an eyebrow at Nick, "if you graduate in January, when it's just cold and snowy — nothing blooming. And here's Founder's Hall — it's a copy of the Parthenon. The Greeks built the Parthenon on the Acropolis, a hill overlooking ancient Athens, and dedicated it to Athena, their protector Goddess. You'll study the architecture when you get to Middle School and even get tested on it," he said, starting up the broad steps.

They stood on the wide marble landing and looked out over the trees in the Circle and the gates and iron fencing. "That," Matt continued, "is Corinthian Avenue. It begins in front of the Hum and runs down to Fairmount Avenue 'way down there. The street that runs along the Hum's walls as I told you, is Girard Ave." Girard Avenue was alive with cars and trucks and people. A trolley car, stopped at the corner of both streets, suddenly began dinging loudly and disappeared behind the school's stone Wall.

"That's old number Fifteen. It runs the length of Girard Ave. Starts down by the waterfront, crosses Broad Street, then past the Hum here, and the Zoo in the park and goes 'way out to the edge of the city. The Hum campus was once a farm in the country. Can you imagine how small Philadelphia was then? We can walk to City Hall in about twenty minutes now. It was called Peel Hall farm for the owner, Oswald Peel, who bought it from Richard Penn, Billy Penn's son. Do you know who William Penn is?"

"Yes, Miss Frazier told us. He owned the whole state and called it Pennsylvania. It means Penn's Woods."

"Correct. Have you seen the statue of Billy Penn on top of City Hall? You'll see it when they take you to see the Toy Day parade. It's the tallest statue on any building in the world." He waved at some Biggies going by the base of the steps. "This is starting to sound like a lecture by Miss North, our art teacher. All I need is her clicker." He caught Nick's eye, "Get ready, you'll get it, too; Michaelangelo, Gainsborough, Winslow Homer and the rest."

Matt sat, leaning against the column. Nick went to the next column and sat too. Even Matt looked small against the huge, round column base. "First thing is this building doesn't belong here."

"Huh?" said the astonished Nick.

"A rich, powerful banker man named Nicholas Biddle was the head guy in overseeing the building of the school, starting with Founder's Hall. It was a couple years after Stephen Girard died. He'd been to Greece and musta fell in love with their buildings 'cus he directed the architect to design it like one of their temples.

"It has thirty-four of these columns around it, supposedly to hold up the roof. Look up…see those caps at the top? They're not just plain, square, Doric caps or Ionic caps scrolled up with flower stems, they're the fanciest ones, Corinthian Caps. Elaborate, bell shaped with acanthus leaves and volutes."

"Hey, Miss North," he called across the Circle, "How 'bout a grade for this." He grinned at Nick, then held up a finger, remembering. "I said it didn't belong here because Girard would never have allowed it for his orphanage. He was a modest guy, even though he was rich. He admired the Friends Society, y'know, the Quakers, for their thrifty ways and how hard they worked and the plainness of their homes — can you imagine what he'd say about this marble shrine for his orphanage? Founder's Hall, when it was finished in 1847, was the most expensive building in America. The same Philadelphia architect, Thomas Walter, later designed the Capitol Building in Washington. But it sure is a great building," he exclaimed, as he got to his feet. Nick leaped up immediately.

"What's in there?" Nick said excitedly. "Can we go in?"

"Sorry, those big doors are closed, so we can't go in today." Seeing Nick's disappointment, he added, "It'll be open next month on Founder's Day, when we celebrate his birthday. I'll go down to get Jimmy, and you can come along. I'll take you inside to see his statue standing over his tomb, and we'll go upstairs to the Senior Center and get soda and pretzels, okay?" Nick answered with a wide smile.

The Library was to the left of the main gates, opposite Bordeaux Hall. Matt went in and Nick sat on a bench just outside. Nick remembered the Library had two floors but little kids weren't allowed upstairs; that was for big kids. The Library lady said everyone had to take a book, even if they wouldn't read it, and they should bring it with them when they were brought back in two weeks. Sign your name on the card in the pocket in the back of the book and put it in the little wooden box by the door. Nick liked to read in bed before lights out. Kids who read books borrowed them from kids who didn't, but there weren't many of them. Miss Saunders sometimes made them lie quietly in their beds with their heads on their pillows, while everyone else was reading.

"Okay, let's go." Matt said, as he came out, a book under his arm, "I'm ready to follow Lewis and Clark's trail now." Nick waited again while Matt ran up the steps into Merchant Hall. When he came out, four other Biggies came with him, one carrying a basketball.

"This is one of Jimmy's friends. I'm walking him back from the Library," was enough to cancel the curious looks.

"Where ya from kid," the basketball holder asked.

"Wilkes-Barre."

"Oh, no, another coal cracker like you, Walt. We're getting so many of 'em, the Hum'll probably start teaching us how to be miners in the Mechanical School, soon."

"I'll mine your head with my foot, South Philly dago!" Nick jumped back as the basketball flew past his face. It hit the other Biggie who screamed "Yow!" in mock pain. As the ball rolled onto the grass by Merchant Hall, a whistle blast was heard.

"Great, idiot. You got Stubby Craig after us. Dammit, if he confiscates that ball, it's signed out in my name!" The culprit retrieved the ball and gave an okay-I-know-we're-not-supposed-to-throw-balls-on-the-Main-Road wave to the housemaster, then dramatically tucking the ball under his arm, turned back to face the group with a sardonic smirk.

As they walked, Nick listened, intrigued by their conversation. "I got five hard whacks on each hand for running in the hall and almost bumping Miss Goodrich coming 'round the corner. I said I was late for Spanish 'cus I forgot my homework paper, but nobody believes anybody around here."

"Hell, I got fifteen on the ass Tuesday," sounded like a boast to Nick. "Geez, I couldn't play basketball for two days."

"You got his new paddle, Jewboy. Mr. Conklin made it in his Carpentry Shop for Doc Cooper. Must be almost an inch thick and a foot wide with half inch holes drilled in it. Man, it really stung. When I took a shower, guys were razzin' me about where'd I get those huge raspberries." Nick was surprised to see him laugh with the others. "It's funny now, but it sure as hell wasn't then."

Matt, about to say something to Nick, was interrupted by a female voice. "You boys, stop bouncing that ball." Standing on the Infirmary steps was a figure in white.

"It's Miss Leister, the head nurse," someone murmured. Another wave and compliant expression achieved a satisfactory result.

Nick had been too interested in the conversation to notice the *thunk, thunk, thunk* of the ball on the road. "Whatta place," the kid called Zak said angrily. "For almost eight years, everybody's bossed me. No matter where you are, whatever hour, somebody's always around to bitch or punish you for anything. I can't wait to get out."

Matt turned to Nick. "Better go in the East Wing now and down to the West Wing. You should get there in time to wash up."

When Ned challenged, "Let's hustle, too," they raced away. Nick watched until they got past Good Friends, sorry he didn't say thanks to Matt, and then headed for the East Wing door.

Boxing match and Halloween parade

THIRTEEN

It was the biggest sandbox Nick had ever seen; so big it had see saws, slides, monkey bars and a jungle gym. Atop the jungle gym, Nick could look down at their Juke-Joint. It had a longer line of waiting players than any of the others. He and Henry Wyzykowski and Jerry Magee spent most of Saturday, after lunch, making it. They scooped up a mountain of sand. It had rained yesterday and the sand was still hard. With spoons and knives smuggled out of the dining room, they had carved mini-sled runs. Juke-Joints were gambling games. Kids dropped a marble in the starting groove at the top, hoping it would it run all the way down, missing side grooves that would take them into deadends, and they would lose their marble. If it made it to the bottom, they'd win three marbles and keep their own. Jerry said that was the best deal to get kids to play.

"We've gotten a lotta marbles so far, though," Henry proclaimed to Jerry, as he dropped another loser's into his cap on the sand.

"Hey," Nick yelled down. "Guys, that kid grabbed up his marble from a deadend. Go get him!"

"Yo," Jerry cried, "that's not fair!" and ran after the kid, who was casually walking away. When he touched the kid's shoulder, the kid turned, put both hands on Jerry's face, shoved him hard and turned to walk off. Nick had jumped off the jungle gym and reached the kid in time to shove him hard from behind. He tumbled into the sand, his marbles flying. Jumping up, he brushed sand from his forehead, grimaced at his empty hand and rushed at Nick. A whistle blew — freezing all movement on the huge playground.

"You boys want to fight?" Mr. Hickerson, standing atop the Junior School steps called through his megaphone. "I think we can take care of that." He held out keys. "Someone run and get the boxing gloves." Immediately, the cry went up, "Fight, Fight, Fight!"

Kids leaped off the jungle gym and jumped off swings to run toward Mr. Hickerson. Games ended as players joined the onlookers. They gathered in a circle around him. Others climbed the steps or stood on nearby benches.

Nick and the other boy eyed each other. Through the crowd, held high, came two sets of boxing gloves. "Put them on that boy." Nick's hands were grabbed, shoved into oversized leather gloves and laced tight.

Pushing the thief aside, Mr. Hickerson yelled, "Who wants to fight?" Arms waved from a dozen locations. "Me! Me! Me!" He pointed at a boy whose hands were held out ready to be gloved. He was taller than Nick, a year older, probably nine and he smiled confidently when some onlookers shouted, "Go get him, Taggert!"

"Yeah, kill him!"

"Seckie Four wants a knockout, Tim." A short blast on the whistle, a cheer from the onlookers and the fight began.

Nick edged closer to the boy who suddenly jumped forward and punched him. The thick glove stung his cheek. A roar went up when Nick fell back, but hands caught him and stood him up. The crowd's "Ohh" sounded sympathetic when the boy's next jab glanced off Nick's chin and landed on his shoulder.

"Keep your hands up, Nick," said a familiar voice. Bringing up both gloves in time to deflect another blow, he stepped forward, turned his glove over and struck out from his hip. It landed in the bigger boy's stomach. The crowd cheered again as his opponent *"Whooshed"* and bent over, gasping for air.

Then he rose, leaped at Nick and swung his left hand low. Nick dropped both gloves defensively, but the punch didn't arrive. Looking up, he saw the other glove at his face. *"Whack!"* His nose exploded with pain. His head rocked. Caught again as he staggered back, hands lowered him to the ground on his back. Rolling over, about to push up, he saw blood drops begin to dot the black tar surface.

The circle of spectators, growing larger with each cheer, quieted when he rose, then screamed delightedly as he ran at his opponent, swung with his left glove, stopped it mid-air, and slammed his other glove into the boy's face with all his angry might. An uproar followed when Nick's foe slumped to his knees, his nose in his glove. Mr. Hickerson blew his whistle twice, hard, and stretched his arms over his head. "All done!"

Over the hubbub, he pulled off their gloves, patted each on the head, checked their noses and said something as he pointed toward the Junior School basement entrance. The crowd cheered in appreciation as they pushed their way through. At the first lavatory, Section One's, Nick went to a washbasin, soaked his handkerchief and squeezed the cold water out. Holding it to his nose, he turned and saw the other boy, a few basins away, holding a red and white handkerchief to *his* nose. It just seemed funny to Nick, who smiled. The other boy smiled back. A thunderous outburst could be heard and the boy nodded his head toward the door, his eyes widening in question.

"Let's go!" Nick said and off they went. Pushing through the animated throng, Nick saw the thief standing in the center of the circle. Who was he fighting? Facing him was an even bigger kid, ten for sure, probably in Fourth Grade about to go into fifth. He looked big enough to be in Good Friends.

"Nick," Jerry called over the din, "you did great. And look, that bastard from Section Eight that stole his marble back is getting the shit beat outta him by Seckie Two's giant!" And he was. The kid was so tired he could hardly keep his gloves up to defend himself. The crowd erupted with laughter every time the giant punched the cheat's glove, which then punched *him* in the face. Nick, maneuvering forward to enjoy it even more, was still confused as to why everybody was fighting the wrong guys.

When the kid dropped to his knees a second time, Mr. Hickerson blew his whistle and stopped the fight. The crowd quickly scattered back to their games and sand tent play.

◆

Waiting in line to go to dinner that evening, flush with praise and friendly pats on the back from admirers, Nick gently blew his nose on some toilet paper he'd put in his pocket.

"What happened to your hankie?" Miss Saunders asked, as she started checking outstretched hands.

"Please, Miss Saunders, he got in a fight with some boy and Mr. Hickerson caught him and made him box." Jon Gray was considered guvvie's pet.

"Well," she said, smiling at Gray and looking again at Nick. "Your nose is bleeding again. Get your towel in the lavatory, soak the edge in cold water and hold it to your nose 'til the bleeding stops. Give it and your old handkerchief to the seamstress after breakfast when you go to get a new one."

"Please, Miss Saunders," Nick called after her, "I didn't fight the right boy. I fought some boy from Section Four I never saw before and the kid I was mad at — the thief, he fought a different, great big kid."

"Antoine Zerby, Miss Saunders," said Gray, ever informative.

"I think Mr. Hickerson suspects who might be acting like bullies or troublemakers," she replied with a hint of a smile, "and tries to teach them a lesson."

FOURTEEN

The Junior School was throbbing with excitement. All East Wing boys who were to take trains or buses home stood in a long column stretching down the hall along the sections. Mr. Netherman, surrendering to save his voice, stopped shouting for quiet. He was about to lead the swaying column, staggering with their black suitcases, up the Main Road. At the circle, they would join the bigger Hummers on Founder's Hall steps, waiting for the Martz Buses to come through the open gates. Others joined the crowd about to be transported to the train station.

When the grinning Mr. Netherman, himself infected by the unflagging enthusiasm, finally blew a long blast on his whistle to begin the march, the youthful clamor became earsplitting, resounding off the walls as they exited onto the Main Road. It electrified everyone waiting in the West Wing section rooms, confirming to the young ears that summer vacation had officially begun.

Miss Saunders just couldn't speak harshly to the boys. A glance around the room at them squirming in their chairs and chattering away with others was enough to keep them at their desks. They stacked their suitcases on their desks, and on some were perched square white cardboard boxes, lunches for those traveling a great distance.

After checking the lock on his suitcase for the third time and then opening the box to find two baloney and cheese sandwiches, a hardboiled egg, an apple, an orange, a Hum Mud and a paper napkin, Nick noticed Hennessey, sitting two rows away. He didn't have a suitcase on his desk and his coat was hung behind him on his chair. Nick waved, even yelled his name, but Hennessey, leaning back, seemed disinterested in all activity and conversations around him. Nick tapped Dennis Freeman, sitting between them, on the shoulder and signaled he wanted to change places. Everyone did it when they wanted to move from desk to desk to talk to a friend.

71

"Bob, where's your suitcase?" Bob didn't even look at him.

Freeman, watching them, called out. "He doesn't get to go home."

"Nah. Can't be," Nick said doubtfully, "he went home for Easter."

"But not for summer vacation. Right, Bob?" Freeman said.

"Right," Hennessy looked down at his hands clasped on his belt buckle, "only Easter and Christmas."

"That's crazy," Nick said, "I don't get it. Are your grades that bad?"

"It's not my grades. It's where I live."

"Huh?"

He kept looking at his hands. "They told my mom that we lived in a bad neighborhood and I couldn't go home."

"Then how come you went home for Easter?" Nick questioned.

" 'Cus they think its okay for two weeks at Christmas."

"Didn't your mom do something?"

"She said she couldn't. The papers your mom signs when you come here means they can do anything with you."

"So you won't go home today?"

"No, not this year. I'll go to Hum camp for the first session and then come back here. It's not bad. My mom's allowed to come in on weekends and take me out for a while, but she works lotsa weekends. They told my mom I could come home for summer when I get to the high school."

"That's so rotten," Nick slammed a fist down on Freeman's suitcase, "that'll be about five years. Somebody ought to…" He turned his head and saw Miss Saunders watching him, not mad but not happy, slowly turning her head from side to side. Then the lights started going off and on. Mr. Dunkel, by the door, waited until it was quiet.

"I want all boys who are going by bus or train to line up in twos in the hall. The rest of you stay right here until your mother comes."

72

Nick rose and put his hand on Bob's shoulder, then squeezed the lunch box under his arm, grabbed the suitcase handle and ran for the door. He was going to ride a bus home and see his mom and sister!

◆

Head resting against the window glass in the darkened bus, Nick considered his vacation, as Hummers around him animatedly described theirs. Everyone treated him as though he was different, special — his mom and aunts, the neighbors, even the kids he played with on the street. Lots of questions: Why was it called a college? What was Philadelphia like? How many boys were there? Were teachers mean? What did he study? If you did something wrong, what happened? Did you ever see girls? What did you eat? It went on and on, everyone so interested in him and the Hum. And, he had bacon and toast and a chopped up soft boiled egg with butter in the morning, and Welsh Rabbit and Mom's meatballs with rice in them — he called them porcupine balls — whenever he wanted, and sometimes a bottle of Squirt when he came in from bike riding. When his mom asked, he said yes it was a fun vacation and she smiled, pleased. Suddenly, it was the end of August. Packed in his suitcase were two boxes of chocolate cherries from Aunt Edith and an envelope with dollar bills given with handshakes or hugs from uncles and aunts. He felt sad when his mom and the other moms at the bus station waved and began crying, as the bus started up. He swept the carpets and dusted the furniture when his mom was at the silk mill. Now he couldn't help her. He tried not to cry but couldn't smile, just waved back at her. Mr. Harmon once said, Junior School Girardians had to be little men and men don't cry. Everyone quieted down. The bus was quiet. As he lay back in his seat he wondered how he could feel sad to leave Mom and Janet and yet feel excited, too, about going back to the Hum.

FIFTEEN

Far off, Nick could hear a bell ringing. He was at Harvey's Lake. It was a family picnic. He and his cousin, Eddie, had gotten their legs over the slippery telephone pole chained in the water and were trying to stand up without falling in. The bell kept getting louder, then a bright light wakened Nick.

"Nick, get up, get up." Someone was pulling at his foot. "It's an air raid. Everybody's gotta get up." Sitting up, he rubbed his eyes hard and looked around. Kids were out of bed.

"Waken every sleeping boy," he heard Miss Saunders say. "Section Eleven, put your shoes on, no stockings, and your coat over your nightshirt, quickly." Each boy soon stood at the end of his bed, most leaning on its railing, some with heads down. When the bell in the hallway stopped ringing, Miss Saunders silently waved them to the door and put the light out. They followed Section Twelve down the stairway, other sections in front of them. The stairwell echoed with the shuffling feet of over three hundred eight, nine and 10-year olds, half awake, making their way down to the basement of the Junior School. Lights were being turned off behind them.

Below ground, both West and East Wing landings began at far ends of the building and sloped down to meet in a flat area by the auditorium doors. There were no windows and the lights were out. A few small emergency lanterns hanging on the walls provided a dim light. Along both sides of the entire hallway sat boys, backs against the tile walls, knees up. Nick could just make out the faces of some of the Section Twelve kids across from him.

A loud "Ow!" startled everyone and a housemaster's flashlight shone on someone's face. "Get your legs in, blockhead, do you want a governess to trip over you?" Leaning out, Nick could see Mr. Hickerson near the auditorium doors, holding a flashlight to his face.

74

"Boy, he really looks scary now," Ned Stanton said aloud, raising a chorus of shushes. Mr. Hickerson's strident voice carried down the long hall.

"You boys did fairly well tonight. President Roosevelt would be proud of you. Housemasters are walking up and down, so there's nothing to be afraid of. Put your heads back and try to rest, you still have school tomorrow." Then they heard Mr. Netherman's voice nearby.

"A boy just asked me how long we've been at war. Since it's 1944, this is the third year and we all hope it will end soon." The hall was still except for an occasional cough. Then Mr. Hickerson said, "Miss Piatt has been kind enough to bring along her radio, so I'll plug it in and we can listen…quietly." After a few seconds, Gene Autry's soulful singing rose out of the distant dark, "*Back where a friend is a friend . . .*" but a wave of approving murmurs brought an immediate response. "If you can't keep quiet, I'll turn the radio off."

◆

"The last thing I remember," Nick was digging at his orange half, "was some lady singing about a nightingale that was singing in some square somewhere. I don't know how I got back to my bed."

When the waiter brought the toast to the table it was barely warm and cooled quickly as the plate was passed. Nick lifted a slice and brought it to his nose. As he took a deep sniff, someone said, "Look, Nick thinks he's some sort of a gourmet, I think that's the word."

"Why don'cha lay on the table like one a them Romans eatin' grapes?"

"Yo, Nick," Dylan Finnegan said, holding his plate out. "If you don't want that toast, heave it over here."

Nick gave him a friendly sneer. Even the white Bond Bread from the Shurfine Market at home was better, not just because it was hot, but the way it tasted. Just slightly singed, his mom said, the coal brings out the sweetness in it. He'd poke a long fork in one end of the

75

slice and out the other so it wouldn't slide off. Standing in front of the broad stove with its black top, he'd fit a black iron handle into the slot of one of the six heavy round lids in the stove surface, lifting it and setting it to one side. Leaning forward, he lowered the bread over the hot coals close enough to entice the blue flames that sprang up from the shining anthracite coals to lick it away from him. Sometimes it did in a blazing flash, twisting the slice into a curled black hand. When it was brown and smoking a little, his mother would say, "Quick, let's cover it with a blanket of cheddar cheese before it gets cold."

"Nick's gone crazy, look at him smiling at his toast!"

"Naw, he's just rememberin' something," Tony Cline observed, "what the teachers call 'wool-gathering.' And didja ever notice after grace, when all the Hummers butter their dry toast at the same time, it sounds like Old Marley dragging his chains across the floor in Scrooge's bedroom."

"Stop all the borin' talk." Barr griped, "and eat, though most of this Hum food's awful."

Charlie Mangione answered woefully, "Poor, indentured orphan, what else don't you like?"

"Lots of things around here besides some people. The mushy peas and watery corn niblicks…the string beans are so limp they won't stay speared on your fork. And 'sparagus is something I never saw before and I ain't gonna eat it."

"They don't cut the bottoms off so it's like chewin' on a tree root," Newman added; a country boy who knew every vegetable.

Barr continued, "Has anybody ever eaten mashed potatoes without tough little lumps in 'em? And the Harvard beets taste like candy but I'm sick of 'em."

"So, how come you never give me your peach or pear half?" Mangione asked. "I see you gobble down rice pudding and Jello, too."

"You kin have any of them," Barr said, "if you'll promise to eat my liver next time we get it."

76

"Ugh! No! Never!" The cries were sincere and unanimous. Nick sensed how the dining room clamor quieted when the waiters came out through the swinging doors loaded with those dark brown slices.

"I'll take your liver gravy, though," Mangione offered.

"No way!" was the quick response. The first time Nick tasted liver was the last time. He didn't notice the guys watching him cut it, which took some effort. But the look on his face when he began to chew and got its full flavor was what they were waiting for. Since then, like probably everyone in the dining room, he never again tried to eat the liver. For some unknown reason though, the gravy tasted great on mashed potatoes or bread slices.

"Hurry up, Nick. Take more than one slice on your plate so we can empty the platter and send back for seconds." After stacking the slices on his bread and butter plate, Nick carefully scraped the gravy off each one onto his boiled potatoes. Then spreading his handkerchief over the linen napkin on his lap, he carefully placed the slices on it.

"Smokey, don't put your cleaned ones on the platter. If they see that coming back they'll know what we're doing," Sarky Surgeoner said. He showed Nick how to bundle up his slices and pocket them "Rinse your hankie out 'n hang it on your washbasin railing to dry out."

"Whatta ya do with the slices?" asked Nick.

"They're too damned big and tough to flush down the toilet," Lazarra answered. "We learned that and had to quick mop up the mess. Go outside and throw each one behind a bush. If bushes are taken, throw them over the wall." "Yeah." Bob Kase was watching the tutoring. "Remember when Jim O'Neill said he musta hit somebody, because a piece came flying back over the wall?"

The group laughed so hard they got a stare of suspicion from Miss Saunders at the next table.

SIXTEEN

"Geez, Nick, what happened to you?" Nick looked up from his bowl of tomato rice soup, squinting his bloodshot right eye, flinching when he tenderly touched the swollen arc of red below it. "Looks like you're using that rouge stuff like Miss Steiner, cutie, you really should spread it all over your cheeks." Nick kicked hard under the table, but Cohen, opposite, had already tucked his legs behind his chair.

"You got your laugh, Cohen, go suck up your soup."

"What happened, Nick?" Sam Thomas asked, "You usually come outta fights pretty good."

"I didn't see it coming. Does it look bad?"

"Yeah, it's gonna be black by this afternoon." Nick scowled disgustedly.

"If any teacher asks, just tell her you caught the ball with your eye, instead of your mitt." Nick nodded grimly, accepting Cohen's excuse.

Looking around for a governess, he dropped a slice of white bread in the bowl and began wiping up the remaining tomato and rice soup. Curiosity swept the table when he said, "I don't even know the kid who did it. Coming down the stairs, I got to the landing and this kid was so slow like he was a cripple or something, so I shoved him to one side to get to the door and he just turned and punched me. I couldn't believe it, 'cus everybody pushes and shoves on the stairs. I stopped because my eye really hurt and I got shoved aside, too." Holding the dripping tomato soaked bread over the plate, he pledged angrily, "I'll get even with that little bastard when I see him in the halls. I'll know that walk."

"Don't do it, Nick. It won't be worth it." Cohen said, smiling, "He might bite you this time."

"Sirkeed!" Barr called to nods of approval from others at the table. "The guy just got sirkeed — no wonder he punched you!"

"What?" Nick asked nervously, "does every newbie get…sirkeed?"

"Only if you're not neat." Smokey began jabbing with his knife in little circles, delighting everyone at the table. "You know how they want us Girardians to be," he sang the words, "little gentlemen, so-o-o perfect and so neat at everything."

♦

In the middle of the long first floor hall between East and West Wings was a telephone booth. Inside, Nick sat crouched on the floor, knees up, one foot holding the door ajar so the overhead light wouldn't come on. He had waited a long time after the lights went out before he slipped out of bed, nervousness keeping him awake. Deliberately stepping, heel first, then lowering the rest of his foot, he eliminated the slapping sound feet made on the tile floor. Even the swishing sound of his white nightshirt against his knees seemed to echo down the silent hallway. At the stairs, he held the heavy door until it closed softly, the cool breeze lifting his nightshirt up to his knees. Holding the railing in the darkened stairwell, he made his way down two floors to the first floor where he peered out. That main hall was always brightly lighted, day and night. He saw no one, heard no sounds. As he hurried toward the phone booth, he glanced at the wall clock above the dining room doors; it was almost ten o'clock.

His left hand ached a little from gripping eight quarters so tightly. Peanut Shoell said it'd only cost him seventy-five cents when they let him call his mother because his vacation train ticket to Harrisburg didn't come, but Nick wanted to be sure he had more than enough. He'd asked a lot of kids in the section before he found two with enough change to trade for his dollars. Larry Edelson wanted to know why he needed the quarters. When Nick said he wanted to call home, Edelson said. "Nobody calls home. That phone's off limits, Dumbo Crossan tried it and got caught and was on the grudge line forever. You're gonna get in big trouble!"

Larry didn't understand — he had to do it.

Rising up above the wooden booth walls, he could see through the glass an empty hallway. He carefully placed the quarters in a row on the little shelf. Standing up, his foot still holding the door ajar, he dropped one quarter in the slot. He anxiously shook his head as it clanged loudly all the way down. When he spoke too softly and the operator asked him twice for the name of the city he felt sweaty. I'm gonna get caught standing here. Finally she said, "Please deposit another fifty cents for your first three minutes." He dropped two more quarters in the slot, heard the okay-to-talk hum, dialed the number and kneeled down on the floor, holding the receiver.

"Mom, is that you?"

"Nick, is that you?"

"It's me, Mom, I'm calling from a phone in the Junior School." He tried to keep his voice down, but it seemed loud.

"What's wrong? Are you alright?"

"Yes, I'm okay, but I want to ask you a question."

"Nick, they said I couldn't call you and you couldn't call me."

"I know, I know we're not allowed to use a phone unless it's an emergency. But everyone's asleep and," with another deep breath, "I really need to ask you something." And he blurted it out, "Was I ever sirkeed?" There was a long pause at the other end.

"What? What do you mean were you sirkeed? I don't understand." Nick could hear voices in the background. It was Saturday night, so everyone was at the house. "Uncle Ralph wants to know why you called. He says it must be important to call this time of night. Why did you call?"

Nick could see them all: Mom, Uncle Ralph, Aunt Arlene, Aunt Nannie, Uncle Bill, sometimes even Aunt Edith and Uncle John. They were sitting at the kitchen table. Each had a soup bowl filled with tiny clams, an eggcup full of hot butter, a glass and a bottle of Stegmaier's Gold Medal Beer. In the middle of the table was a basketful of crackers

80

and a big aluminum pot for the empty shells. His cousins, Eddie and Ralphy might be there, too. Nick always sat with them at the newspaper covered dining room table where they had cherry soda with their clams and read some of Eddie's comic books. It was one of Nick's favorite times at home. He blinked hard, picturing them.

"Nicholas, you have to be clearer about your question. What do you mean "sirkeed?" Nick's face felt hot.

"When I go to the bathroom and pee — is my thing, is it sirkeed?"

"Huh? Hon, I still don't understand?"

"Like, cut with a knife like they do here to kids and they walk around like cowboys. Ed Rosen says like Smiley, the funny guy with Gene Autry."

The phone was quiet but he could hear his mother's breathing and conversation in the background. "Like, are they going to cut my," the guys used words he could never use with his mom, then he thought of…"my weenie?"

"Oh — OH!" she said, "you mean are you circumcised?" Laughter flooded Nick's ear. He could hear the word "sirkeed" being said over and over.

"Oh, honey, you were circumcised when you were a baby."

"And," Uncle Bill called out, "they can't do it again, Nick, even if they want to!"

"Poor boy," he heard Aunt Edith say over the uproar at the table.

So happy, so relieved, Nick stood up in the booth. "Mom, I have to go. Thanks for telling me. I had to know. I won't call you again and I'll write you a letter tomorrow."

"All right, luv." He could feel the smile in her voice. "Now you go to bed and never worry about that again. We all love you very much."

"Goodbye, Mom."

Nick hung up, silencing a chorus of good nights. "Whew," he blew out a deep breath, "I don't have to be sirkeed! I don't have to be sirkeed!"

What he had learned earlier scared him so much he wasn't even hungry at the dinner table, but the guys didn't notice. Frank Newman explained that every time new kids came in, whether six-year-old West Enders or guys even nine years old, they were sent to the Infirmary and didn't get back to their sections for over a week. When Nick heard a few were getting their tonsils out, he gleefully announced "Mine were taken out last year at the General Hospital back home."

"All the other guys," Furmanski directed his comments to Nick, "were there to be sirkeed, and that really hurts." Nick put down his silverware and listened. "There were about twenty kids in the ward, all crying every time they turned in bed and at night there was moaning and stuff and kids in other wards coming down and yelling at us to be quiet."

"Tell him about the operation, Frank," Barr said eagerly.

"You go in alone, everybody else sitting outside on benches, scared and trying to be brave. There's a bed in the middle of the room and next to that a table with shiny knives on it. You lay down under a bright light and they pull up your nightshirt. All the people looking down at you have their faces covered. It's scary and nobody talks. Then someone puts something to your nose and holds your mouth closed. You have to breathe it and everything disappears."

"So, you don't feel the knives cutting?" Nick asked.

"No, but it sure hurts when you wake up. There's a nurse sitting right there by your bed and she's real nice but grabs your arm when you try to reach down. She doesn't let you turn or anything; just lie there still, staring at the ceiling and listening to other guys in the beds crying for their mommies. It pains so much ya gotta cry."

"How long did you stay there?"

"Over a week, an' every morning they come and put medicine on. But taking them bandages off — does that ever hurt." He reached under the table, remembering.

"Ya get mad at the tonsil guys when they cry 'cus they get ice cream the next day and we don't. And even when you come back to the seckie, it's painful for a long time."

"Yeah," Jack Pace said, "and guys do funny things around them because it hurts sirkees when they laugh."

When Nick announced apprehensively, "I don't want to hear anymore," everyone did laugh.

Knowing now that wouldn't happen to him, he took another deep breath of relief. He wished he could call his mom back and thank her. Then he realized he was standing up and the booth light was on; turning, he saw Mr. Netherman down the hall by the East Wing, beckoning to him. Nick walked slowly toward the housemaster now standing by the stairway door. Stopping in front of him, Nick looked up. Mr. Netherman was a big man with powerful shoulders and the rest of him was like a tree trunk running down to the ground. Andy Bressi said he was built like Babe Ruth. Nick lowered his head when he saw a rose colored anger flush the man's broad face.

"I can't believe it!" His voice boomed down the empty hall. "You actually came down here in the middle of the night and made a phone call?"

"Yes, sir."

"What's your name?" Nick told him and added, "Section Eleven, sir."

"Well, isn't Miss Saunders going to be happy to hear about this."

"No, sir." He didn't want to look at Mr. Netherman; the housemaster's tone seemed angrier with every response. "Sir, Mr. Netherman, sir, the reason I came down and made a phone call, even though I know it's not…"

83

"Excuses, too?" he bellowed.

"Ow!"

Nick was shocked, more than pained, by the hard slap on his forehead. He stumbled back, then stood up and moved again in front of Mr. Netherman, snuffling his nose to prevent crying.

"First, you were out of bed after lights out. Then, you left the dormitory. THEN you came down and used the phone!" He could hear Mr. Netherman's breathing now.

"Miss Saunders, when she hears about this, will probably make you turn over in bed with your head down so you can't read books at night. And you'll sit alone at your desk in the section while everyone goes down to cartoons on Saturday nights. I don't know what else she'll do, but I'm going to make you so tired you'll never want to leave your bed again. Find me on the playground and you can run around the sand tent until you drop; then stand on the grudge line. That's every afternoon until I think you've learned to follow the rules. Do you understand me?" A silent nod was what he got.

"Go — get to bed!" Nick turned slowly, then jolted forward to escape the kick Mr. Netherman was famous for, racing with slapping feet toward the West Wing stairs.

◆

Mister Netherman followed Nick and knocked on Miss Saunders door, describing the misconduct. After he left, Nick explained why he had to call home and Miss Saunders just told him to go to bed. When she motioned him to come up to her desk that morning, she didn't look mad.

"Nicholas, you explained what you did last night and you know it was against the rules. But I also understand how important it was for you to talk to your mother. You're a good boy and we'll just let this drop and not hear of it again. I also told Mr. Netherman I would take care of punishing you." She smiled at him. Nick smiled back at her, turned and headed toward a Monopoly game just getting underway.

SEVENTEEN

George Green waved a dauber in his face.

"No, no!" Nick threw his arms up, "I don't want to be a hobo!"

Miss Saunders was shaking her head as she watched Green, Loder and some others brush their cheeks and foreheads with black polish. Sleeves up, they wiped it on their forearms, before rolling up their pants a little and blackening their ankles. Torn notebook paper, covered with brown polish was rolled to look like a cigar. Miss Saunders said they could do it, but "no crying" when they had to scrub it off — "all off, including fingernails."

Nick asked Duke Carl, one of the tallest kids in the seckie, not to throw his old nightshirt out in the hamper after showers the night before. After he explained why, Duke gave it to him and he hid it under his mattress.

After hanging his tie, vest, coat and shirt on a lavatory clothing hook, Nick pulled Duke's white nightshirt over him, Miss Saunders having gone out in the hall.

"Great!" It dragged on the floor, covering his brogues.

Next he took his washcloth, soaked it and squeezed it out. He'd waited until most boys had gone outside, then stopping in front of several washbasins he took down toothpowder cans. Shaking powder in his hand, he dabbed the washcloth in it and began patting his arms and hands. When they were white, he patted his face, caking his eyebrows and lips and damped his sideburns before whitening them. Satisfied that most of it was sticking, he went back to his washbasin, took his white towel and pulled it tight over his head, covering his hair and tucking it tightly around his neck.

He was a ghost.

Outside on the playground, hobos, bums, tramps, even a few kids who looked like black-faced Al Jolsons, were loosening laces and dirtying brogues; some adding water to make mud.

Nick saw cowboys and Indians and clowns and skeletons and soldiers and even a few brave kids in dresses and skirts. Hennessy told Nick some mothers who lived around Philadelphia could drop off costumes at the Lodge with the kid's name on it. From a distance, music was heard.

"The band! The band!" hundreds of kids cried joyously.

Quickly, they lined up in columns, section by section. When the band, in Battalion uniforms, halted in front of Junior School, Mr. Hickerson lined the sections up behind them. Moments later, the band stepped out and the ragged throng began marching up the Main Road to "Anchors Aweigh." Mr. Dunkel barked at some kids from Good Friends and Lafayette who stood by the curb, amusing themselves by yelling nasty comments.

Nick heard Mr. Dunkel tell Miss Saunders later that the twelve sections became a bee-like swarm of revelers, some dancing like Mummers, forward and backward, some chasing others, pulling down masks to identify them and waving at onlookers.

Nurses and youthful patients stood on the Infirmary steps; others waved from crowded windows. As they paraded past the halls, Nick saw Biggies watching, some pumping their arms high in approval. Around the Circle past Founder's Hall they went and then back down to the Junior School. When the band suddenly halted and the music ended, everyone collided into others. Nick saw a few were crying or nursing scrapes, having been knocked down and trampled on in the moving fray. As the band marched off silently, a loud cheer went up.

"What's that all about?" Nick asked Leo Troy.

"That's the bonfire!" Troy said, grabbing Nick's arm and pulling him. They followed the mob as it rushed onto the playground and surrounded a pyramid of cardboard boxes. "That must be two stories high!" he exclaimed.

"Stand back, everyone, stand back," Mr. Hickerson cried out. Around the circle, Nick could see Mr. Netherman and Mr. Dunkel waving kids back.

"C'mere, guys," Mike Light called, pointing a thumb at Mr. Hickerson. They squeezed through just in time to hear Mr. Hickerson say to Miss Satherwaite, "Time to let the pagans loose."

With that, he lit a newspaper torch in his hand, held it high above his head and threw it onto the mountain. After a shrill cheer arose, the crowd quieted, bewitched by the spectacle: the whooshing sound of the blaze, the radiating heat; the engulfed boxes, now an orange pyramid, sending fiery fragments into the night sky. When there was nothing left but a seething pile of embers, everyone was ordered inside to wash up for dinner.

◆

"My plate's clean, Miss Saunders."

"Don't tilt your plate, Nicholas, I can see. Yes, go up and get more, though I think they may be out of meatloaf."

Miss Saunders told the section before they went in to dinner that tonight would be a short night. "Some boys asked if we would bob for apples the way we did last year, but we won't because so many of you have used shoe polish this year." Ignoring the low groans, she said "We're going to have an early shower tonight because you have a lot of scrubbing to do. And there will be an inspection when you come out."

Standing in a long line, waiting for seconds, Nick got nudged from behind. "Some fire, eh?"

"Yeah, Bozo, that was great. This was my first one. Do they have a bonfire over in Good Friends?"

"Dunno, my brother's up in Banker and he said some guys used to get dressed up in Good Friends and even in Lafayette. In the halls no one gets dressed up — but they play tricks on guys. Some guys got up in a tree after dark and got another guy to call a kid over and they

87

dropped out of the tree on top of him." He snorted with his nose, "They said the guy almost pooped himself."

"If you two want to talk, go back to your table."

When Mr. Dunkel walked away, Bozo said, as Nick stepped up to the serving cart, "If you think Halloween's great, wait'll winter comes and we got lots of snow on the playground."

"What happens then?"

"That's when the big snowball fights start. Mr. Hickerson and Mr. Sparks call all the sections to line up."

"An' when they say," Jim O'Neill had joined them, "we're gonna have a snowball fight, everybody starts cheerin.' Mr. Sparks goes across the playground, halfway to the sand tent. When he gets there, Mr. Hickerson says 'West Wing, you go over to Mr. Sparks.'

"All the seckies, seven to twelve, run to him and start making snowballs. That's when all the East Wing seckie guys start making snowballs, too, and when Mr. Hickerson yells 'Charge!' everybody starts throwin' snowballs as soon they get close to the enemy. The East Wing governesses," O'Neill added, "go into the West Wing seckies and stand with our governesses and watch from the windows. Miss Saunders said last year, with about four hundred kids, there must have been two hundred snowballs flyin' in the air the whole time."

"I hope we do better than last year," he said glumly. "It only lasted about fifteen minutes, but they drove us all the way down to the railing at the end of the playground by the Mechanical School. Then Mr. Sparks started blowing his whistle to stop. When we lined up in seckies again, Mr. Sparks said he had to stop some real fights. Said we can't be bad sports and if it happened again, there'd be no more snowball fights this winter." Leaning over to Nick's shoulder, he whispered, "It's a lotta fun, but I'd rather be a Biggie. They probably have really good snowball fights."

"Someday," Nick replied.

Enjoying a Hum Mud

President Harry Truman
surrounded by young Hummers

Hum Muds

Girard had its own currency and it was edible. Edible, that is, for the first few days you possessed it; after that it required a therapy treatment to make it toothsome again. At lunch on Fridays, every Hummer, from six-year-old newbies to seventeen-year-old Biggies pondering what will they do after their upcoming graduation, found their bread and butter plate hidden under a dark brown discus. It was a Hum Mud. Five inches in diameter, more than a half-inch thick; it was a dark brown ginger cookie. It could hardly be called a cookie, nothing like those dinky toy ginger snaps so popular at Halloween!

They were rarely eaten at the table; that would be like chewing up a dollar bill your mother enclosed in one of her letters. Hum Muds were money — used as a reward for being the shoe, towel or equipment monitor, for running some errands for a governess or housemaster. And you traded them for anything, from comic books to illegal cigarettes. They were usually stored in desks and lockers to be eaten at leisure in your section room or on the playground or for later use as payment in purchase agreements.

After a few days' storage, Hum Muds lost their hearty ginger aroma and began to harden and within a week they were impenetrable. Smuggled dinner knives were bent in attempts to cut them. There were tales of those in the past foolishly venturing to gnaw on them and ending up in the dentist's chair. You could rap a Hum Mud hard on the corner of your desk, but never do more damage than a dent or two in its uneven surface. If a governess were present you were yelled at for mistreating the furniture.

I believe our obsession with Hum Muds went beyond their value as a currency and delicious confection. We admired their amazing durability, their toughness under all forms of stress and their loyalty in letting us enjoy them long after the desirability of ordinary treats would have expired. Months after they left the oven they could be resurrected and that mystical act could be achieved wholly or piecemeal. The magical potion to accomplish this was not some exotic witch's brew; it was the only one available to indentured orphans at all times — water.

90

Girard College had water fountains everywhere. From child-sized ones throughout the West End and Junior School to adult ones in the Halls, the Infirmary, the Middle and High School, the Library, the Armory and on all playgrounds, water was always at hand.

So, it was normal to find kids lined up at water fountains, waiting to hold a Hum Mud under a restorative soaking of water. You had to wait patiently because it took several minutes before the downpour softened it and renewed the ginger flavor. You usually wet only a portion, since they were almost too big to eat at one time. And what you didn't eat could be stored again. There must have been thousands of partially eaten Hum Muds sitting with whole ones in desks or on locker shelves awaiting their owner's next craving. By your teens you were less enthralled with them, not hoarding as much, more inclined to eat them in a few days while they were still enjoyably al dente.

I was pleasantly surprised when my wife discovered Hum Muds described as Girard College "gingies" in Betty Crocker's classic cookbook. But Frank Sabol, a classmate, said the recipe couldn't be correct. Frank was on the Reserved List with a heart condition and it seems he could roam about, after class, almost at will, and spent lots of time at the Infirmary and in the Dining & Service Building. There he became a friend of Billy the Baker. Supposedly, Billy created the Hum Mud although some say he got the recipe from Charlie Hummel, considered the originator. When the school closed the bakery, Billy retired. He told Frank he left something out of the recipe he gave the school and, like a true German baker, would give the real recipe to his family or take it to the grave with him.

Saving them up before Founder's Day, instead of eating or trading them, could be very a profitable pursuit. Inevitably, old grads, wandering up and down the Main Road, would venture into Junior School or onto the playground.

The typical scenario: Budding entrepreneurs, waiting on the building steps or benches just might have some with them when old grads asked, "Hi, Hummers, do you guys have any extra Hum Muds?" Fresh ones had to be on sale somewhere on campus, but it must have meant something special to get them this way. Years later, I knew how the old guys felt.

A Hum Mud would be thrust out with a generous, "Here take one," followed up with a feeble "Oh, no, don't pay me." The transaction usually concluded with a sheepish acceptance of a dollar and both parties pleased.

And it wasn't unusual to find two or three grandfatherly types bending over a miniature fountain, soaking their Hum Mud to make it edible, their laughter reverberating down the Junior School hall, just as it did many years ago.

Archive photo of The Circle
with Founder's Hall and The Lodges

EIGHTEEN

"Yow!" Cold water spilled out from under the white china cup as he turned it over, splashing down from the shelf onto the washbasin and his bare chest and shoulders.

"A cupee!" McKnight, on his right, declared joyfully. "Somebody set it up last night and really gotcha this morning. Perfect!" McKnight, clearly awed at how well someone pulled a damp washcloth out from under an upside down mug and kept all that water inside, ignored Nick's angry stare.

Fully awake now, Nick looked down the line of washbasins and saw Scanlon, leaning way over past other faces, with a broad smile, his eyes bright with satisfaction. Scanlon was one of the seckie bullies; laughed at onlookers after he shoved little newbies around and taunted them, like it was a joke, not mean at all. Even Miss Saunders knew it and sometimes seemed to punish him for no reason.

When Nick was standing in line waiting for seconds on pancakes, Scanlon came up and shoved Nick aside and stood in front of him. Nick said "Hey, wise guy," but didn't do anything. He knew he had to at least shove him back, but Mr. Holman came up to the line just then and it'd look like he started it. When he got back to the table, Cohen announced, "Guess what, guys, Scanlon's after Nick now."

Nick already knew it. Last Tuesday, on his way up the stairs to class, his books were poked out from under his arms, falling down the steps, homework papers flying, guys stepping on them. He knew Scanlon, the only one looking down from above, did it.

On the playground, Nick and George Green were sliding like snakes down the monkey bars, when someone yelled, "Hey, look up at that zeppelin." He did and sand rained down on his face. His eyes hurt with grains in them and his tongue, coated with sand, made him cough when they stuck in his throat. Green helped him climb down and led him to the fountain.

"Who's on the monkey bars!" Nick cried as he splashed water in his eyes.

"No one's even near it," Green answered, stepping back as Nick spit out a mouthful of water.

"Hey, you!" It was some kid they didn't know. "I seen that big kid that's so pushy when your seckie lines up throw sand up at you and run. See, he looks like he's waitin' for stilts at the equipment tent…with the blue vest."

"Scanlon," Nick added softly, and cursing for the first time in his life, "that sonofabitch. I'll get even with him."

◆

At dinner, Nick was still seething. Pulling his white linen napkin out and banging the dull nickel ring down on the table, he had everyone's attention. Even "stoker" Wyzykowski, usually wolfing food while watching for the waiters to come swinging through the kitchen doors with seconds, turned to watch. Nick saw Cohen, across the table.

"So, what's with the smile, Rabs?" Nick knew it was short for Rabbi and it bothered him when it was used, but he was so mad.

Cohen smiled back scornfully. "Nick, I actually like you, you'll be a good Hummer someday, which is why I'm gonna save your life." His comment brought group moans, until he said, "I don't like guys like Scanlon," to everyone's approval. "But physically you can't win. You're not big enough…and you're too nice." More groans. "You need to do what I suggested Lenny Rubino do."

"Lenny Rubino, wasn't he the kid who hated milk? Only drank water. What happened to him?" Andy Bressi asked.

"He was so mean to Rubino, he made him drink his milk, and sometimes Scanlon filled his own glass again and made him drink that." Nick's hands, under the white napkin on his lap, were clenched.

"Norm, tell me what it is — I gotta do something."

Norm leaned toward Nick. "Okay, here's what I'd do."

Scanlon took his time descending the stairway to the lavatory. He'd be a little late for lunchtime wash up — he was a little late to everything, just to show them they didn't own him. Turning at the first floor landing, he didn't look at the small window in the door where an eye in the lower corner blinked excitedly. A few steps later, he heard the door open and the normal start of a stampede as Hummers raced on the stairs.

"What the . . .?" he yelled, as his mackinaw was pulled over his head. Then he was pushed. "Ow!" he banged his shoulder on the railing and rolled down the last few steps, his head wrapped in the coat. "Ow!" he grasped an ankle. "Yow!" He reeled from a punch in the shoulder. "Ouff!" as a knee to his back slammed him to the floor.

It was a scene of heavy breathing and vigorous motion, but not a word was spoken. As Scanlon lay whimpering, head still covered, Conradi pointed at Nick and then at Scanlon. Nick made a short kick, just as the victim rolled over. The toe of the brogue met a kneecap and an anguished scream echoed in the four-floor stairwell. After an arm wave by Lazarra, the gang scrambled up the stairs and out the door.

◆

Fifteen minutes later, Mr. Durkin, who was overseeing Sections Eleven and Twelve that day, came into the lavatory. "Hurry it up, Eleven, it's almost time for lunch."

"What in the hell happened to you, Scanlon?" everyone heard Mr. Durkin ask. Nick joined the group waiting near the door. Scanlon, crouched down in front of Mr. Durkin, clutched his knee, a red scrape on his cheek. Looking up, he revealed a darkened arc below his left eye.

"Pick up that overcoat!" the housemaster said sternly. "We don't drag our good coats around like that, boy." A surge of enjoyment swept over the small crowd. "Yeah, you should know better," a voice called out, taking advantage of the situation. "Hang that up right now," another ventured, spawning quiet laughs. Watching the big kid hobble toward the hook where his mackinaw belonged, Mr. Durkin said. "I asked what happened to you?" Scanlon didn't even look at Mr. Durkin.

"I tripped over my coat and fell down the steps, Mister Durkin." Nick felt a light poke in his back. "That bastard's lookin' for sympathy, can ya imagine that?" Nick could sense O'Neill's grin and couldn't subdue his. Mr. Durkin scratched the back of his head. "As soon as lunch is over, find me. I'll give you a pass to the Infirmary."

"Aw, Sir, I'm okay. They'll keep me 'til dinner and I'll miss swim class and playground. Please." But Durkin was already in the hall, announcing "Okay, Section Twelve, start up the stairs and no running."

◆

The next morning, Ed Swartz approached Nick at his washbasin. "Hey, tough guy, whatta ya gonna do when Scanlon comes after you now? Everybody knows what happened, somebody leaked it."

Nick had thought about this possibility last night after lights out. What I gotta decide is — should I fight him? If I just ignore him, he'll probably start a fight and I'll hafta fight him. But if I don't say anything, he'll probably start a fight anyway, thinking I'm afraid of him. Either way, I'm gonna hafta fight.

Somehow, he felt relieved knowing what he'd have to do. But what was he going to do? He wouldn't bite, but he'd kick, and pretty quick too. Scanlon was bigger and fatter, so maybe he couldn't jump away too fast. Remembering Scanlon's wheezing he thought, I'll have to keep circling and try to punch him in the gut. Pressing his head a couple times deeper into the pillow, he decided he'd better start practicing moving his head up and down fast like boxers in the movies. Tomorrow, on the playground, he'd practice with Reds Eckard, the best fighter.

"Okay, okay, ya don't hafta shove!" Swartz said, as he was pushed to one side. Scanlon's face appeared in the mirror, right next to Nick's. Geez, Nick said to himself. Taking a deep breath he hoped nobody would notice, he thought, here goes. Turning, he leaned against his washbasin, dropping his hairbrush casually over his shoulder into the sink and crossed his arms on his chest. He looked into Scanlon's eyes and made his face as intimidating as he could. Holding his breath, he just stared. Very slowly, like that scary guy who plays vampires in the movies, he squinted, slowly closing his eyes, but not all the way, just part way, and keeping them like that. Lips pressed together, he hoped his mouth looked mean.

The bully stared back and didn't seem affected by Nick's go-ahead-and-do-something-and-see-what-happens look. He's not even blinking, Nick thought. I can't keep this up. Then, after what seemed *so* long, Scanlon squinted his eyes at Nick, turned and walked away.

NINETEEN

Several boys were ahead of Nick, walking down the steps to the basement level entrance and the West Wing lavatories. Suddenly the two doors burst open. Everyone had to jump back; one of the boys, stumbling over the bottom step, sat down hard. "Dammit!" he cried angrily, quickly putting his hand over his mouth when he saw Mr. Hickerson inside holding both doors open.

"Did anyone," Mr. Hickerson paused, annoyed that he had to take a deep breath, "see a boy run out of here?"

"No sir," one boy said. The others, like Nick, shook their heads also. They watched in quiet trepidation as Mr. Hickerson quietly rubbed his moustache, surveyed the noisy playground and said, "I saw a boy run down the hall — no one's supposed to be in the building, everyone should be on the playground. I chased him down the stairs from the first floor and he had to come out here. Line up. Someone must be lying." The boys and Nick hurriedly lined up side by side on the bottom step. They watched him, at attention, wide-eyed, as he searched their faces for suspiciousness.

"I want to know who that boy was." Hands on his wide hips, he waited, but the only sound was of playground clamor. "Tell me and you'll be better off," he said in threatening tone.

"Honest, Mr. Hickerson," the smallest of the three said, "we," he pointed to the other two, "were just coming from the monkey bars. We didn't see anyone."

"What about you?" His face loomed in front of Nick's.

"No, sir." Nick's voice seemed creaky. "I was just gonna run in quick to the bathroom." Stepping back, Mr. Hickerson looked quietly to one side for a few seconds, then shouted angrily, "Someone's lying! I can't stand liars."

"Sir, we really didn't . . ."

"All of you go stand at the wall by the water fountain." They scrambled up the steps and over to the stone wall, watched with interest by others. Spacing themselves by holding their arms out, they formed a line, arms length from the stone wall and arms length from each other. After a few minutes someone glanced furtively back and announced, "Hickerson's over by the Main Road with Mr. Wileman." Nick turned to see the others looking at him. One said, "Are you the kid he's looking for? Maybe you ran out and then turned back to act like you were with us."

"I didn't do it, guys. I really was just behind you."

"Well, we didn't do it, either." Heads nodded. Nick nodded, too. He believed them. "Ow!" Someone got slapped on the back of his head.

"I could see you were talking from over there. Now, all of you — around the Sand Tent, go!" The group broke into a run. The Sand Tent was a thirty foot square pavilion of sand, edged with railroad ties, with a high metal roof over it. It was located in the far corner of the playground, the greatest distance from the Junior School west entrance. Racing along the concrete sidewalk, they called out "Watch out!" or just "Move!" to unsuspecting walkers or bystanders, weaving around them, sometimes pushing off them or knocking them aside to the accompaniment of angry cries and curses. Circling the Sand Tent, they headed back, drawing taunts as they crossed through two soccer games.

Lined up again, breathing hard, they heard, "That wasn't good enough — do it again and run harder or you'll keep doing it!" When they returned this time, they were bent over, holding their knees, heads down, gasping loudly; someone was coughing. "Straighten up. I hope you're satisfied with the consequences of your lying." They stood upright again, arms down, studying the ugly gray stones in the wall. After about twenty minutes one boy checked his watch and announced the time quietly. Hearing Mr. Hickerson's voice far away, someone felt it was safe to talk. "Geez, they're always telling us in class and chapel that we have to be fair and honest and not cheat and —"

"And ya gotta take whatever comes like a man."

"You mean like a Hummer?" Nick asked.

"Yeah, right, like a Hummer," the kid on the end replied.

A whistle blew. Then it blew again. "You four," Mr. Hickerson called, "over by the wall, you're dismissed." He waved them away from the wall, turning back to a boy standing in front of him, head down. A small crowd had gathered around them

"Let's go see what happened."

They rushed off toward Mr. Hickerson while a resentful Nick slowly sauntered toward the lavatory steps again. As he started down he heard "Hey, you." He turned to find one of the guys who'd been punished with him, a sneer on his face, "Guess what, buddy? That old bastard just caught the kid coming out. He said he was hiding behind the shoeshine rack in Seckie Nine's lavatory, 'n we got punished." With that, he pushed past Nick, slamming the door so hard Nick expected the window to shatter. But it didn't. As Nick pushed the door open he thought, I guess these skinny wire strings that run through the glass must make it a lot tougher. Maybe that's what Hummers should have.

TWENTY

"How long have you been here?" the weak little voice asked. "Almost a year and a half." Nick looked back at the tiny kid trailing him, his cheeks tear-stained. Probably seven, maybe six, Nick thought.

Miss Saunders asked Nick if he would take the new boy up to the seamstress and shoe shop. When they got to the seamstress' room, the woman said pleasantly, "Ahh, a new boy ready to be dressed like a Girard gentleman. Do you want to wait?" she directed at Nick.

"Outside, please," he answered, where, after a drink from the hall fountain, he sat down, his back to the wall. "Poor kid," Nick murmured aloud, recalling those days, "when he comes out I'll tell him it won't be long until Christmas vacation." Head resting on the cold tile wall, he thought of his vacations.

I've been home for six vacations so far. Some guys go to the Hum camp in the Poconos, especially ones that don't even have a mom. I'm just glad to get home. Easter's okay, but so short. One week. You get home and it's time to come back. One thing I hate about vacations, as soon as people say how glad they are to see you they ask, "When do you go back?" His reverie was interrupted by a loud whisper.

"Hey, Nick." Frank Caruso's head tilted out from the hallway that ran down to the shoe room. He wasn't allowed up here right now, Nick knew. "We're playing Seckie Nine today at 4-o'. You gonna play outside, right?" Nick nodded yes emphatically and Frank's satisfied face disappeared.

Seeing Caruso made Nick think of all the new things at the Hum that nobody knew about at home. He remembered the first time he looked out the seckie window and saw kids chasing a ball and kicking it. Four groups of them were playing on the huge playground. When it rolled across a white line, everybody stopped, someone picked up the ball and threw it and they all started kicking it again. One kid stood in a wooden frame with a net attached to it. When they kicked the ball at him, he grabbed it and kicked it 'way down the field over everyone's head. And when the ball went past him, the other team cheered. He asked Frank, who'd come over and stood by him, what they were playing.

"Are you crazy, that's soccer — that's our best game! The Hummers, that's what they call our team of Biggies in the newspaper, are the best around. Mr. Sweigart says they almost always win the city championship. He said Hummers went once for five years without losin' a game."

Caruso explained the game and once Nick started playing it, it was his favorite thing to do after school. This year he played a couple times each week on Section Eleven's team. He described soccer to the kids on the street at home, but nobody ever heard of it. Evan Evans made fun of it, said it sounded sissy compared to football. That didn't bother Nick; Evan was a bit of a bully and everyone knew it, so he didn't have any real friends. Nick didn't feel sorry for him because he always made fun of Nick's knickers. Nick hated them. Everyone at the Hum did. And you didn't get long pants until you were fourteen years old and went up to Banker or Merchant Hall. Or you were five foot, six inches and there weren't many kids in Junior School that tall.

The door opened and the newbie came out, looking like a midget Hummer.

Hummers all look alike, Art Felberman once grumbled to Miss Saunders when they were getting measured for new suits. "With our shirts and ties, and coats and knickers, and our mackinaws and watch caps and gloves . . .and our brogues…ya gotta look somebody straight in the face to find out who he is, even kids in other seckies look just like your friends."

Nick didn't mind wearing them in the Hum; it was when he was away from the Hum, knickers made him look so different. He felt people looking at him, especially other kids.

"Now we have to go to the shoey," he said to the kid, who was studying his knee length, argyle-patterned stockings. "Listen, kid, I've been here a while and one thing ya gotta learn," he raised his hands in front of him, palms out — "if somebody pushes ya, ya gotta push him back, and just as hard." A response, if any, was muffled. The newbie's mouth was buried in the arms of the raincoat and overcoat he was carrying. Guess I scared him now, Nick thought. His eyes look like a boiled egg at breakfast, except with tiny, blue marbles for yellow yolks.

After stacking the coats on a chair by Miss Saunders' apartment door in the dormitory, they went down another hall. "Here's the shoey. G'wan in, he knows what to do. I'll wait out here for you."

Normally, kids aren't allowed to sit in hallways, but it was empty and quiet and everyone was in their sections downstairs, so Nick sat down. He yawned, yawned again and stretched his arms out. He was tired. Some guys were talking after lights out last night and didn't own up when Miss Saunders came out. So everyone had to get out of bed and stand at the ends of their beds. It must have been over an hour before she let them go back to bed; and there would be no radio tonight at bedtime.

A door opened and a voice wakened Nick. "Polish them every day and if the heel comes off or you start to see a hole in the bottom, and you can't find the shoe monitor, get a pass, come here and get in line." The boy came out in brogues, hands together holding a pair of oxford shoes everyone wore to Chapel on Sundays. Nick led him to Section Eleven's dormitory again and told him to put the shoes with his other clothes by Miss Saunders' door and she'd assign him a bed after showers.

"We can go back to the seckie now, newbie," Nick said. As they started down the steps, he wondered, should I tell him his mother won't be there?

GOOD FRIENDS
Bon Ami—Stephen Girard's Favorite Ship

Grades 5-6 Ages 11-12
1946 -1947

TWENTY-ONE

In a corner of the dormitory a small group stood discussing their impending doom. "Geez, ya work hard to get promoted to Fifth Grade and look what ya get, split up," Barr wailed.

"I think they do it on purpose," Jim Swahl said, "splitting up guys from the same seckie. It's like they don't want friends to have friends. 'Betcha I won't know anybody in Section Eighteen."

"Maybe they think kids'll be less trouble if they're not with their friends," Tony Cline ventured.

"And with the grade divided up into three groups, we probably won't be in class together," Barr said, then added hopefully, "but we can see each other on the playground."

"Sure," a sullen Nick answered, "you'll be playing on Fourteen's team and I'll be playing against you on Twenty's."

◆

"You boys have had it very nice so far." The man looked huge and threatening, his tone harsh, mean. He stood on the curb, across the Main Road from the steps leading to the Junior School's main entrance, the wide steps crowded with about ninety boys, jostling nervously.

"When you were at the West End, you were six and seven and had a governess who was like a mother to you. Then you came up to the Junior School and another governess. You did everything in one building: eat, sleep, go to school, see cartoons in the auditorium and play games outside and relax in your section rooms. Now, it's time for you ten-year-olds to test your ability to become self-reliant, which is what Girardians are supposed to be." Nick looked to see Hennessey's response. His expression was stern.

"When you cross the road to Good Friends today, you're entering a new life. From now on, every year or so, your life will change. You'll leave friends behind, and teachers and governesses you

105

know. Everything will be new. You'll have to live and get along with boys you don't know and you'll answer to new authority figures." Nick couldn't hear any undertone conversations, no smart-guy remarks or jokes, no sneaky poking, just shifting feet.

"You'll have a bit more freedom here, but it comes with more responsibility…and tougher punishment."

"What Mister Dorrance is saying," boomed the voice of a man who had been standing quietly by his side, "is that in these buildings, Good Friends this year and Lafayette, where you'll be next — with probably fewer of you — we have a reputation. This is where we take the child out of you and prepare you for manhood." The youthful gathering was stone-still; most faces downcast, a few defiant.

"Now," the first man said, "you've already been told your new section number. When I call your names I want to hear a loud 'Here!' Then cross over and go to your new section and be quiet. No talking. When everyone's in your section, your new governess will come in and tell you what you will and what you won't do. Okay, let's start with . . ." a few papers slipped from his hands; he retrieved them, looked at the top sheet and said, "Bressie, . . ." A moment later, Hennessey yelled "Here!" swinging a goodbye elbow into Nick's side before running off.

There he goes to Section Seventeen, Nick thought. Don's in Fourteen. Jock's in Twenty-Three and I'm in Twenty. Friends for almost two years and they take them away. Sometimes I hate this place. I wish I could find some way to get even with them. Then his name was called. Racing across the road and up the steps, into Good Friends' wide hall, he noticed a boy just inside the doorway. "Hey, do you know where Twenty is?" The boy turned to Nick with a surprised look.

"Gosh, I don't know. I walked over a while ago 'cus I'm on the Restricted List and can't run. I'm looking for it, too. Where's everybody?" The boy smiled when Nick said the man must have dropped his papers again and everybody's still outside. Then he nodded over Nick's shoulder. "Let's ask that kid by those stairs. Looks like he's waiting for somebody."

"Yeah, he should know," Nick replied. Sprawled across the bottom step, the boy blocked the stairs with his legs. His look told them he knew they were dumb newcomers from Junior School.

"Down the end of the hall," he snapped at the question, throwing an arm in that direction. As they got to the end of the hall, a man appeared, another big man.

"Where do you think you're going?" he demanded in a gruff voice.

"To Section Twenty, Sir," said two voices in trembling unison.

"Turn around and follow me. You're at the wrong end of the building."

They followed him, and as they stopped at the doorway to Section Twenty, he said, "Who told you to go down there?" They pointed tentatively to the boy at the stairs who was calling up to someone. As they watched, the man went over to the boy, grabbed his tie, lifted him up in the air with one arm and began shaking him vigorously. Nick and the other boy inched around the door until they could no longer see what was happening. In the still empty room, they stared at each other with fearful eyes, paralyzed by the choking sounds.

TWENTY-TWO

"You'll have to move a lot faster than that!" Her tone was menacing, and after a few seconds she delivered, snapping, "That's a demerit for you back there. No, two demerits. When I speak I expect your full attention."

Nick recognized the terrified kid's face from Section Twelve. He hadn't been clued in. Nick felt lucky. An older kid sitting near him said, before she came into the room, "Listen, Buddy, if Lockwood speaks to you, jump up quick and stand at attention — and look straight at her, or you'll get a demerit, and maybe a whack on the side of the head if she's near enough to you."

Later, after she dismissed the section and everyone surged out onto the playground, Nick searched out that same kid. He was talking with two other kids. They're all probably twelve years old, Nick thought.

"Thanks," Nick said, walking up to him. He nodded and seemed pleasantly surprised by the remark. After asking Nick's name, he said, "My name's Blackwell, Ed Blackwell," and pointed a thumb at the others. "This is Tony. Tony Campo." That kid was even taller, but kind of big in the middle; everything about him seemed brown; his eyes, his hair, his skin. Nick had to grin back when he smiled broadly and his white teeth seemed to leap out of his bronzed face.

"Hi, kid, welcome to Good Friends and the Middle School. If there's anything ya want to know, go to him." He jabbed his thumb at the kid on his left. That kid was just a little bigger than Nick. Hair almost white, freckled face and white skin. He was one of those wiry, full of energy guys Nick had come across playing soccer in Junior School. "He's Mick, Mick Ward," Campo went on, "Yur guy if ya like trouble and wanta spend your time tryna talk your way outta U's and VO's...and getting your hands and ass paddled once a week." Blackwell nodded, approvingly.

"Ha!" Mick said smugly, "These guys get their share of grudge lines and red bottoms."

"C'mon," Blackwell said, walking away, "let's go."

"Thanks, again, Ed." Nick called after him.

"Don't call him that, unless you want a busted lip. "His real name is Edgar," Tony said, "but he hates it. 'Course, everybody over here calls everybody by their last names, so he gets Blackwell. We call him Blackie."

"Let's go, Campo," Blackwell insisted, "I wanna go down the end of the playground by the Armory. Somebody said there's a chunk a rock missing and it's easy to get a foothold for hoppin' the wall. Let's check it out."

As the trio went off, Nick roamed over to the benches lining the Main Road side of the playground. He could see across to a soccer game on the Junior School playground. Gabby Purkis threw the ball in and Dick Baumann gave it a good boot. It was his team, Section Eleven, playing another seckie. Excited, he sat down to watch, even cheering, "Good try, Sam," though he knew Thomas couldn't hear him. When Dar Klinger trapped it, passed it to Bob Nordstrom, and everybody began racing downfield, Nick was suddenly surprised to find he was feeling sad. His eyes felt tired and he needed to take a deep breath, then another. Maybe they'd all come over next semester. Standing slowly, he turned, stepped over the bench, and sat down, his back to the game.

His world, the one he had known for over two years, the only one he knew, was over there. He was used to everything there: what you did every day; watching buddies pulling tricks without getting caught; having close friends you could say anything to. He had gotten used to, most of the time, being away from home. He liked hearing about home in his mom's letters and got homesick for a little while when he came back from vacations, but that didn't last once he got back to the seckie and all the guys. Now he could never go back. Never play on Eleven's teams, swing on the swings and wrestle guys in the sand, even ask Miss Saunders what might be a dumb question...Junior School might as well be a thousand miles away.

He knew it the first time Miss Lockwood strode into Section Twenty. Tall, with wide shoulders and long arms, she was a lot younger than Miss Saunders and moved very fast. Her shiny black hair was cut short in what his mom called a page boy, but pulled into a knot at the back. She wore no lipstick and her cheeks weren't powdered, so her face seemed hard, not soft. Her dark blue dress hung straight down on her, seeming to know not to sway when she moved.

"You Junior School boys who just came over know the demerit system. That goes on here, too. But here we expect you to do things a lot faster, and you're only told once, that's it. Don't plan on using excuses. Your imaginations aren't good enough to fool us over here. We've heard them all, and they'll just get you additional demerits. Behavior-wise, what does start here, and will go until to the very day you graduate — though some of you won't have to worry about that — is that bad behavior will not only get you the grudge line, it will get you sent to Dr. Cooper for a physical reprimand and...it can get you a U or a VO."

Waving down some upraised hands, she went on, "A U stands for unsatisfactory behavior. You can be awarded that for a variety of reasons. Breaking things, constantly getting into fights, being caught somewhere where you're not supposed to be, not being in class or coming in late, not doing your assigned chores, smart-alecky responses. You usually won't get one with the first infraction, just some demerits or a paddling. Do it often enough and we decide this last time earns you a U. It goes on your report card, a letter goes out to your mother or guardian, and you get punished, losing passes to go home on weekends or out to the park, lots of grudge time and an unforgiving paddling by Dr. Cooper.

110

"A VO is for Very Objectionable behavior. That includes such no-no's as getting caught smoking, on campus or off, and going off-campus illegally by climbing the wall. Get three VO's in one year and you'll go off campus for good, through the front gate." She turned, walked to her desk, and as she sat down, said, "Three VO's, like three strikes in baseball, and you're out. Sometimes, a few U's and VO's over several semesters, they'll decide you'll never become an acceptable Girardian, and your poor mothers will have to take you back."

She gave a brief description of how life was to be lived in Section Twenty, ranging from personal cleanliness to language; about the dress code, dining habits, punctuality and chore responsibility. "Your homework is between you and your teachers. Do it or don't — it's your responsibility, not mine." Kids who were beginning their second semester in Section Twenty sat quietly, watching and listening. No one moved even when she stopped talking.

Taking the lid off a cardboard box at the edge of her desk, she said, "All you new boys come up and take a lock out of this box." As Nick and about a dozen others lined up and picked out locks, she pointed at a boy. "Deibel, show them where our dormitory is. You boys pick out a bed that doesn't have a pillow and find yourself a locker. Then go back to your old section, gather up your clothing, hang it in your new locker and go out to the playground. The rest of you — dismissed."

Following Deibel up two flights of old, wide wooden steps, they entered a large, open dormitory room. The walls had a few small windows and were lined with green, metal lockers. There were four rows of beds — two along the side walls and two rows, head to head, down the middle of the room. Nick walked fast to the far end of the room and sat down on a bed, until the clanging of locker doors alerted him. He ran to the nearest wall, checking to see if each was locked. Another kid got to one just before he did. The one he did find wasn't very close to his bed, but he decided others might be even further away.

A kid nearby said, "Great, even with all our clothes there's lots of room."

"Well," said Nick, to a round of nearby laughter, "maybe we'll need that room to stack all the demerits we're gonna get."

After retrieving his clothing and shoes, he put his only possessions up on the lone shelf: an empty chocolate cherries box filled with letters and birthday cards from home and a thin, square wallet his Aunt Nannie gave him at Christmas. It held pictures of his mom, his sister and his dad and a picture of Jesus in a garden. As he closed the door he thought, maybe next time I go home I can get a big picture of Mom and Janet and stick it on the inside of the door.

"Hey guys," the Deibel kid said in a loud voice, "don't lose your key or you'll have to saw the lock open and the guvvie will make you grudge and she'll find work for you to do to pay for a new lock. You can't go out and buy your own. See how these beds are made?" he went on. "Watch guys near you and make your bed exactly like that. Not just covering the bed, neat like, like in Junior School. You're supposed to be able to bounce a quarter on it. She comes through sometime during the day, we don't know when, but you'll know you got two demerits if you find your bed tore up."

"What the hell is this," someone asked, "an Army camp?"

"Yup, that's what it is," Deibel affirmed. "Guys say she got out of the Army when the war ended, and came to work here at the Hum. She was some kind of WAC officer and musta liked it, 'cus she still acts like it, and we gotta live with it."

Junior School's not a thousand miles away, Nick thought, it must be a million miles away.

TWENTY-THREE

"Where you going with your first Pass Out, Nick?" Walt asked. He was the kid in the next bed, with the funny last name, Uebele. "You're lucky. I've gotta go home. But your mom lives upstate so you get to go anywhere you want to."

Nick heard in Junior School that one of the benefits of going over to Good Friends were Passes Out. They were actually passes to the park or to go home, but nobody knew where you went after you went through the gates. You got them on Saturdays after lunch and had to be back and washed up for dinner at 6 o'clock. And next year, in Lafayette, you could go out on Sunday afternoons, too.

"I've never been outside before, so I'll probably start by…"

"I want all of you to stand by your lockers," Miss Lockwood, in the center aisle, demanded. Conversations stopped and bustling was heard as newcomers rushed from their beds to their lockers. "When I call your name, you answer with the number on your locker. Deibel?"

"Nine Eighteen, Miss Lockwood."

"Whitmire?"

"Nine Twenty Seven, Miss Lockwood."

Nick answered to his name, "Nine Thirty Nine, Miss Lockwood," and sat down on his bed.

"Hold it right there, Mister, I'm not finished yet." He stood up, stiff, at attention. "You probably all know about Pass Outs to the park and home. If your mother has sent a letter saying she wants you to come home on Saturday afternoons and she'll be there, she'll have to give you the money to take the trolley or subway and you'll have to be back by 5:30 to wash up for dinner. Turn up later and you won't get out next week. You can call your mother and tell her why."

"Can we go home every weekend?" someone asked, hand raised.

"It's a privilege and I decide who deserves it. You can request one on Thursdays or Fridays. Anyone who gets three demerits in a week, don't waste your breath. As far as these locker numbers go, don't forget them. From now on, here, and in Lafayette and all of the halls, you'll have a number, the one on whatever locker you get. It's for Check Ups, to find out if you're where you're supposed to be."

"Geezus," a skinny kid named Toizer whispered, "we're prisoners."

"You, Mister Bigmouth," she pointed at him, "can see me downstairs and get in some grudging to start life here. And forget about getting out this weekend."

"All of you," she continued, "sometime this week find your way to the seamstress, during your playtime and with a pass from me, and take your coat, overcoat and vest. She'll put your number inside. That way, if the Housemasters find anything hanging on a playground railing, soaked after a rain or snow, they can locate the culpable one and take suitable action." Picking up the clipboard, she said, "You're dismissed. Everyone must be out on the playground. No one better be in the building."

◆

Walking alone along the edge of the huge playground where four baseball games were underway, Nick saw Bob Hennessey at bat and cheered when Hennessey whacked the ball. The left fielder, standing near the shortstop in the next game, was half watching that game to make sure he didn't get hit, and Hennessey's ball went by him. The first baseman in the other game picked it up and very casually threw it back, drawing curses from the left fielder who was being vilified by his team. Hennessey easily raced to second base and, hearing Nick yell again, waved back.

Nick turned away when he heard his name. "Yo, Nick!" It was Hoppy, Bill Hopkins, a kid he'd met for just a short time in Seckie

Eleven. He was just a year or so older than Nick but he was in Lafayette, already.

"Hoppy, how'd you get to Lafayette so quick?"

"When you came in, I was almost eleven and went to Good Friends, and now I've been twelve for a while and they sent me to Lafayette."

"Guys in Lafayette are supposed to be thirteen and go up to the halls when they turn fourteen, right?" Nick asked.

"Yeah, but between when the school year ends, twice a year, and your age, it's just crazy. Plus, as Mr. Fretz said, it depends on your maturity, too." With that, Hoppy stuck his thumbs into his belt and started raising his shoulders up and down, like he was a big deal. Nick punched him on his shoulder and Hoppy laughed. "Nick, nobody can figure it out. It's the Hum's way. Whatever they do, that's it. I hope you can come over to Lafayette while I'm still here. 'Course if you're not in my seckie, you're an enemy."

A whistle sounded. Then a few more blasts, more insistent. All movement stopped, then instantly erupted from all corners of the huge playground, carrying bats, balls, gloves and tetherball paddles, boys began running towards the lone figure standing by the outdoor toilet building. "Mousey Elman's pulling a Check Up," Hoppy said.

"Guvvie Lockwood said something about that. What's a Check Up?"

Everyone was running toward the housemaster. Some, tripping on others, were pushing and punching. Four or five separate lines were forming in a circle around him. He'd move occasionally from line to line.

"Don't run," Hoppy said. "Let's just walk over. It gets so crowded. A Check Up is to find out where everybody is. If any guys hopped the wall or if they're roaming around down by the Mechanical School or anywhere they're not supposed to be, this will mean big trouble for them."

115

"You don't know when Check Ups are coming?"

"No, that's the purpose of it."

The line they were in gradually moved them up to Mousey. Now, in front of him, Hoppy called out, "Twenty One Seventeen." He glanced at Hopkins for a second and then made a check on his clipboard. "A new boy. What's your name, your section and your number?" Nick told him and he nodded, writing it down.

"Hoppy," Nick asked as they walked away, "what happens to anyone who doesn't check in?"

"When you turn up at your section, you're sent to the housemaster to tell him where you were — with proof."

"Proof?"

"A pass, you better have a pass, signed by someone with the time and date."

"If you don't have one?" Nick asked, knowing the answer.

"You're in big trouble. And no matter what you say, they won't believe you. So, you try to say the best thing. I told them once I just got bored and went down by the back gate, just to snoop around. But you only get to say something like that once," and he laughed. "My bottom can prove that."

"What were you doing?"

"I hopped the wall with some other guys and went to the big F to see what movie was playing that weekend, and we smoked some cigarettes. When I got back over the wall, Todd Ross told me there'd been a Check Up, so I hid my ciggies and brushed my teeth before going to the seckie."

Nick gave Hoppy a friendly punch. "This is like listening to the bad guy confess to the Shadow on the radio," Nick said. Hoppy grinned and give Nick a faked punch to the stomach. "And?" Nick asked.

"And he made me empty my pockets, which were empty, of course, and got close enough to smell my breath. Then he said, 'I know

116

how you orphans do things — next time I'll give you a U.' But he did give me four demerits, two hours to work off on the grudge line. Yeah, and when Bull Fretz found out, he put me on latrine duty at the playground toilets. I gotta sweep up all the loose toilet paper and paper towels every morning before breakfast. Forty johns and pisspots. Some of these guys are so damned messy, sometimes I can hardly eat."

"Do they really keep doing Check Ups until you're a Senior?"

"I don't know, maybe they do. We're prisoners for a long time. And from now on, I'm gonna buy some a that SenSen stuff the real smokers buy and chew that before anybody gets to me.

"C'mon, let's go down by the Armory and get in line to play tetherball."

Whistle Power

If a Hummer's school colors were Steel and Garnet, his song, "Hail, Girard," and his verbal catechism, Please, May I, Sir, Ma'am, Miss, Mr., Doctor, and Thank You, and his visual perspective an ever-present ten-foot stone Wall, then his most ingrained physical reflex was to pause instantly at the sound of a whistle.

Every day, after school and on weekends, the Junior School resonated with the cries, screams and yells of over 300 young Hummers. With the sound of a whistle, everyone was expected to freeze; every face turned toward the whistling housemaster.

Silence was also expected. Talking boys could be punished, although those at distant ball fields could protest the game's pause without fear of being heard. The housemaster would bellow while pointing at the miscreants who would begin running towards him. When they got to him, he blew the whistle again and waved everyone back into action.

When, in late afternoon, a whistle blew, it meant time to wash up for dinner. Everyone raced to form twelve single files, starting on the left with Section One, facing the building. Stragglers were sure to be sent "around the sand tent! Go!" returning exhausted. If their section had already gone in to its lavatory, they were admonished by their governess for being loiterers, possibly awarded with additional punishment.

This shrill decree held true across the Main Road in Good Friends and Lafayette, where hundreds of youths, 10 through 13 year-olds, ran or walked very briskly to register themselves legal at Check Ups or to their buildings for ablutions before meals.

When you migrated to the halls and became a Biggie, you found more individual independence, albeit with the millstone of even greater personal responsibility. Whether a 14-year-old Freshman or a 17-year-old Senior, many of your activities and behavior were to a great extent still monitored by a whistle. It continued to mean "stop" until a situation was resolved and a signal given to resume whatever you were doing. The spontaneous Check Up whistle became an even more indispensable tool for housemasters charged to oversee the whereabouts of the older orphans, more imaginative in their misdeeds and detection.

In the Halls, the sound of a whistle was often directed at an individual as much as at a throng.

"You, stop throwing that baseball!" (or kicking that soccer ball or dribbling that basketball) on the Main Road or some place deemed inappropriate.

"Stop that roughhousing right now or I'll come over there!"

Or "You boys know better! No shortcuts allowed, get back on the walk!" provoking a subdued, barely lip moving chorus of, "Get off the grass, get off the grass, or old Doc Cooper'll burn your ass!"

A whistle could be accompanied by silence. Even at a distance, someone might dramatically point at you and then at your feet, questioning the absence of raincoat and goulashes. If you were walking anywhere on the campus when classes were underway, a whistle directed at you included a gesturing finger meaning come here, tell me where you're going and prove it with a pass. The only places I never heard whistles were inside Founder's Hall or the Chapel.

And yet, as much as our lives were directed by the harsh sound of the whistle, it never seemed tyrannical to me, bothering me only when it ended a game or when I was participating in a satisfyingly unauthorized diversion.

Pavlov would have admired the school's use of the whistle; he may have had his dogs, but Girard had a thousand indentured orphans.

TWENTY-FOUR

"What happened to you?"

"Nothing, Mister Sanford."

"Doesn't look like nothing."

"I was running on the playground and tripped and fell."

"Okay," he answered, though Nick knew he knew. Earlier, in the empty lavatory, in front of his washbasin, he leaned down and splashed the blood off his chin, then carefully wiped the end of one eyebrow with his damp washcloth. In his mirror he saw Spider Demchak watching him.

"He got you, but you sure got him!" Nick smiled a satisfied smile at Demchak, who went on, "His housie made Jamison go to the Infirmary 'cus of his bleeding nose and his teary eye. Made another kid go with him and that really made him mad."

Patting the red scrape on his cheek dry with a damp washcloth, Nick said, "Maybe he thought I wouldn't fight him. He's been picking on Tim Roberts for the last few weeks. Before that it was some kid in our art class."

"Well, that kid has a brother who's a Biggie, and he was waiting for Jamison when he came out of the Middle School. Put him up against the wall and talked to him, banging the back of his head on the wall a couple of times. Some housie was in charge of the playground and he watched but didn't stop it."

"Didn't stop Jamison, either. That's when he probably started on Tim."

"Yeah, and sometimes there are two or three guys, like a gang. That's tough," Demchak said.

"I heard they split 'em up when they send them to the Halls. Some go to Banker and some go to Merchant and the guys are bigger there," Nick said, hanging up his washcloth. "I bumped Jamison by accident on the way to Miss Knapp's room, yesterday. Everybody rushes to class. Said 'Sorry,' and he gives me a dirty look."

"He was sure after you today, Nick. When he tripped you roundin' third watchin' for Smitty to wave you home, you really went down. Phil Bartow was umpin' the game and said Snake Yotty put his whistle to his mouth, but didn't blow it when he saw you get up and go after Jamison."

"I was never so mad in my whole life! I'd a killed him if I had the bat. He doesn't deserve fair play."

"He got you a couple times, but you sure got him. He was scared of you at the end, when Mr. Yotty broke it up. What'd Yotty say to you?"

"Did I want to go to the Infirmary. When I said no, he said to go in and wash up."

"You gotta feel good. You don't get into too many fights."

"Yeah, but you learn in Junior School ya gotta fight back so's they know you will."

Inspecting his face in the mirror, Nick said, "My family would never believe it. Now, it's time to go show off in front of the guys at the table."

"Right." Demchak grinned.

TWENTY-FIVE

"Anybody going with me to the Infirmary after breakfast?" Mike Light asked.

"I will," Jim Falen said eagerly.

"Me, too!" Denny Freeman added, then turned to Nick, "C'mon with us!"

"Why? I'm not sick."

"You don't have to be sick."

"Huh?"

"Just come and you'll get a nice surprise."

"Right, Nick, it's such a cold day…perfect for the Infirmary."

Curious, Nick said, "Okay, I'll go."

At the section door, Mike held up his hands, stopping them and then instructed everyone.

"Denny, you sniff. Jim, you cough a couple times. Nick, you sorta close your eyes and breathe through your mouth. I'll go first and sneeze and nobody look at me when I go by."

The line moved slowly toward Miss Lockwood at her desk. Each sufferer was scrutinized before he was handed a pink slip. Nick began breathing noisily out of his mouth as he stepped forward, lowering his eyes, afraid he would laugh if he looked up. Pink pass in his hand, he joined the trio in the hall where they waved the passes and made faces at each other, silently celebrating.

It was a cold November morning. A light snow had fallen the night before and the wind, racing down the Main Road, shivered the bare tree limbs. Venturing out into the dark, the four made their way toward the Infirmary, wrapped in blue and brown plaid mackinaws, peaked caps pulled down to cover noses, mittens covering mouths. From the small landing at the Infirmary's narrow doors, the line of patients arriving from Junior School, Good Friends and Lafayette ran down the steps, across a broader landing, then down more steps and along the walk to where latecomers were joining it at the edge of the Main Road. Huddled together, faces buried in the backs of those in front of them, there was very little conversation.

The four looked up when they heard loud voices. Nick saw two tall kids standing at the doors, looking down at the crowd.

"Did you see that," Mike grumbled, "those Biggies pushed aside those other kids who were first on the steps and now they're first!"

"Happens all the time, Mike," Denny said. "They say they can't wait. They have important things to do — like we don't do anything."

Mike said to Nick, "The West End and Junior Schoolers go inside and get treated first, anybody from Good Friends, Lafayette or the Halls is supposed to wait outside."

Just then a housemaster came out followed by a group of little kids, hands in their pockets. Then the line started to move forward and as the quartet of pretenders got close to the doors, Nick could see kids going one by one into a brightly lighted room. Soon the first ones came out and burst through the door, crying to the waiting crowd, "Chinese Whisky! Chinese Whisky!"

Like a gigantic sleeping caterpillar suddenly wakened, the long mackinaw line began swaying as hundreds of chilled feet stomped. Animated conversations began, inspired by news of the anticipated medication.

"Chinese Whisky," Falen said, holding a pretend mug up high in front of him, "a Hummer's favorite drink."

"Is it like honey? I heard about it but I've only gone to the Infirmary for shots like everybody gets."

"No, no, Nick, it's the opposite of honey. It's a magical cure for the cold," he said, throwing his arms up to the great outdoors, winking at the others.

"Heck," Light announced loudly, "Chinese Whisky makes winter seem like summer."

"Right, right!" others echoed.

123

The door opened again; and they went in and joined the line. Each one, Light, Falen and Freeman, made a happy expression at him as they came out of the treatment room and passed him. Nick stood before the nurse who held out a tray with little white paper cups on it. He took one, looked in at the yellow liquid and drank it. He coughed. Then he coughed again and slapped his chest. It burned all the way down his throat.

"Hey!" someone behind him shouted, "This kid can't even drink Chinese Whisky." That brought jeering laughs from those just outside. As Nick turned to the door, pausing to look at the kid, the nurse picked up a different tray and offered that to the joker. "Oh, no, please?" he whined, as she dumped a large brown pill from a little paper cup into his hand. "Open," she said firmly. He did and put the pill in his mouth. "Now swallow." Casting a nasty side glance as Nick went by, he gulped, then groaned as the disgusting taste rose in his throat.

Nick joined his waiting friends in the hall. He announced, "That kid just made the nurse mad and now everybody gets pills." The outcry among the waiting brought a nurse into the hall. "Quiet everyone! We have some really sick people resting here on the benches. You!" she pointed at a tall Biggie standing just inside the door, "Don't let anyone leave. Everyone's getting the pill." Outside, the word "pills" had a potent effect, instantly curing many of the "sick" as the long line began dissolving in the dark.

As the quartet sauntered back, Falen asked, "Ain't it great, Nick?"

"Yeah," Nick said, unbuttoning his mackinaw, his tongue stuck out as he breathed in, "it feels like I've been toasted from the inside out."

◆

As they sat down for lunch, Tony Cline caught Nick's eye. "So, how was your Chinese Whisky?"

"Good. I didn't feel cold all morning, even walking up and back from the Library."

"That'll have to hold you for a while," Dale Heffner said. "Once a guvvie or a housie suspects you're fakin' it, you'll have to die before you get another pass."

"Ask Frank Caruso," Joe Camperson said. "He was really sick and didn't get one. Had to go help shovel snow and go to Morning Assembly. When he got to first class, Miss Goodrich noticed him, felt his head an' quick wrote him an Infirmary Pass."

"When I said they were giving out pills, everybody ran."

"I'll bet," Jim Broussard said. "Did you ever taste one? No, of course you didn't. But I've got one if you want to."

"How'd you do that?" Cernicki asked.

"Yeah," said Ricky Bauer, " 'cus they watch you put it in your mouth and it gets too soft to take out."

"I did it with Smitty," Broussard went on, "a couple weeks ago. Smitty was coughing and hates the pills and you know how smart he is. Smitty says Miss North told them in Art Class, use your imagination in everything, so he did." They watched Jim take his linen napkin and fold it into a horizontal U-shape. "We tore pieces of paper from a Life magazine in the Library and folded them like this, into little U-shapes."

"Don't get caught doin' that."

"I know, but it wasn't the news. It was the edge of a page with some movie star smokin' a cigarette."

"So, how'd you do it?"

"The first time we didn't need it. We got Chinese Whisky."

"How do you get to go so often?" Nick asked.

"They're on the Reserved List," Bauer said. "They have some kind of heart or breathing thing and can't play sports or sweep steps. Or even be in the Battalion, someday. So guvvies and housies believe them all the time."

"We were trapped inside last week when they switched over to pills. So," he spoke slowly and proudly, "we pulled out our paper and just before we went in we put it in our mouth.

"It was that slick, shiny paper," he responded to Cernicki's questioning eyebrows. "You put it in your mouth and stick the top piece to the roof of your mouth and the other to your tongue. Then close your lips and puff out your cheeks a little like a chipmunk."

"Like Tubby Fusco."

Reaching in his vest pocket, Broussard took out the pill and held it up. "You open your mouth," he acted out the scene, "put the pill in and quick close your mouth. Press your tongue up against the roof and pretend a big swallow and fake a gulp. I showed her my empty hand and when I got outside, I spit it out, nice and dry."

He sat back and folded his hands on his lap, enjoying the admiring glances.

"So, whattya gonna do with it?" Heffner asked.

"I don't know." He peered around the table as though trying to decide. "Maybe I'll put it in somebody's glass of milk."

"Why dontcha give Nick a taste, instead?" Cernicki asked.

"No thanks," Nick answered. But with all the coaxing and berating Nick finally agreed to it. "But just a little piece."

Broussard pressed down hard with his knife. Snap! Plink! A piece flew across the table and hit Mike's milk glass. Nick took it and dramatically held it in front of his mouth.

"Hey, it's like Communion!"

"That's sacrilegious, you heathen!" Light snarled at Cernicki.

Slowly extending his tongue, Nick solemnly placed the pale brown piece on it, then drew it back very slowly, closing his mouth, then his eyes and bowed his head, everyone enjoying the theatrics. A few seconds later they heard, "Uhhhh—ughh!" as Nick spit it into his napkin. "That stuff's awful!" he cried, grabbing at his glass of milk and taking a long swallow. Hands were clapped while others howled at Nick's sour face.

"Is there a problem at this table?" Section Twenty Two's housemaster asked, curiously watching Nick wipe his tongue with his napkin.

"No, Sir," Nick answered, carefully clenching his napkin, "something started going down the wrong pipe."

As soon as he left, Cernicki said, "That's a great Chinese Medicine trick. I'm going to the Library this afternoon. Who wants to try to do it with me tomorrow morning?"

Broussard waved his hand in objection. "Forget it, Chink, it's too late."

"Why?"

"Smitty told some guys he knew. But the dope who tried it coughed and the pill came flyin' out in front of the nurse. An' he had to take the paper out, too. Now, you have to look at her, open your mouth real wide, drop it in and swallow. Then open your mouth again."

The disappointed "Geez" and "Darn's" coincided with the ringing Mr. Dorrance made on a glass calling for silence for the remainder of the meal.

Snowy day on the Main Road
Christmas Concert in the Chapel

TWENTY-SIX

Nick turned over, punched a hole in the middle of his pillow and buried his head in it, his eyes closed the whole time. Opening his eyes, he could see, from his bed near the end of the middle aisle, the distant red exit sign above the fire escape door. He studied it for a moment as he pulled himself upright. Reaching to the chair by his bed, he found his watch, and, holding it up, read the luminous time — 4:17. Putting the watch on, he fell back and stared at the black ceiling. Miss Lockwood wouldn't put the lights on until 6:30. With a sigh, Nick sat up again and rubbed his eyes. He couldn't last until 6:30! He had to go to the bathroom but the dormitory bathroom was locked. Every bathroom in Good Friends was probably locked.

That's what I get for playing Zorro with Sabs coming back from showers, Nick thought. I shouldna' flicked my towel at him. Nick rubbed the red spot on his thigh where Sabol got him a good sting. Shoulda' got in line to use the bathroom.

The only bathroom that couldn't be locked was the playground toilet. A narrow building about sixty feet long, it was built up against the Hum wall with open hallway entrances at both ends. It was lined on one wall with johns and the other with urinals. But it was three floors down and far away from Good Friends. Well, at least it's dark, he thought. Some guys got caught because it was starting to get light out and a night watchman saw them. And it was almost summer then, not the middle of February. Nick sighed again. It was bad enough to be caught out of your bed after lights out, but out of the building meant real trouble. Getting a paddling and lots of hours standing on the grudge line, not playing soccer with the seckie team. And they might tell your mother.

He sat up, rubbed his eyes hard, and remembered the paddling he got for helping John Martin. He had held his hands together. palms up, so John could put a foot in it and spring up to grab onto the top of the wall Thursday afternoon. Before he even started to raise John, a whistle blew.

He was just helping John and wasn't going over himself. "No excuses," Mr. Fretz said whenever he paddled the hell out of someone. And he often called kids out after showers in the hall for everyone to hear. Bent over, your nightshirt lifted to uncover your butt for that stinging paddle. The first hit hurt most; then the second. After that you knew the rhythm of his swing and could sense the paddle coming. So you gritted your teeth, and though you made a painful grunt, you tried not to cry out. "Flinching and yelping is okay," Charlie Wakerics said at the table once, "but crying was not what you did."

Nick was buoyed by the thought that this was the first time a housemaster caught him at anything else so far this term, especially when he got even with those loudmouths in Section Twenty One, always boasting about what great athletes they were. Leaving the shower room, Nick reached under his towel and gave the big iron wheel a twist. He almost made it to the dormitory when the cold water turned them all into screamers. Mr. Fretz, who'd wandered away for some reason, came charging down the hall followed by some governesses. The uproar brought guys from every dormitory swarming out into the hall. Miss Lockwood stood there, mouth open, before walking down the hall to calm Miss Boyd, Twenty One's governess.

"Someone," she said, surveying her Section Twenty crowd for a telling face, "someone turned the cold water on Section Twenty One".

The boisterous laughter made her very angry. So angry that she ordered everyone to bed and turned the lights out right then, half an hour early. After a few minutes, Ed Rosen sat up and said in a whisper loud enough for everyone to hear,

"I know who did it. He had to do it 'cus he was the last guy out, right behind me. Nick was the guy who iced those bastards." Low calls of "Good work, Nick" and "Great trick" and some subdued clapping brought Miss Lockwood to her door. She stood listening to the silence before closing it quietly.

Nick smiled, remembering how guys patted him on the shoulder the next morning as they passed. But that was then and now he felt his problem return. He had to go to the bathroom. Throwing off his covers, he got out of bed and pulled on his pants and then his coat over his nightshirt. Shoe in each hand, he made his way down the aisle past sleeping forms. Most were silent. Occasionally a murmur could be heard or some peaceable snoring. After putting a bare foot in each cold shoe, he pushed the heavy metal door open and positioned the wooden wedge that was kept hidden in the old iron radiator. Just the tip, so he could get back in. On hot nights after lights out, it was used to keep the door open.

Gripping the cold railing at the edge of the third floor landing, he looked at how the fire escape made its way down to the wide concrete walk. The landings and steps were made of black metal with little holes poked through. From the playground below, it looked like a giant creature clinging to the gray limestone wall of Good Friends. What did Dylan Finnegan call it? A Giant Black Thousand-Legger, hanging on the building, waiting at night to suck the blood out of anyone who ventures out. Nick shook his head to erase the image. As he started down the steps a gust of wind whipped the bottom of his white nightshirt back and forth like a loose sail, wrapping it around his ankles. Scrunching his shoulders, he pulled the lapels of his coat up around his neck. If it weren't so darned windy, I'd take a leak up here, he thought. Shivering, he reached for the railing and gingerly placed his foot on the first step. Painstakingly, he started down. The two thick iron pipe railings on both sides of the fire escape and the wide steps between them, shone with an icy glaze. He blew on his fingers with his warm breath every few steps; they were starting to turn white and hurt. His gloves were in the pockets of his mackinaw hanging up down in the lavatory.

Nick just stepped off the second floor landing when one foot slipped on the icy metal. He fell forward. As he starting plummeting down the steep steps, he lunged to the right and grabbed the top railing with both hands. His body swerved as he hung on. Now he was sliding feet first toward the open space below the lower rail. His hands slipped off the top railing. The back of his head hit the metal landing. "Ow!" His legs went under the railing and out over the pavement two floors down. He threw his arm up and it hooked over the lower railing, his hip slamming into the thick iron post. "Ooof!" Air rushed from his lungs. He grimaced as a sharp pain raced across his chest where the post had stopped him.

Locking his hands on the lower railing, he sat on the edge of the icy landing, breathing hard, puffing white clouds. He looked down at the snow-covered concrete walk below; his legs, encased in the soaked white nightshirt, felt numb. He swung them gently back and forth like a corpse that'd just been lynched in a cowboy movie.

Gripping the top railing, he slowly worked his way down, putting his weight on each foot for a few seconds before taking the next step, each time lowering himself onto the next frosted step. This railing is my life preserver he thought. Finally, he stepped down on the snow-covered walk.

The trick is to stay close to the building so you're not seen, he'd heard someone say. A gang of watchmen roamed the school at night, checking doors and locks and making sure all was secure. They looked for strangers, outsiders, or kids hiding and smoking. John Martin said he hopped back over the wall one night, and a watchman tackled him and beat him up in the dark 'cause he thought he was a robber with a gun. And watchmen always turned you in, and that meant lots of trouble with housemasters and guvvies, and sure punishment for a long time — a U maybe even a VO and a letter to your mom.

Nick crouched down, cautiously making his way along the limestone building until he came to the corner. Squinting as he leaned out into the wind, he saw the playground toilet. It seemed so far away. A black shape by the distant white stone Armory moved, but it was just one of the small gingko trees bending in the wind. Taking a deep breath, he rushed out in the dark, running as fast as he could, head down, watching for ice patches. He felt as though he was moving in slow motion. And then the moon pushed through the clouds and it turned the night into day. He was sure to be seen! Finally he reached the end of the long, stone building and leapt into the dark entrance hallway. Leaning against the moist tile walls, he caught his breath.

Suddenly he felt the need again to relieve himself. That puzzled him. Why didn't I feel this way on the steps, he wondered. Or running across the pavement? That's strange. He turned the corner into the restroom. His footsteps were deafening on the tile floor, echoing off the tile walls. The room became brighter. The moon must have come out from behind the clouds again. He made his way to the nearest urinal and, as he turned to face it, he heard footsteps. The night watchman! Kneeling, he pushed himself up against the white tile wall between two urinals. He pulled his feet close to the wall, and held onto a wet water pipe. A crazy thought passed through his head: This is like being in the swimming pool about to start a backstroke race. A flash of light passed overhead on the walls. Don't move! It snaked back and forth along the line of urinals, brightening the room as it came. He knew his curved back stuck out a little too far. Reaching back, he pulled his nightshirt up as far as he could over his brown coat, pressing his head forward against the wall. The light came, brightening his hiding place and moved on. Thank God, my nightshirt is so wet it stuck to me.

The light went out and feet shuffled toward the far entrance. Nick quietly pulled himself up and stood there. After waiting for what seemed like five minutes, he relieved himself, trying to hit the side of the bowl as gently as possible to cushion the sound. Maybe I shouldn't flush it. But his hand was on the cold, chrome handle and habit made him push down on it. The loud flood of water sent him to the entryway. Seeing no movement, he darted out, hop-scotching his way over icy patches. The fire escape looked good to him now.

Tightly holding the railing and concentrating on each step, he made his way to the top landing. He opened the door wide and stepped in, along with a blast of chilled wind. "Geezes Christ, close that goddamned door!"

"It's freezin' in here, you sonofabitch!"

"Everybody, shut up and go to sleep!" another voice yelled.

Nick rushed down the aisle, threw back the covers and jumped into bed. As he covered up, the dormitory lights went on and a cranky, female voice said, "Okay, I want to know who's making all the noise?"

Nick turned on his side so his shoes wouldn't be noticed. The dormitory was quiet, but Nick felt sure everyone could hear his loud breathing. "Well," she said, "everyone up. You can stand at the end of your beds until someone comes forward." She turned and went back in her room, leaving the door open.

Kids were sitting up, rubbing their eyes. Some were standing, poking the sleeper in the next bed. Nick, trying to keep his covers on him, dropped his shoes on the floor. When he took off his coat and hung it on the back of the chair, though, he could feel eyes on him. A voice hissed, "Own up, Nick. It's your fault!"

From the other end of the room, "C' mon, you guys. Own up! I wanna go back to bed."

"Yeah," other voices chimed in, some ominous.

By now everyone, cold and sleepy, stood in front of his bed. Forty some unhappy boys. Some were weaving, trying to stay awake. Others slumped back, leaning against the bed railing.

Returning to the doorway, Miss Lockwood ordered, "Stand up straight!"

Nick felt the chills coming on and tried to pull his damp nightshirt away from his body. Staring at the floor, he considered his choices. If I don't own up, and some guys know it's me, they'll tell everybody and everybody'll be pissed at me. I don't mind the names but it's a good way to get pushed down on the steps or shoved hard into your locker. Some guys might gang up on you. Nobody likes guys who don't own up or guys who rat on others to housemasters or guvvies. And they're right. Hummers own up.

He looked down the aisle. A lot of bleary eyes watched him. Podagrosi, that Italian giant, made an inquiring face. Guys who were friends were looking away. He stepped out into the aisle and made his way toward Miss Lockwood's room, hearing sighs of relief. "About time," Mark Maslow, always hostile, snarled.

Rapping tentatively, he heard movement. Then the middle slice of Miss Lockwood's face appeared in the slightly opened doorway. Her shiny black hair, usually molded to her head like a soccer ball, was askew.

"It was my fault, Miss Lockwood." Be sorry, but not too much, he thought. "I went to the bathroom and rattled the doorknob — and woke people." She shook her head, side to side, mouth pursed. He could see her bed behind her with lots of pillows. Hope she's too tired to notice my damp nightshirt.

"You know bathrooms are locked. You had a chance to go. You never did this before." She paused. "Use the one by the shower room, I forgot to lock it." She opened the door wider. "Section Twenty, go back to bed. And you," she spoke sternly, looking at him, "report to me after class tomorrow."

Nick raced down the hall, his damp footsteps on the linoleum floor echoing after him. Closing the door, he waited for a few seconds before flushing the toilet. Then waited a few more seconds, long enough to wash and dry his hands, in case she came out in the hall. When he got back to the dorm, it was dark and silent.

In bed, he was awake thinking, I only wanted to relieve myself once, but I got relief three, no, four times! Once with the playground toilet. Then, not getting caught by the night watchman. I owned up to Miss Lockwood, but I know she won't punish me much, I'm really such a "good" boy! And I didn't slide off the fire escape and kill myself.

Rolling his damp nightshirt up under his arms, he tucked the blanket tightly around his nude body. That was kinda scary, but I did it. I'll hafta tell the guys about it at breakfast. He yawned. But never my mom.

TWENTY-SEVEN

Pulling out his chair to sit, Nick felt happy, but hungry. The letter from his mom said his little sister had gotten over a bad cold and was breathing okay at night so she and Aunt Nannie got to sleep, too. And she said they would try to go to Harvey's Lake when he came home on summer vacation.

"Am I ever hungry!" he said aloud as he spread his white linen napkin on his lap.

"Yeah," said Log Richan, "you guys played a good game beatin' Seckie Twenty Four. They're last year's soccer champs." An arm placed his dinner plate in front of Nick. Thin slices of beef with gravy running into thick asparagus spears. He could see the dark lumps inside the mashed potatoes. As Nick began pouring a glass of milk, someone called out, "Snitchees 'n Snares!" Quickly putting down the pitcher, he reached to protect his silverware, but he was too late. His knife was gone. He turned to the culprit, Magee, on his right, but brought his left hand up and took Bob Kase's knife. But Kase grabbed his hand and yelled "Snared! I want your peach slices!"

"No, no, I got first dibs, but you can have them," Magee said. "I'd rather have our Nick provide some entertainment tonight, right guys?" with agreeing nods from around the table.

Nick put his dessert dish next to Kase's, figuring you don't get mad, it's just another crazy Hummer game. Sometimes they don't even expect anything, just want to see if you can get through the meal without getting caught.

"Have some bread, Nick." Don Barr offered in a conciliatory tone. "Go ahead, take two." Nick took a slice, checking to see if any governess or housemaster was watching. He moved his bread and butter plate closer, pushed some butter off the edge of the plate onto the bread with his fork and began spreading it with the back of his fork handle.

"Geez, I wish we had Jello for dessert. Nuthin's funnier than a guy trying to keep Jello from jumpin' off his fork when his spoon's gone," Ken Mazak said. "Ever try eatin' it with your fingers?" Nick, biting into his bread, ignored him.

The meal was unusually quiet, everyone observing Nick's performance, amused by his culinary creativity. Eating the potatoes with his fork was easy, so he did that first, looking up constantly to scan for trouble. Asparagus was next, a least-liked vegetable. The fork worked fine cutting off the tender tips but the woody bottoms were hard to cut even with a knife. Finally he trapped each one with the overturned spoon, stabbing the fork into its base. Eating it popsicle fashion drew some appreciative comments. He'd leave one spear on the plate; any more and you got yelled at. After several tries, though, he knew the fork would not cut the beef slice. He heard disapproving grunts when he put the fork down and picked up his spoon. "So," he barked, "the spoon edge might be sharper."

One extra hard push down with the spoon sent a small meat slice spurting onto the white linen tablecloth. Angry at the result and the laughter, he shoved the bread and butter plate over the blotch before grabbing up the slippery slice with his fingers and just about had it to his mouth when he heard, "What great manners."

He recognized the voice of one of the Good Friends' governesses, Miss Courtney. Standing behind him, she hit Nick hard on the top of his head with a fist. "African gorillas eat with their hands." His tablemates relished the moment, especially when Kase reached out for more bread, purposely bumped the plate and uncovered the dark brown stain. "And you've made a mess of the white linen tablecloth."

"Ow!" Nick grimaced in pain with the second, harder hit. "And I see you can't even tell a knife blade from a fork handle." He turned and looked up. "Miss Courtney, the reason I didn't..." He knew he really couldn't explain.

138

"Out, out! Get out! Come back when you can eat properly." Nick rose to low mutters.

"Stop back for breakfast, Nick."

"Enjoy the water fountain."

Miss Lockwood, at a distant table, glared at him, sure to ask for an explanation later. Unnoticed by the crowd, he left the noisy room. The clock in the tranquil hallway showed about fifteen minutes left before dismissal. Sitting down, his back to the wall, Nick considered how he might get even with Magee, clearly the culprit.

The door opened and Miss Courtney came out. "Go back in and finish your meal. And Miss Lockwood would like to see you after dinner." That meant grudge line demerits for sure and no Pass Out this weekend.

Everyone looked up when he approached the table. It was quiet time and Nick responded to the phony welcome back faces with a scornful stare. "Y'know," Richan said, "some guys say that the guy who snares someone gets to pick whatever he wants of their food *and* he gets to give them a punch on the arm — really hard."

"Well, if anyone wants to try it," Nick scowled, "he'll be sorry." He picked up the knife, now bright and shiny by his plate but saw he had no use for it, at least not for his meat. The beef slices were gone. And his single asparagus spear was now hidden under a mountain of newly donated ones.

A glass dinging was heard and kids began rising. Everyone was dismissed, but no one at Nick's table rose. "You better eat some of those green Sequoia sticks, real quick," someone said, "or some housie might see your plate and give you hell."

"Thanks for the contribution, guys," Nick said, standing up and shoving all the asparagus back on the serving platter, "but I'd like to share my good fortune with you and let him blame the whole table. See ya later." His laugh was masked by the scraping of chair legs as the table was abruptly abandoned.

TWENTY-EIGHT

Section Twenty guys, sitting on their beds or standing in the aisle talking or rummaging through their lockers along the walls, were all acting as if nothing was going to happen. Conscious of the trio kneeling behind a bed at the far end of the dormitory, they knew something *was* going to happen.

"Where the heck is he?" Dylan Finnegan asked Nick. "I saw him washing his face in the lavatory."

"He'll be here, just wait," Mike Betts reassured him. "And why are you so anxious. Nick's the guy behind this to get even with Magee for the demerits he got in the dining room."

"Yeah, but I showed him how to make a weakie."

"Big deal, it just took the three of us to pull the metal railings up from the little notches they're in and set them balanced on the edges."

"Shh, here he comes," said Finnegan.

Jerry Magee and Tom McCleary came in, laughing about something. McCleary went over to his locker. Magee went down the middle of the aisle and set his books on the edge of the bed. Sitting down, facing them, he put his hands to his face and rubbed it.

As Nick yelled out, "Poor guy's tired. Needs to take a rest," Magee swung his legs up on the bed, put his arms behind his head and announced, "Right, and don't anybody wake me 'til dinnertime."

Then the bed fell. It went down with a loud crash, metal bars thudding and springs twanging when they hit the floor, with Magee flopping awkwardly on the thin mattress, his arms and legs splayed out. The foot railing tilted forward on the wooden floor with a loud bang. And the tall head railing fell forward, landing hard on Magee's head. His mouth opened, followed by a whooshing sound and a loud "Ow!" Guys scurried to see the scene close up while others stood on their beds clapping and whistling at the performance.

"A weakie! That was beautiful. Hey, Jerry, do it again." Finnegan cried.

"Okay, guys," Nick said, rising, "let's go help him put the bed back together."

"What? Why would we do that?" Betts asked, "When he sees us he'll know for sure we did it. I'll give it away when he looks at me."

"Now, now," Nick spoke with a calm, tutorial tone, "remember, every day the adults instruct us so we'll become proper gentlemen with strong moral fiber and a sense of fair play — like Tom Brown facing some a those English lads."

Striking a pompous pose, one arm behind his back, the other held out in the direction of the still struggling Magee, Finnegan declared, "Let us proceed, then, to aid our enemy."

"Good man. Spoken like a noble Girardian — and," Nick lowered his voice, "it's not as much fun getting even with somebody if they don't know you did it, but we'd better start testing our own beds before we sit on them."

TWENTY-NINE

"Hey, kid, ya got a cigarette?" Nick, Reds Eckard and Ernie Podagrosi froze; they hadn't noticed the man sitting, his back against a tree, knees up.

"Nah, he doesn't, but I do." Reds went over to the man and leaned down, holding a pack of Luckies. The man reached up and took one. Then he took another. Reds turned back to the other two with a did-you-see-that look.

They continued walking along the railroad tracks on the ballast stones. Reds said, "He's a hobo. I seen them near the repair works at home in Altoona. My uncle says they hide down the tracks waiting for a train to start out slowly so they can hop on it."

"That's right, boys, that's how we get around. Free and easy." The trio stopped short. He was right behind them. "Sorry I scared ya. I'm goin' this way, too. An' thanks for the Luckies."

Nick studied him. He wasn't very old, about thirty maybe, like his cousin, Ralphy. His face was rough looking; burnt dark brown and unshaven, with deep creases around his mouth and eyes. Thick shoots of hair like straw stuck out from under a black cap like the ones Nick noticed on cab drivers. Ernie, one of the tallest kids in Good Friends and Lafayette, had to look up at him. Maybe he seems taller, Nick thought, because of the way his clothes hang on him. The shirt must have been bright blue when he got it; now it was dull, stained darker in different places with one side of the collar torn and hanging down. Loose on his narrow hips, the black pants had long stains of gray running down them reminding Nick of a watercolor he'd messed up in art class.

White skin showed through the kneeholes when he shifted his weight and the pants cuffs had worn off. Thin strands of fabric, curiously white, were fringing down over his black, scarred boots; what

Miss Dyke, who taught Art, would call an elegant tasseled look — well, maybe not elegant.

"Let's go, guys," Reds said, starting in the direction they had come from.

"Why ya goin' that way?" the hobo asked.

"We're showin' our friend the bridge," Ernie said defiantly.

"Bad idea. That's a dangerous spot." As they walked off, he called, "That's the Pennsy Main Line. Busiest tracks in America. From Boston, through New York, Philly, Baltimore, Washington and sometimes all the way to Florida." The trio kept walking.

"Don't look back," Ernie said.

Louder, they heard, "The passenger trains that come through here are pulled by GG-1's...streamlined, the front and back look alike. They're the fastest trains in the country. Don't get caught on that bridge no matter what you do. They'll drag you in." They turned to look back when he yelled, "Here she comes!"

Nick was surprised at how the train, so far away, became so big so fast. It caught up to them, two sets of tracks away, the sleek locomotive a runaway monster, sucking in and out breathlessly. Reds yelled something but it couldn't be heard over the hissing roar. Passing, the GG-1 threw up a cloud of dust and gravel, the boys holding their arms over their faces. Passenger cars went by in just a few seconds, fleeting images of faces in flashing windows.

Ernie shook his head in admiration as the last car disappeared around the curve beyond the bridge. "That GG-1 is some locomotive." Nick was in awe. The Black Diamond that came through Wilkes-Barre seemed like a grandmother locomotive, now.

"Well, that means we should be safe for a while," Reds said.

Nick followed the pair along a side track to where they stopped in the middle of the bridge, got down on their knees and hung their arms over the low crumbling concrete wall. Nick felt dizzy for a moment, it was the highest he'd ever been. He could hardly hear the horns of the toy-like cars and trucks on Girard Avenue down below. Another busy street crossed it and ran right under the bridge and out of sight under a cover of trees.

Way back from the street corner was a tall, black fence like the one at the entrance to the Hum. A banner across it read: "Philadelphia Zoological Society — America's First." People were lined up at a little gatehouse to pay, then crossing past the tall iron gates into the Zoo. Nick could see families with kids standing at a balloon-seller and an ice cream stand.

"Problem is, from up here the trees cover the outside cages so we can't see any animals, not even Monkey Island," Reds complained, then brightened. "Look, see that yellow dot? Betcha' some kid's cryin' like hell down there." The dot grew larger. It was a balloon. Swirling in circles, it rose fast toward their side of the bridge. "Get it!" Reds cried. Grabbing up stones, they turned, arms cocked, but were too late; the yellow circle was already too far away and too high, getting smaller and smaller. "Then I'm going to the other side and throw stones at something." Ernie followed Reds. Nick said he'd catch up to them.

Watching the crowd, he could make out a lady with a baby and wondered what his mom and Janet were doing right then at home. Wish we could come to the Zoo someday, he thought. Trolley cars were clanging to a stop, people getting on and off. Two men came out through the open gates, calling to three boys running in front of them, waving pennants. Nick turned and sat his back to the wall. Wonder what it would be like now to have a father? His dad died when he was five. He knew his dad a little bit, but it was getting harder to remember him. And now, at the Hum, he didn't think of him. When he got home again, he'd ask his mom about him. No one at home ever mentioned his dad, maybe because they didn't want him to feel bad.

A crow landed on one of the rails. How could it find anything here to eat? He leisurely threw a stone that landed near the bird. It tilted its head at him, cawed once and flew away. It made Nick smile.

144

"C'mon over," Reds called from the other side of the bridge. "You can see skinny boats racing on the river."

"Next time," Ernie said, "we'll go behind the zoo and climb trees there. When nobody's lookin' we'll drop down and get in free. Hummers do it all the time."

Nick began picking his way across the four sets of tracks, making sure he didn't step anywhere near where short curved rail pieces were attached to the main rails the train rode on. Ernie'd pointed out the switches after they hid their shirts, ties and coats behind a little storage shed. He'd said switches only made a quiet "shooooop" when they suddenly slid over, like a big silver scout's knife blade closing up. "If you get your foot caught in there, it'll break it and you'll never get it out. And it means there's a train crossing over to that track." He'd just gotten to the other side when Reds pointed at the nearest track.

"Hey, that thing just switched. A train's coming!" Looking back, they saw it come around the curve, a GG-1. Like a one-eyed black snake it seemed to slither over the tracks and, growing bigger every second, came right at them. "Run, run…it's gonna get us!"

They scrambled along the low concrete wall. Reds tripped on the gravel and fell. Ernie hopscotched over him. Nick, last, caught up with him as he rose and shoved him forward, hard.

"Run!" Nick screamed, but he couldn't hear his voice. The roar of the GG-1 was growing so loud, it must be catching up to them. Reds looked back, his mouth open, his face twisted in fright. We're gonna die, Nick thought. My knickers are slowing me down. It's gonna suck me into the wheels! He saw Ernie, at the bridge's end, jump, Reds right behind him. Then thunder exploded right next to him. It shook the ground. It blew hot air in his face and flung gravel that stung his arms. Then a dark shadow spread over him and something black edged into the corner of his eye.

145

"Jump, jump!" Headfirst he did, just like in Gym class. Tumbling, he landed upright, but his brogues slid out from under him and he began sliding on his back down the muddy slope. He could see Ernie, just beyond Reds, sliding down, too, nearing the bottom. "Catch a weed patch!" one of them yelled. That effort flipped all three on their sides, creating a human log roll. "Oofing" and "Oowing," they bounced over small rocks and dirt mounds, Nick finally rolling to a stop in tall, uncut grass at the edge of a field.

Nick, breathing deep, staring at the sky, heard Ernie curse. Raising his head, he saw Ernie rubbing the side of his head. Nick leaned on an elbow, winced in pain and fell back. The skin was scraped off his elbow and it was bleeding. He rolled forward, sat up and tried to wrap it in his handkerchief, but couldn't tie the knot. Reds, holding a muddy shoulder, hobbled over and leaned down to tie it. Ernie joined them.

"Hope I don't get a black eye out of this. It'll mean demerits." Nick got up slowly. "Look at our knickers? All mud and grass. We're gonna get killed!"

"Yeah," Reds added, as they brushed dirt off their bare chests. "But we're lucky it's so hot we took our coats and shirts off." Walking in circles, Reds lifted his legs high. Each brogue had a thick coating of mud clinging to the soles. "It rained yesterday. I kin hardly walk. Let's go find some water and wash off. Looks like this field goes all the way down to the Schuylkill."

Part way across the field they came on a small pool of dull gray water. "Must be a little stream running off the river." Reds stepped into it, his shoes sinking out of sight. "It ain't clean, but it's water," he said. Ernie joined him, then Nick. Soon they were laughing and splashing each other.

THIRTY

"This proves we're indentured orphans!" Ernie shouted from the far end of the playground toilet building. Someone at a urinal yelled back, "Quiet, willya? I can't hear myself piss!" Nick laughed with the toilet's current occupants, even though he was on his knees, too, pushing a mop behind a commode. "Shouldn'a got caught," another voice said dictatorially, fostering more chuckles.

"You guys just do your business and get outta here or I'll mop your privates with this thing." Reds' threatening tone brought silence. His reputation as a hot head, always looking for a fight, was well known. The trio had been cleaning the playground toilet for well over an hour.

Mr. Fretz had been waiting for them outside the dining room. They followed him to the toilet building where he unlocked the hopper room and set out supplies. After a few instructions, he left them. Agreeing on what made up a third of the room with 40 urinals and 40 toilets, they began to work. They poured chemicals in the johns and urinals, used small mops to clean and then flush them, and started to mop the floors. Nick finished dry mopping out to the open entryway then, leaning on the mop handle, watched a nearby soccer game. Mr. Elman, whistling at somebody, glanced over, so Nick backed into the shadows.

"I still say we shoulda hopped the wall," he heard Reds say firmly to Ernie.

"Well, you agreed not to hop the wall, so don't complain now." Nick considered what had happened.

Following their escape from the GG-1, they splashed in the dirty water, rinsed their knickers and draped them, with their long, argyle stockings and underwear on some bushes. Dousing their brogues until they seemed mud-free, they tied the laces together and hung them from the low branches of a tree.

147

"Let's go over there where the ground's dry, between those shrubby things. Nobody'll see us there. "

"Good, maybe our underwear will dry out."

On their backs, nude in the sun, they relived their escape from the GG-1, turned cloud forms into housemasters, sang "Hail, Girard" and, as loud as they could, the obscene version of "My Grandfather's Clock."

Later, with damp clothes clinging to them, they carefully scaled the hill, put on their coats, shirts and ties behind the storage building, and started up Girard Avenue toward the Hum. Walking along the ten foot high stone wall, they passed the Armory on the other side and then came to the roof of the playground toilet.

"Let's hop the wall," Reds said, kneeling at the curb, ready to rush at the wall, "Ernie, lift me up."

"No. We don't have to. We're going back through the gates the way we came out. We've got passes to prove it, even if you can't read them."

"Are you kidding? Lookit the green and brown spots on your pants and socks. If any housemaster sees us, we're in big trouble. What do you think, Nick?"

Looking down at his still mud-slicked shoelaces, Nick suggested, "Why don't we just wait where the wall ends and the iron fence begins by the main gates. When we see a gang of Hummers going in, we run over and get in the middle of them."

"Yeah," Ernie added, "and when we get inside we'll quick run back along the wall, behind the high school and the chapel…and into Lafayette, through the underground passageway into Good Friends and we'll be home. In the lavo we can wash everything out again. Tell them we had a dirty water fight and we'll just get a couple a demerits for that."

"That's a great idea!" Reds slapped Nick on the shoulder. Now, Nick thought, it doesn't seem like such a good idea. Joining a crowd of

Biggies going through the gates worked fine until one of them said, "Hey, who's making that squishy noise?"

"Maybe one a these little twerps from Good Friends is peeing in his knickers."

"Right, these little Hummers haven't been taught proper manners yet. Be quiet around us…and show respect for your elders."

"Look at their shoes — and their knickers."

"Were you guys fighting the war, today?"

"I hope they weren't on our side, 'cus they lost."

Knowing the laughter would just start more jeering, Ernie broke from the crowd, the other two behind him, and raced along the wall by the back of the high school. When they reached the Chapel, Reds called out hoarsely, "Stop running, stop running. This isn't even a normal place to walk when there are no classes. We don't want to get anyone's attention by runnin'."

Ernie slowed to a fast walk. "Right, we already got enough of that from those big bastards back there, yelling after us."

At Lafayette, they went down side steps to a basement door and into a long, dark corridor. It was lighted only when the sections from Good Friends came from their lavatories to the common dining room upstairs in Lafayette. Hurrying down the darkened hall, Ernie stopped short, Reds colliding with him. "Wha?" Reds exclaimed. A large silhouette filled the exit.

"That sloshing sound reminds me of poor Jean Valjean, slogging his way through the sewers of Paris." It was Bull Fretz. "Come closer, so I can see who you are." He moved aside and they stepped into the light forming a semi-circle. "Well, well. No surprise with you two. But you," he pointed at Nick, "you're a new one…about to learn a hard lesson these two still haven't learned. Girard gives you ungrateful orphans the best quality clothing and just look what you do to them. Get up to my office."

149

"Ow!" As Ernie went by he got a whack on the back of his head. When Reds bent his head down to miss the strike, a hard kick sent him sprawling to his knees. He scrambled up. No one said a word. Nick was waved by with a hard look. He hunched his shoulders, waiting for something, but nothing happened.

Outside his office, Mr. Fretz said, "Stand out here facing the wall. I need to file a report to Mr. Davis and Dr. Cooper, so they can decide the punishment you deserve."

"Godammit," Reds whispered when he left them, "it was the Lodge man. He heard those damned Biggies and called down when we ran."

"How'd he know where we belonged?" a puzzled Nick asked.

"By our knickers," Ernie said, "we had to be Lafayette or Good Friends."

Out came Mr. Fretz. "Go to your sections. Your governesses are waiting for you."

Miss Lockwood, Miss Courtney and Miss Irving were standing by their doors. Nick heard Ernie get hit again as he passed Miss Courtney. Nick followed Miss Lockwood and stood in front of her desk. "Phew. You smell like a swamp. Go stand by that window." She dropped down in her chair. "I'm exhausted with punishing people today." Nick grew hopeful. "After breakfast tomorrow, go to the seamstress for clean clothes. Then take your shoes to the shoe shop and see what he says. For now, I want you to take a shower and put on your Sunday pants and good shoes. Now go." He went, head bowed, trying not to smile. As he reached the door, he heard, "After class tomorrow, you can begin working off ten demerits on the grudge line. And Mr. Fretz will probably find some things for you to do, too."

He wouldn't mind sweeping steps or something, but, ten demerits — that's wasting play time, five hours of grudging, probably walking around two lampposts. He liked to do things with Reds and Ernie. It always seemed to get him in trouble, but it was fun, too.

150

When the lights went on the next morning, Nick leapt out of bed, dressed, put on his Sunday oxfords, washed up and ran to the seamstress who took forever giving him new pants and stockings, shaking her head disgustedly all the while. The shoe man held up his washed off shoes and said to come back in two days to see if they were wearable. He didn't seem to care.

A flood of kids burst through the door as Nick got to the dining room. Breakfast was over. "Nick, hey Nick!" Don Loder worked his way over to him. "Thanks," Nick said gratefully, as he took the sandwich of two slices of buttered bread. "And Bull Fretz put this on your plate." The blue pass, dated and signed by Mr. Fretz, said Nick was to report to Dr. Cooper, the Middle School Principal, today at 9:30 a.m. In the Reason space below was hand written: Complete disregard for personal property. Ruined pants, stockings and shoes. Careless, irresponsible behavior. Needs lesson.

He couldn't find Reds or Ernie in the Middle School halls and finally went to his first class, Social Studies. When the bell rang, he pushed his way out and ran to Dr. Cooper's office in the Middle School. Knocking, he heard, "Enter," and found Reds and Ernie standing at attention, side by side, before a huge desk. Nick stood next to them.

Dr. Cooper seemed big, though he wasn't tall. Somebody said he was a giant bullfrog with a desk instead of a lily pad, eager to pounce on lawless Hummers. He was thickset, but not fat, and the way he moved and spoke, slowly, deliberately, calmly, seemed to make him all the more frightening, like something terrible could happen at any moment.

He held up the three blue passes in his hand like playing cards. "I don't think any discussion is necessary. I don't need to hear any excuses, especially from you two." On his desk was a paddle, twice as wide as the ones in the ping-pong room and a lot thicker. He reached for it and, rising, pointed at a console table against the wall. Ernie approached it, hitched up his belt, gripped the table edge and then backed away from it until his head went down and he was facing the floor. "You two, turn around."

As Nick watched Dr. Cooper move to one side of Ernie, he remembered what Mort Walstine once said. "Doc Cooper positions himself next to the poor Hummer just the way my uncle tries to get me to address the ball at the driving range."

"Whack!" The shiny wooden paddle struck Ernie on his bottom. "Ow!" Ernie cried in pain. He straightened up a little, but bent down again. Nick counted the swings, squinting each time the thick paddle slammed into Ernie. Each time Ernie cried out a little louder, but Dr. Cooper ignored him, continuing to swing again and again with the same force, four more times. "Enough," he said, after the fifth hit, "for now." Ernie stood up slowly, breathing hard. Rubbing his bottom gently, he limped back to the desk.

It seemed to go faster with Reds. Hitching up his belt, too, he strode over and bent down. The first hit brought a loud "Ouch!" Then Reds was quiet. He gasped each time as though he was being electrocuted, and squirmed but didn't say a word.

Then it was Nick's turn. Dr. Cooper stood silently as Nick leaned down and lowered his head. Suddenly, not expecting it so soon, he was hit. The paddle's stinging pain spread down his legs and up into his back. "Yow!" he cried out, his head jerking up. He was on fire! He started to reach back, but stopped. "Whew!" he said to himself in amazement as the pain softened, leaving a warm, glowing feeling. He took a deep breath and waited for the next blow. How was he ever going to get through four more like that without crying? But the second blow never came. The edge of the paddle tapped him on his back. "Stand up and join your pals."

Dr. Cooper returned the paddle to the middle of the desk. "This will be waiting right here for each of you. I expect to see the two of you again, although, if you keep getting into trouble, I may never have to see you again. Now, go back to class and behave."

"And you, get better friends," he pointed at Nick. "You're lucky today, mister. The next time I see you, I won't stop at one."

◆

The class was singing one of Nick's favorites, "Cielito Lindo," when he quietly closed the door to Miss Frame's room. Everyone sitting in rows behind him knew exactly what happened when he held the desktop with both hands and slowly lowered himself, shoulders high with pain. Miss Frame noticed but didn't interrupt the singing. Nor did she say anything when the bell rang and class was dismissed for lunch.

Ernie and Reds were waiting for him outside the lavatory. Something's wrong, Nick thought, they're looking at me so strangely. "What's up, you guys?" They looked at each other sheepishly, and then Reds said, "Nick, we feel real bad."

"Yeah, we really do," Ernie said, "We're sorry about what happened to you."

"What?"

"Getting paddled."

"So? So did you." A bell rang and Ernie said, "Gotta go to lunch. We'll be by the steps and we'll tell you."

"Sorry, Nick, sorry," Reds called as he rushed to catch up with his section.

Nick spent so much time shifting around on his chair at lunch trying to get comfortable, he forgot about his buddies' mysterious apologies. Miss Lockwood didn't speak to him, but her look said maybe what just happened will teach you to be responsible…if it doesn't, expect more pain.

Everyone had fifteen minutes to get to class after lunch. Nick saw them under the steps to the Middle School, by the entrance to the swimming pool. "We meant to get to you before you got to Cooper's office, but we couldn't find you." Reds still sounded regretful to Nick.

"What the heck's wrong with you guys?" Nick asked.

"Our paddling didn't hurt as much as it hurt you." Ernie answered. Now Nick was really confused. "See," said Reds, his animated self again, "We've been paddled so much, we came up with a system to beat it. Feel my bottom." Nick stepped back, but Ernie grabbed his hand and pushed it against Reds' knickers. It was soft. Nick couldn't even feel Reds' butt. "We're wearin' extra underwear. Told the seamstress a long time ago someone stole ours and we keep it in our locker."

"And," Reds boasted, "we swiped napkins from the dining room. Put 'em both on and we're all ready."

"Other guys just put their hankie in their pants, but they're too small and make little squares. Open 'em up and they're too thin. It still hurts."

"Ha," Nick said, suddenly understanding, "that's why you guys hitched up your pants . . ."

"...to get everything neat and ready, 'n we pull them up tight under our belt, too."

"We're really sorry we didn't help you, buddy, but if next time you get the underwear, we'll get you a napkin and you'll be like us!"

"...we'll be just like the three fearless musketeers," Reds waved an imaginary saber in circles above his head."

"No, No. Reds," Nick, patted his bottom and grinned back at them, "we'll be smart-assed Hummers!"

"Yeah!" slapping their butts together, they crowed in sing-song tones, "We're three smart-assed Hummers!"

"I think the Hum drives some kids crazy," a passerby said to his friend.

The Unspoken

Life at Girard was an eternal round of questioning and answering, listening, overhearing, discussing, sarcastic repartee, heated arguments, threats and responses, continuing day after day for years, at meals, in hallways, in classes, on playgrounds. Your introduction to this conversation carnival began, simply enough, on your first day when a Hummer asked a newbie, sensing they might become friends, "Where are you from?"

It made you feel good, perhaps for the first time in this new world, to learn someone was familiar with your Philadelphia neighborhood — Olney, Overbrook, Fishtown, South Philly; or suburban Darby, Ardmore, Norristown or Willow Grove. When I replied, "Wilkes-Barre," I usually got a blank stare and a "Where's that?"

On a few occasions, I was told, "Hey, I know where that is — I live just outside Wilkes-Barre in Plymouth," or "I know Wilkes-Barre, sometimes the bus stops there first, then goes to Scranton where I live."

This was usually followed by detailed research: exactly where the two of you lived, what places you've been to — The Orpheum Theatre, Harvey's Lake, Nay Aug Park or Artillery Park to see the Barons baseball team play their archenemy, the Scranton Miners. It also meant you might take one of the same Martz buses for vacations, perhaps in seats not far from each other and could talk back and forth. It was very reassuring to a newbie to learn not everyone around him was a stranger from some foreign land.

It also seems curious now, looking back over all those years, from newbie to graduating Hummer, how some topics never came up: no child or youth, none of the classmates you grew close to in the last year or two, and no teacher or housemaster ever asked, "How did your father die?"

I would not have felt bad if someone asked me, but they never did. And I never thought to ask that question of the hundreds of guys I came in close contact with over the years. Perhaps being raised to be self-reliant fostered such a sense of aloneness in us that it prevented us from asking personal questions. No one ever talked about his mother or brothers or sisters or problems at home. We never invaded the privacy of others and they never invaded ours. I figured most guys from coal country lost their fathers because of a mine accident, like I did.

Whatever the reason, it was years later in private moments at reunions that I learned how several of my classmates' fathers died of heart attacks, auto accidents, one murdered as a cab driver and another by suicide. They answered briefly, without emotion or detail, and I changed the topic.

Another unspoken topic was Brotherhood. As a newbie, looking out over the huge Chapel, it was comforting to join a thousand voices singing Hail Girard, a verse ending "One in voice and heart and will, Brothers of Girard." In such a masculine community, however, the word was never mentioned. Classmates or buddies might be best friends, but never considered brothers. Yet brotherhood did exist. Biggies played peacemakers, breaking up fights of younger Hummers and you felt they were keeping an eye on you when you were outside the wall buying candy at Gates' store or the Dugout. You truly believed Brothers of Girard existed when, at twelve or thirteen, in Good Friends or Lafayette, returning alone or with a buddy or two in the late afternoon from a Saturday or Sunday Pass Out, you saw trouble on the horizon. Approaching at a distance was a gang of outsiders, possibly members of the Green Street Counts or Taney Street Rams, most out of high school, some in their twenties; they liked to gang up on Hummers when they came upon them. Looking behind you, you surveyed both sides of the street, hoping to find a group of Biggies also returning to the Hum for dinner. If you were fortunate enough to see some Biggies, you zestfully called out, "Yo, Hummers!" and, seeing them casually wave back, affected fearlessness as you continued towards the enemies.

You moved to one side of the walk, but not so much as to show trepidation. They passed with dirty looks and some muttering, knowing you had protectors coming up behind you. You didn't know those Biggies, but that didn't matter. At that moment you knew the value of "brothers of Girard." Of course, if you didn't see any potential protectors, you took your chances, *darting across the street at the last second and making a run for the open gates.*

Growing up together and learning to cope with each other, living through the same experiences, we were in a sense all brothers, except in blood. During my first semester in college, I observed fraternity life. I couldn't afford to join had I wanted to, but I didn't want to — the focus on their social life seemed frivolous to me after eight years of unspoken brotherhood in Girard's fraternity.

THIRTY-ONE

Nick leaned down and lowered his glove just as the ball smacked into it. A long whistle blew; then a series of short, insistent blasts. "Yo!" voices bellowed, "Not again!" Other voices echoed the cry across the huge macadam playground. Mitts were thrown on the ground, as were caps. "Let's go, so we can get back and keep playing," Ray Smyth yelled as he stood up behind the batter, pulling his face mask off. Nick stuffed the ball behind his belt. It dropped into the circle of fabric formed where a black garter held the top of his stocking and the bottom of his knickers, just below his knees.

Hundreds of eleven to thirteen-year-olds rushed to form a long line that led to Mr. Sweigart. Players, loud and argumentative, pushed forward. Hearing their locker number, Mr. Sweigart checked their face to confirm, nodded, and off they flew. Others, alone in their thoughts, were swept along to the head of the line where, recognized, they wandered away.

Nick rejoined his Section Twenty team at the farthest of the four baseball fields. He was covering third base and Section Eighteen's team was up.

"Hey, Nick." Ernie and Reds were standing just over the foul line. "C'mon, we're gonna do something."

"I'm playing! Can't ya see?"

"You guys winning?"

Annoyed, he said, "They are, five to one."

"And they're first in the league. C'mon, we'll do something exciting. You already have a hankie so we swiped some extra underwear for your next paddling," Reds teased.

Section Eighteen's batter struck out. Nick considered the situation thinking, this is no fun and it'll be forever before I get to bat again. "Green, hey Green!" Leaning against the fence railing was

George Green, a kid who was on the Reserved List, not supposed to play sports.

"What?" he answered, then looked behind him, thinking a foul ball went by him onto the Main Road.

"Take my place." He scrambled over to Nick.

"Really, kin I borrow your glove, too?"

"Okay, but lock it in your locker, I'll get it later."

"See," Ernie put an arm around Nick's neck, "you made the kid happy and nobody even noticed the switch."

They waved off the threats and curses as they made their way across the middle of the playground, the outfield of the four ballgames. As they approached the far end of the playground toilet, Nick asked, "What are we doing here? Somebody gotta go?"

"No, something better than that," Ernie said. "We're gonna do a little wall hoppin'."

"What?"

"We ran outta cigarettes last night," said Ernie, "and Sweigart just had a Check-Up. He won't have one for a while now."

"Anyway, we shudda hopped it last week and we wouldn'a got caught," Reds said. "Besides, it's a fun thing, ya gotta live a little." They were now at the end of the building. "Is he watching?"

"Naw, Reds, he's talking to some kids. Hold it. Hey, you guys stop that and go away." Two kids, probably new in Good Friends, stood on the concrete walk edging the playground, watching them.

"You guys are gonna tip off old Sweigart," Ernie cried, stuffing his cap in his pocket. When he started toward them, they flashed five fingers on their noses but moved quickly away.

Reds suddenly ran, put his foot on an outcropped wall stone and leaped up. Grabbing the smooth stone cap, he gave a loud grunt and pulled himself up, swinging one leg over the wall. He lay on his stomach for a second and then dropped out of sight.

159

"You next, Nick." Nick pushed his cap down in his pocket and ran at the wall, but he put his foot too low on the wall and fell back, caught by Ernie. "Damn!"

"Aw, beginners always do that, unless they're real tall. Try again and this time I'll really push you up hard." Ernie, bent down, his back against the wall, his hands, clasped together, hung in front of him. Nick ran at him, put one foot in Ernie's hands and was lifted up. He grabbed the stone cap, swung his legs up as Reds did, swung his other leg over and dropped down. Reds threw his arms around Nick's shoulders and steadied him as he landed.

"Watch out, below." Ernie landed next to him, tripped, ran forward, hugged the trunk of a sycamore tree by the curb and stood up. "Let's get moving," he puffed.

"Why? Aren't we safe out here?"

"No way. Hear that clanging? At Assembly the other day, John Martin warned me. Said last semester Jim O'Neill, Joe Camperson and Bob Sterling, real big messers, hopped the wall."

"And nobody saw them go over," Reds said, "…and nobody saw them come back over."

"Then they got passes to Doc Cooper," Ernie continued, "got their butts beat red and got VO's — didn't get off campus for a long time."

"Huh?"

"Seems Doc Wolf, the world's most boring teacher, was going home and saw them from the Fifteen trolley. And here it comes, run!" They ran ahead of the trolley, along the wall as it curved with Girard Avenue at the end of the campus. It then made a sharp left continuing on Girard Avenue, moving toward West Philadelphia and away from the school. Nick followed them into Gates' Candy Store entryway, where they stood, talking quietly by the door, watching for the Fifteen to pass by and making old Mr. Gates, behind the counter, eye them nervously. It was rumored, Reds said, that the old man, who acted

160

grouchy even when you bought something, was gypping little Hummers. "A couple of them complained to some big Hummers they saw going by. The Biggies brought them back in and said 'Our little brothers didn't think they got the right amount of candy.' Old Man Gates didn't say a thing, he just glared at them; but his big fat wife, always sitting on a stool behind him, jumped up and yelled 'Get out!' When she said, 'Those little orphans are lying. I ought to call the cops and have you all kept back behind the walls, where you belong!' the Biggie nearest the long glass display case leaned against it and it tilted. Different kinds of hard candy began to bounce around in their glass dishes, some spilling out. 'Look,' another Biggie said, 'those sweet, little prisoners are making a break for it.' Then another Biggie started doing it with another case, and candy bars started jiggling. They said the old lady screamed and then shut up, and she and old man Gates watched, hands to their mouths. Somebody said 'Okay guys, that's enough,' and they lowered the cases. 'Gyp any of our little brothers and we'll be back,' another said."

"Now," Reds said, "whenever any a them go by, they tap on the window with a coin to remind him. The Gateses hear them but don't look out."

Reds went inside and bought a Turkish Taffy from Mr. Gates who was expressionless. Outside, he slammed it down, unwrapped, on the top of a fireplug and offered pieces to Nick and Ernie.

"Isn't it great being out here, Nick?" Ernie said expansively. "It's like being on vacation — doing what you feel like doing and knowing all those guys back there are doing exactly what they're supposed to be doing."

"It's like beating the guvvies and housies at a kind of a game," Reds concluded.

Continuing down Girard Avenue, they came to the Big F, The Fairmount Theater, where they looked over the current and coming attractions. "Can't go in even if we had the money," Reds said to Nick, "gotta be back by 5:30 to wash up for dinner."

Being the tallest, Ernie went into the drug store at the corner of 29th Street and came out with two packs of Lucky Strikes. He and Reds lit up and took turns blowing smoke at Nick.

"Yo, Reds." Four guys across the street waved, obviously Hummers by their knickers.

"Geez, half your seckie must be over the wall," Ernie called. The group crossed over, and one started dancing around Reds pretending to box. Another held out a big white bag. "Broken donuts from the German Bakery." Nick pulled out a handful and said "Thanks."

"We were out in Fairmount Park, tryna set off some rockets. But we're headed back now. What're you guys doing?"

"We needed ciggies. Showin' Nick here the art of how to hop the wall," which brought favorable grins.

"Well, we're legal today. Got passes to prove it. See you back at the Hum. Good luck at the wall." And off they went.

Ernie, Reds and Nick wandered down the avenue to the edge of the park before starting back on the other side of the street, waving at strangers in passing trolley cars.

At the EZ Wash, Reds made eyes at a girl sitting on a dryer, but Ernie wouldn't let him go in. "We gotta get back."

Hiding behind one of the sycamore trees that lined Girard Avenue, they waited until the Fifteen trolley passed, then rushed across the street to the wall. Nick admired how nimbly Reds went over. "Okay, Reds? Ernie called but didn't get an answer. "Great, he ran off to the seckie already," Ernie said with disgust. "You're next." Nick flew up with help from his friend, rolled over the wall and landed on both feet, but it wasn't Reds who stabilized him. It was Mr. Sweigart who shoved him aside to where a dismayed Reds stood. They watched as

Ernie dropped down facing the wall and turned to the unthinkable scene.

♦

"Back here so soon? You must like pain." Dr. Cooper rose from his desk and came around to them, paddle in hand. "Mr. Davis and I decided, for going over the wall and having cigarettes in your possession, you will get VO's, a Very Objectionable rating on your record. You two won't last long here at Girard. And you," he looked at Nick, "I told you to find better friends last time, and here you are again, another slow learner."

He tapped the paddle gently a few times on his hand, almost caressing it, and then said to Nick, "Only because you didn't have cigarettes on you, you're going to get a get a U for Unsatisfactory Behavior. Letters will go home to your mothers, making them unhappy. Get ready to explain your conduct to them. They sent you here because they care about you, and this is how you reward them, worrying them. Since you all live far away and don't go home on weekend passes, you will not get any passes to leave the campus or even to special events with your class for a long time. You'll be spending your free time on the grudge line and doing some less than desirable chores." Heads bowed, the three gazed dolefully at the oriental carpet.

Smacking the upper part of his leg several times rather sharply with the paddle, Dr. Cooper continued, "I guess I'm going to have to make a stronger, more lasting impression on the three of you." As they turned to bend down, their extra underwear padded with thick linen napkins, Nick saw Reds glance knowingly at Ernie.

Then Doctor Cooper said, "Hold out your hands."

163

THIRTY-TWO

Carefully pulling the rubber band off a neat pack of letters he'd taken down from the shelf in his locker, Nick found the one with stamps inside. Taking one of the three left from the ten his mother had sent, he licked it and pressed it gently on the envelope he'd gotten from Miss Lockwood. Sitting on his bed in the quiet of the empty dormitory, he looked down at the palms of his hands, the fat part by his thumbs still swollen and reddish. He didn't want to send the letter; he'd lied to his mother in it. Told her the reason his writing might seem hard to read was because he hurt his hand playing tetherball. That he even went to the Infirmary — she'd want to know that — and they said it wasn't broken. He'd just have to soak it in cold water three times a day, and it was starting to feel better already.

Thinking back, Nick thought it strange how, after the first two hits, the ones that stung so much, his hands seemed kinda dead and unfeeling. The last four paddles hurt, but not as much as the first ones. Electricity seemed to explode in his fingers and shoot up his arms into his shoulders with the first whack. His legs felt wobbly. He felt dizzy. Crying a shrill "Ow!" he pulled his right hand back, pressing it to his chest, but it was pulled away and back and he was struck again. Nick shrieked. His hand was now in flames! Closing his eyes tightly, he tried to press back the tears but they coursed over his cheeks onto his upper lip. Then his left side was flooded with pain when Doctor Cooper made the last three paddles on his left hand. He stood, swaying, looking down at his scarlet hands, afraid to clasp them together hoping to comfort them because it might make them hurt more. Doctor Cooper jabbed him in the back with the paddle's end and said, "You don't have to wait for these two. Go."

◆

No one at the table razzed him, not even Gene Custer, when he lifted his glass of milk with both hands and gripped his fork like a

164

shovel to push at his mashed potatoes. Al Smith made a general announcement that Doc Cooper's hand paddling was worse than Mr. Davis's.

"It's like he pours gasoline over your hands and then lights a match to them," John Martin, one of the best known Good Friends "messers" said. "Believe me," he cupped his hands and blew on them, "I know."

Dinner over, Nick stood on the grudge line, his back to the playground. He knew he had to write home. Martin said his mom would get a letter saying his behavior was unfavorable and it would go on his record and that some privileges would be taken away temporarily. "But they won't tell her what you did wrong," Martin had said, "they leave that up to you."

He wished he could just go home. He'd like to hug his mother and just tell her he didn't do anything really wrong. No one got hurt. Nobody did anything bad. She always said, "Don't be afraid to explore and try different things; you can't get anywhere just sitting on the porch playing cards with Charlie Bevans and Meredith Griffith and Jackie Fisher." That's why she let him ride his bike with Carl Reisinger, a Hummer who lived in South Wilkes-Barre and was more than a year ahead of him at the Hum, all the way over to Harvey's Lake, thirteen miles away, when he was home on summer vacation. Nannie, his maiden aunt, who lived with them, said his mom was sending him out to be killed; hit by a car or run over by a truck. But Mom always let him go with enough money to buy hot dogs, french fries and a bottle of chocolate milk when they stopped at the amusement park, halfway around the seventeen mile lake. It took all day and, when he got home, too tired to eat, she let him go right up to bed without even washing. Now he had to tell her what happened and why he was punished.

Though my hand hurts a little now, it is getting better. My next letter will be easier to read.

You are going to get a letter that I did something bad. I'm sorry about it, but it's not really that bad. I went to the park with some friends. We tried to go down a hill and slipped and fell in mud and got our clothes all dirty. The guvvie yelled at us. It's called messing around when you do something they say is wrong. Messers stand on the grudge line and do dirty jobs. The seamstress gave me new knickers and I promised not to climb there again. Another thing happened when I left school without a pass with friends. I got a C in Math and a B+ on my English composition, which was about waking up in my bed at home and smelling bacon in the kitchen. Thank you for the letter with the dollar. I bought some black cherry soda and pretzel sticks at the Hum store with it. Lots of boys get U's on their report cards and are still here. I don't want any more. The bell rang for dinner so I have to go. I still say prayers every night, but I get in bed before I do it. Give Janet a kiss and hug for me — and for you. I love you.

Nick reread the letter. He saw where Mr. Tolson would give it a C-minus, maybe even a D and tell him to rewrite it. The sentences were not well thought out and the topics weren't organized in what he called a logical order. I don't want to rewrite it. I don't even want to look at it, he thought. I'm already lying to my mom.

Licking the envelope, he remembered what Bob Furmanksi, another big "messer," told him one day when they were facing the wall on the grudge line, "It's like playing a game, us against them — getting away with stuff instead of doing the same old thing over and over like they want. I think most guys smoke and hop the wall 'cus they're not supposed to. It's fun to do something and not get caught."

I don't want to get in such big trouble again 'cus it hurts Mom. Maybe I just better be a smarter Hummer and learn not to get caught.

THIRTY-THREE

"Where are we?" high-pitched voices sang out in planned unison from the back of the bus. "Will we ever get home?"

"We just went through Mt. Pocono," a Senior announced. "We're headed for Tobyhanna, then Bear Creek and we'll be in Wilkes-Barre in about an hour after that. Now, quiet down back there, you guys. Some of us are trying to sleep."

The snickering from the response, "I thought you Seniors were always asleep," ended abruptly when a large silhouette rose from a front seat and looked back. Nick felt sleepy too, about to close his eyes when he felt a gentle tap on his shoulder. "Hey, Nick. You awake?" It was Joe Camperson, sitting on the armrest across the aisle. Everyone kidded him because he looked so Irish. White hair, fair skin, blue eyes and always a grin. They became friends in Section Twenty until Joe had to move to Lafayette. Now that Nick was about to turn thirteen and go into Seventh Grade, he'd move over to Lafayette after vacation. But Joe, like Vic Tunila, a little older, was going into Ninth Grade and leaving Lafayette for Banker or Merchant Hall.

He remembered in Junior School when Pete Bracken complained to Mr. Dunkel. "It seems soon as I start to feel guys are buddies, they get sent over to Good Friends." Mr. Dunkel told him not to expect to have close friends again until he got to, maybe, Mariner Hall. It happens all the time, Nick knew. You're either moving away from friends or trying to catch up to them. "Yeah, Campy. What's up?"

"I was just wondering what shop you were taking first, Sheet Metal or Foundry or what?"

"I picked Foundry, but I don't want to work in a foundry forever."

"You don't have to. It's just to show you what it's like to do it. Then you might take Carpentry or Pattern Making. You take a shop for a while then you switch and take another one."

167

"Hell, I heard they even grade you," Froggy Remaley cried. He was standing in the aisle, swaying, his arms hanging from the luggage railing. "I just wanta get through English and French and all the rest of the class stuff and get out."

"It's the Hum's educational curriculum, dumbo," Camperson continued. "You were told; you just didn't listen. Stephen Girard said every Hummer should have a vocation to fall back on. So, even though we have to go to regular school, we all have to go to the shops and choose one. But you can choose Business, too, Typing and Office Machines. This year, I'll be in 9A and take Drafting, then Mechanical Drawing. Then we split the term again in 9B and I'll take Printing and Electric. There's Auto and Machine Shop, too, but ya don't take 'em all; you'll be here forever."

Nick turned to Vic Tunila who said, "I'm taking Cabinetmaking for my trade." Vic had moved to Section Twenty Eight in Lafayette when Nick arrived at Good Friends. They didn't see each other much on the playground, but Nick never forgot how Vic taught him to tie his tie and always tried to save the seat next to him for Vic on the bus.

"Business means typing, shorthand and office machines. That means I'm gonna turn into some kinda twerp that gets his hands dirty with carbon paper," said Froggy.

"Look who's afraid to turn into a twerp!" someone cried and everyone awake within hearing laughed.

Black forms rose from the front of the bus. One shook a fist in the air. "If you blockheads from Lafayette and Good Friends don't shut up, we'll come back and close your mouths the hard way. And if any of those little bastards back there get sick and start running up front, somebody'd better yell and let us know."

"Yeah," one of the Seniors crowed, "somebody vomited on Lover Boy's shoes last year and they still smell so bad he can't get a girl to dance with him at the Proms."

"Shuddup, Brownie. I'll kill anybody who gets near me if he's puking!"

With that, the remainder of the trip was tranquil, until someone spied the Mobil gas station, where the buses start braking down the mountain into Wilkes-Barre. The excitement level rose until the driver finally put on the interior lights and the luggage racks were attacked. Soon, all except the nonchalant Biggies crowded the windows in coats and hats, homemade gifts on their laps.

Another vacation was about to begin.

**About to board the bus
with their box lunches**

Vacation Travel

Exhilaration filled the air as a vacation was about to begin! The length didn't matter — a week at Easter, two weeks for Christmas or the whole summer — the euphoria was the same, especially for those who lived far away and didn't get home on weekends. Youngest Hummers woke up about a week before the start of vacation infused with the much lauded Spirit of Christmas the world wishes would continue all year — an aura of general friendliness toward your adversaries; tolerance of weird kids from other sections in the hallways; even opponents on the soccer field, though you still wanted to win. Everyone seemed to move faster, even the customary laggards. Everyone talked faster and the decibel count got higher as the Vacation Day got closer. Everything was funnier — all jokes laughed at heartily, sarcasm was softer; tricks played on others were accepted with good humor. There was an unspoken cease-fire on pushing and shoving.

This Vacation spirit with its "good will" for others was at its purest in the littlest guys. Still young, their bond to their mothers and family was strong, still dependent though distant. The curve of vacation excitement didn't quite reach those heights as you grew older. Having moved through the Junior and Middle schools to the High School in Banker or Merchant Halls, as a Biggie, you had vacationed many times. And, as you became a Hummer, you became more independent. Although you looked forward to seeing your family and friends, you also looked forward to temporarily escaping some conditions and individuals controlling your life at Girard.

Vacation Day turned the Main Road into a river churned by bodies streaming in both directions. Hundreds of young mothers with happy, tear-stained faces rushed to retrieve sons from West End and the Junior School; trailing behind them like kite tails were hand-holding, wide-eyed siblings. Racing out of Good Friends and Lafayette and staggering upstream with suitcases and shop-made gifts of wood or plastic, freed youths made their way up the road, calling goodbye to friends as they plunged down streets to catch a trolley car or subway. Biggies casually sauntered out of their five Halls in small groups, breaking up when they went through the gates. Others found their families parked around the circle, waiting to drive them home to West Chester, Wilmington or Toms River.

You could tell those who lived far from the Hum because of the boxes set down in front of them during breakfast. Tall, white cardboard squares with their names scribbled on them. Box lunches with a chicken or ham sandwich, a hardboiled egg, an apple or orange and a ginger cookie, a Hum Mud. And you could tell how far away kids lived by the number of boxes they got. Included with their boxes were train tickets, paid for by their mothers. The youngest train travelers were led to the front gates where they joined the older boys and were transported to the Broad Street Station. It must have been a curious sight for other passengers to see the group, different ages, each with a suitcase and white boxes, swarming aboard the last car on the train. Like a Milk Train, it made countless stops beginning at suburban Paoli, then on to Downingtown, Coatesville, Lancaster, Mount Joy, Elizabethtown, Harrisburg, Duncannon, Lewistown, Johnstown and, finally, Pittsburgh. At Harrisburg, when the train stopped to switch engines, it had become a tradition to open the back door, stand on the little observation deck and try to hit the switching crew as they passed by with the unappetizing hardboiled eggs. When some of the older guys became too boisterous, they found themselves sentenced to "Siberia" by the conductor, where they were crouched among mountains of mailbags in the windowless mail car. The switch at Harrisburg was from electricity to coal. With the kids keeping the windows open, everyone soon had a light coating of soot. The trip to Pittsburgh took about seven hours. Jock McKnight got off at Lewistown; Reds Eckard at Altoona and Ernie Podagrosi at Pittsburgh. After the war started, the trains were crowded and Hummers lost their private car. Even the youngest sat in the aisles on their suitcases, eating from their white lunch boxes, often sharing with GIs.

But train travel was luxurious compared to traveling by bus to Wilkes-Barre and Scranton. It was unforgettable, in the worst sense.

171

Gathered on the steps of Founder's Hall, everyone cheered when the Martz buses drove through the gates. The Biggies got in first, Seniors taking the front rows with the best views and a chance to talk to the driver. The seats behind them were filled with other Biggies, then kids from Good Friends and Lafayette. The littlest ones ended up in the back of the bus, which was unfortunate for all. They were most affected by motion sickness and the venomous heated exhaust from the rear engine that seeped in whenever the bus stopped at a red light or stop sign — but year after year, noxious trip after noxious trip, the class system remained intact.

By the time the bus made its way up Broad Street and out of the city, many of the white lunch boxes were empty. An hour or so later, leaving Allentown behind, the decibel level began to sink, especially at the back of the bus. Experienced travelers noticed and quickly positioned anyone, suddenly silent or morose, next to an open window. And not just the youngest fell victim to the cursed atmosphere. Because of their past performance, others often got window seats when they boarded — past adventures with the squeamish taught you it was better to give up that prized location than to suddenly find anguished eyes on you, a hand held to a mouth, the other waving you out of the way. Especially in winter, soothing relief was found with pale faces pressed against the cold glass, noses sniffing for fresh air. But it was a losing endeavor. The driver, working his way up the Pocono Mountains, would slow to shift gears, then stomp on the gas, releasing a cloud of acrid fumes often drawn into the open windows.

"Throw-up! Throw-up!" you yelled. You leaped into the aisle, moving far enough back to be out of his escape route. "Throw-up! Throw-up!" was echoed by dozens of shrill voices. Everyone flung himself against his seat partner, scrunching together toward the window. Often the afflicted made it down the aisle and rounded the corner safely and was out the door before exploding.

"Gross! Disgusting! Close the door, driver and get going! Yeah, leave the little bastard here!" They got no sympathy. When he boarded the bus again, the driver often said, "Why don't you just stand down there by the door

until you feel better?" — at which all the older guys in the front rows shrieked, "Get him outta here, he smells! Dope, you shouldn'a ate your box lunch! Don't put that hankie back in your pocket, stupid little jerk, throw it out your window! We can't see around him! G'wan back, damned indentured orphan, before you make us all sick!"

But not all "throw-ups" made it to the door. Many landed in the aisle and some on the arms or shoulders bringing a shower of curses and angry punches from the newly polluted. After several inside "upchucks," as the driver called them, he'd stop at a gas station and return with a bucket of water. Standing as far back as circumstance dictated, he heaved the water. It raced down the aisle, sloshed into the lower entry area and out the door.

I recall standing near the back of the bus on one trip talking with friends when someone nearby started down the aisle. Amid the "Throw-up! Vomit! Vomit!" uproar, one wave of bodies swayed to the left; another to the right. As the bus screeched to a halt and the afflicted staggered down the black metal floor, already gleaming with water, someone observed, "Hey, you guys, look — it's a kind of parting of the Red Sea!"

After a few such episodes, it was standard procedure for a Senior to declare in a threatening tone, "I want every window on this bus opened right now! And I don't want to see anybody hoggin' for air." If it was a Christmas Vacation bus, the aisle was suddenly jammed with kids pulling down mackinaws and knitted hats from the storage racks. No matter the blowing snow or driving sleet, the windows remained open. Even in our mackinaw overcoats, suit coats, knickers, long stockings, shirt, tie, vest, hat and gloves, it was chilly. Some amused themselves trying to make different shapes breathing cold clouds.

The buses eventually got to Wilkes-Barre and Scranton. Without the turnpike, it took from six to nine hours depending upon the season and the weather. There were no bathrooms on the buses — but even the littlest Hummers had been trained for such trips having learned, in their first few days at Girard, that dormitory bathrooms were often locked when the lights went out. The one relief spot was the Gap Diner in the village of Wind Gap.

173

Kids surged into it to line up at the restroom, and some rushed behind the diner to irrigate trees. All ages spent money on sodas, pretzels and candy bars. The counters, laden every foot or two with metal pedestals stacked with Drakes Cakes, were crowded with boys. Among the Good Friends and Lafayette wise guys, the game was to put your knitted cap on the counter and slip a Drakes Cake under it. Some kids would do it and then put the cake back, but most cakes remained under caps, headed back to the bus.

Vacation traveling was the only time Hummers of all ages spent time together, except for chapel services, though even then you were separated by class and distance. The affable atmosphere on a vacation bus, even with the odorous episodes, created a comradeship with kids sitting near you who might be several classes above you. Such friendships could last up to ten years, but were curious, transitory. Three times a year were the only times you might see and talk to them. Each vacation, as you boarded the bus, you looked for their faces. Some were always missing, having graduated, flunked out, been "kicked" out or reclaimed by their mother. And each year you moved closer to the front of the bus, eventually becoming a Senior, claiming one of the front row seats.

Finally, hours after the bus had left the Hum, some big kids, the only ones astir in the darkened bus, yelled, "Everybody up! We're home!" The lights went on as the bus pulled into the station parking lot, followed by much yawning and arm stretching, then the aisle was jammed with bodies pushing toward the exit. The older ones, first out, lined up behind the driver, got their suitcases, met their families with casually placed kisses and quickly departed. The little ones rushed into the arms of mothers, then returned to pick their suitcase from the pile. In a few minutes the crowded station was quiet, with the empty bus, door open, waiting for the clean up crew. Such was bus travel with Hummers, where, in my eight years, the unofficial throw-up record for the trip home was twenty-seven. Fortunately, most were successful in making it out the bus door.

LAFAYETTE HALL
Named for Stephen Girard's young friend

Grade 7
Age 13

1948

THIRTY-FOUR

The bell rang and the class rose as one, lifting their desktops and gathering their books stored inside. As the room began to empty, Mr. Friedman caught Nick's eye and pointed to the front of his desk. Approaching and waiting there, Nick knew this wasn't good. Ken Mazak passed him with a wondering look. When the door closed, Mr. Friedman spoke, not looking up from a paper in front of him.

"I'm sending a request to Dr. Walcott that you be kept in and sent to remedial math classes this summer. Your work has been barely passable. I know you can do better and it had better improve if you are to last here. I also said I think you should be put on probation and dropped from the swim team immediately." Nick's heart fell. It would be better if Mr. Friedman just stabbed him.

"If your grade improves, I'll tell them you can rejoin the team, maybe by the end of October." He paused, still not looking up. "Do you have anything to say?" Nick just shook his head. "Very well," Mr. Friedman said, without any sympathy in his voice, and Nick, books under his arm, left.

◆

"Can you believe it? My other grades are B's, with an A or two and a C-minus in his math class. I'm not flunking. That guy hates me. I'm in the Two group. I'm not in the One group with the brainy guys, but I'm not in the Threes either."

"Nick, that's the way he is. He's a Nazi. Everybody hates him, even Al Smith and he gets straight A's." Joe Tobin, waiting out in the hall for him, gave him a sympathetic poke on the shoulder when Nick told him what happened.

"I just got on the team this season…we got a lot of meets scheduled. It'll be forever when I *might* get back on the team. I wish I could run away from this place," he grumbled to Joe. "It's a prison. Nobody wants to help you. They just want to tell you what you're doing wrong and figure some way to punish you. I'd really escape if I could."

"Why don't you join us, we're gonna do just that." Jim Groome, in the class a half year ahead of Nick's, was walking behind them. Nick eyed him and then, with Joe, turned left down the second floor hall to their Biology class.

While Dr. Presson went on about something in Biology, Nick grew angrier the more he thought about the math. I get the answers right most of the time, but he says I do it by drawing pictures and dividing them up — that if I don't use the formulas, my answers don't count. My mom would think it's unfair, too.

After dinner, Nick roamed along the sidewalk, not wanting to play soccer or even talk to anyone. Groome, tall, gangly and "always ready with a snippy remark," Nick heard Mr. Newhardt describe him, was standing in the shade of Lafayette with some other kids. He waved Nick to come over.

◆

Nick shone his penlight on his watch. 9:30. He was supposed to meet them in the playground toilets at 10 o'clock. Following Ray Corsini's instructions, he undid his bed, propped his old brogues one atop the other at an angle under the covers, shaped his sheets in a long roll, scrunched up his pillow, balled his nightshirt on it and pulled the blanket up over it. In the glowing red light from the emergency exit sign, it looked good to Nick. He hurriedly dressed, pulling his overcoat and cap out from under the bed where he had hidden it after dinner, and quietly went out onto the fire escape, quickly opening the door and closing it gently so it didn't make a sound or blow cold air in and waken anyone.

They came out of the playground toilet when they saw him crossing over the snow-covered walk. He knew the kids, all in the class ahead of him: Toogie Groome, Ray Corsini and Ralph Carl.

With help from clasped hands, Nick was up and over, as was Ray. Toogie and Carl, both tall, jumped up and easily mounted the wall. Jim put a finger to his mouth and pointed at the wall. Nick understood. A watchman might be passing on the other side. They made their way past the darkened Lodge, down Girard Avenue to Broad Street, the city's widest and busiest street, before speaking. It ran from way up north to center city, around City Hall, and down into South Philly.

"See you in a couple years, Billy," Ralph waved a fearless goodbye down Broad Street at the floodlit statue of William Penn atop City Hall.

"What's the first thing you're gonna do when we get to Florida?" Ray asked Toogie.

"I'm gonna buy a postcard and send it back to Miss Hill saying what a good time we're having. I'll get one with an alligator on it and write her name across it." Ignoring the red light, the group danced across the street waving politely to drivers who beeped horns at them.

Half an hour later, nearing the Delaware River where they heard the mournful hoot of boats, the wind began blowing harder and fine snowflakes started pelting their faces. "Jeez, it's cold," Ralph said. Nick felt that way too but didn't say it. "We'll turn down here and go up by the bridge," Ray said.

"It's the Ben Franklin Bridge to New Jersey, Nick," Toogie said.

"I know, I know!"

"Okay, guys, we're tired but let's not get cranky." No one responded.

"Where we gonna sleep? If we're tryna start for Florida tomorrow, we better get some sleep tonight."

"We'll find a place," Toogie said, encouragingly. The bridge looked inviting with lights shining down on its roadway, but they agreed the bridge cops would probably see them.

178

"They probably turn the lights out at midnight. If we cross in the early morning before the traffic from Jersey starts, it's our best chance."

The wind seemed even stronger and colder now so close to the river, and there were no houses or buildings with fences to provide shelter.

"There, we'll have to sleep there," Ralph said dejectedly. Underneath a dark billboard on steel stilts was a lean-to like structure, plywood sheets pitched against a bridge abutment. The ground was uneven with dirt piles and large dugout holes. "Must be a hobo house," Ray said.

"Yo!" Nick kicked an empty beer can and something ran away. "Rats."

"Aw, they're afraid of us," Ray said.

"Phew," Nick blurted, "this is a piss pot for drunks, I'm not staying here."

"Look, this is the best we got. There's some light from the bridge, and at least we're out of that damned wind and snow. I'm freezing like you."

Ralph, rummaging on the other side of the concrete abutment, called, "Here's some cardboard boxes and they're dry. We can sleep on them. The wind's blowing that way, so put 'em here, uphill from the stink."

The boxes were torn in flat sections and the quartet sat down next to each other under the angled plywood, pulled the biggest single piece of cardboard over their feet, bent it up to their knees and closed their eyes. Not a word was spoken.

Morning arrived, the snow had stopped and there was no wind. Nick woke when someone said, "Jeez, that's the coldest night I ever spent." And then, "Why didn't we steal some bread at dinner?" The response was some glum "Uh huhs."

"Look guys," Toogie sat up, "this was my idea, but you all wanted in. We agreed to head for Florida so we can trap alligators and fish all day and just do whatever we want to. No guvvies, no housies, no teachers and no prison wall."

"How'd you find out about it?" Nick asked, stretching.

"I read in a National Graphic magazine at the Library about how great it is, and we're going to the best part — the Everglades."

"An' we're goin' this way," Ray pointed at the bridge, "because my nonnie's got a place in Jersey. They don't use it in the winter so there's lots of stuff to pick from. I know where the key's hid. After we eat and get some bags of food, we'll catch a truck heading to Florida. Lots of trucks go to Florida, we just gotta watch the license plates and wave to them."

It was 7:30, by Nick's watch, when they finally got to the end of the bridge and started up a busy highway. As they approached a diner, the unanimous decision was to not spend any money there. Nick had three dollars and the others a total of ten and change. They continued trudging along, stepping off the road back onto the grassy path as cars, trucks mostly, came up on them.

"See how some of those drivers look over at us?" Nick asked.

"Yeah," Toogie and Ralph agreed. "Maybe it's how we look." After a desultory discussion, everyone agreed if the escape had been discovered and the police alerted, they'd better try to change their appearance. Taking off their garters, they let their knickers hang loose. "Anybody who sees us in knickers might know we're Hummers," Ray said, "and Ralph's idea to cross over to the other side of the road and back every so often is a good idea, let's start now."

An hour later, their pace was slowing and only two Florida plates were seen. Then they heard, "Hey, boys, where you headed?"

The policeman was pleasant enough, Nick had to agree, even asking if they wanted some breakfast. They were too weary and dejected. "Thank you, sir, but no," was the courteous reply.

On a bench outside a jail cell they sat, heads and shoulders against the bars, too tired to be distraught, silent. Mr. Sparks came in and spoke quietly to the policeman, then signaled them to follow him. In his car, with all four crammed in the back seat, he finally spoke. "Where were you heading? Dumb, boys, dumb," when Ralph mumbled their destination.

"Did you think you could disguise yourselves by letting your knickers hang down to cover your shins? What about your mackinaws, caps, and wearing white shirts, ties and a vest...and expensive brogues? All Jacob Reed clothes only rich kids from the Main Line could wear. The four of you walking along a busy highway early in the morning couldn't get more attention if you were riding one of those alligators from the Everglades around City Hall."

As Mr. Sparks drove across the bridge from New Jersey, Nick studied the thick shadows of girders the sun kept throwing across their legs. Nick knew everyone was thinking of Mr. Davis, the disciplinarian. He looked away, covering his eyes with his hand, after rubbing them. His mom would be so upset — that would be the worst — maybe even cry, and ask why he got into trouble again. Maybe it would be better if he just told her that he left the campus with some friends but didn't get a pass first and not go into the details. It would be even worse if he couldn't go home for summer vacation after Remedial School as part of his punishment.

They followed Mr. Sparks into the Middle School, where he waved them to the bench outside Mr. Davis' office, objects of curious stares from passersby. He knocked and went in. Several teachers went by, each conferring a disapproving glance. Finally, Mr. Sparks came out, held the door open, and said, "Mr. Davis would like to see you, now." The door closed behind them.

"Well, here come our world travelers," Mr. Davis said without smiling. The four lined up in front of his desk.

"Your mothers sent you here to be educated; to learn proper manners and the right way to behave. Do you appreciate it? Of course not. This is the way you respond to your care, your housing, your clothing, your food…and all the people trying to raise you above what you would be at home. You are ingrate orphans."

Rising, his arm came over his desk with a paddle that looked like a tennis racket. "Line up!"

Having been paddled once before, Nick went to the table against the wall, gripped the edge and bent over. The others joined him.

Whack! "Ow!" Ray cried out. "Ow!" he cried, each time he was hit.

Finally, it stopped. Then Nick heard Ralph, "Ohhh!" This time Nick counted. Eleven hits later there was a pause.

Suddenly Nick felt a stinging blow. "Yow!" He clinched his bottom. Reds Eckard told him the stinging didn't spread as far as when you were relaxed.

"Yow!" He couldn't tell the difference and he forgot to count. He just gritted his teeth when he felt it was coming. When the pause did come, a hand on his shoulder moved him aside. It pained him to straighten up. Ray and Ralph stood back, both with a hand on their bottoms, grimacing.

"Now, it's time for the ringleader. We know who the instigator was." With that he slammed the paddle against Toogie. "Eeow!"

Mr. Davis didn't stop at twelve, he kept on until Groome was sagging by the twentieth. "Remember this the next time you decide to go against our rules." Toogie stood, swayed and groaned.

"You will find a Very Objectionable rating on your records — a few more of them and I'll send you on an adventure that will be permanent." He opened the door, towering above them.

"Oh, your accomplice, Mr. Broussard, confessed, after all the Lafayette sections were told there would be no passes for anyone for the rest of the semester until we found out who stuffed the beds. He received an Unsatisfactory rating on his record and will spend a lot of time on the grudge line."

No one looked back as they left, but they heard him say, "I told Mr. Keatley to let everyone in Lafayette and in Good Friends know what you did and how you were punished. And that you were so smart you didn't need a compass. He's sure to tell them you were headed north on Route 130, not south…there are no Everglades or alligators in New York City."

THIRTY-FIVE

The two main entrances to the Chapel were flanked by big stone sculptures. On the way to services one Sunday, when Nick was still in Section Eleven, Miss Saunders had stopped the boys and told them about each of the carved animals. Sitting about twelve feet tall, they were the emblems, she said, of the four Evangelists, each holding a scroll that represented the four Gospels. St. Matthew's emblem was a Winged Man, St. Mark's a Winged Lion and St. Luke's a Winged Ox. On this hot July afternoon, Nick sat in the shadow of his favorite, his back against the base of the noble Eagle of St. John.

Nick shoved a letter from home into the book before slamming it shut. He looked up at the bright blue July sky, disgruntled. Bad enough that old Friedman recommended that he go to Summer School and get bumped from the swim team, but the U he got for hopping the wall probably clinched it. Part remedial, part punishment. The hardest thing was his mom's letter. She didn't really yell at him, but he knew she was upset. He'd do anything to make it up to her when he got home. At least they let him go home. Summer school remedial Math class ran from 9 to 11:30 with a temporary teacher. Friedman wasn't even there. At least they gave remedial guys the weekends off — with homework, of course. And I'm supposed to enjoy Pleasure Camp on weekends. Great!

Nick had explained to his mom that Pleasure Camp on school grounds during the summer was for Hummers of all ages; anyone who didn't go home because they didn't have a family or anyplace to go or they lived where the Hum said it was a bad neighborhood. They spent the day playing sports or going to the Library, with movies at night. They could swim every day in the pool. Sometimes they went out on trips. The little kids saw lots of cartoons. From Good Friends on, there were lots of pickup baseball games. But it was boring after awhile, with so many friends he knew gone, at camp or home. The Hum camp was

184

in the Pocono Mountains on a lake and anyone could go for one of the three-week sessions. Campers he knew always wanted him to go.

"C'mon, Nick, it's great. You can be in a cabin with us. We go out in canoes and take poles with punching gloves on them and try to knock everybody in; the last guy standing wins."

"We give crazy plays and act like Indians and stuff."

"We take hikes in the woods and climb mountains and learn things and make fires and eat. You can pick huckleberries and the cook will make a pie just for you. And ya can learn some dirty songs, too. An' it's real easy to get lost in the woods and take a smoke."

Nick never wanted to go. He wanted to go home for the whole summer. Wilkes-Barre was near the Poconos and the family always went to Harvey's Lake and North Lake to picnic and swim.

He still didn't believe what Smokey Stover told him about his brother. He was such a messer they wouldn't let him go home one summer, and made him stay in and go to Hum camp and then Pleasure Camp. He was so mad at the Hum, Smokey said, when he got off the camp bus in front of Founder's Hall, he opened his suitcase, and it was filled with snakes. Smokey said everybody was screaming and the snakes disappeared in the bushes by the Library.

Well, in another two weeks, it'll be over, if they think I learned something. At least I'll get most of August at home, he thought.

He was sitting by the Chapel, where he wasn't supposed to be. Everyone there had to choose between going to the swimming pool, pickup baseball on the playground or basketball in the Armory. He didn't feel like doing any of those things so he drifted off from the group as they trooped down the Main Road. This Chapel entrance didn't face the busy Main Road and the Infirmary; it faced one end of Lafayette and the Hum wall running down Girard Avenue. No one would see him here. He closed the book, the letter from home his bookmark.

185

The only good thing about Summer School, Nick thought, was having lots of time to read. He'd finished "The Man in the Iron Mask" and wondered what would happen next in "The Count of Monte Christo." But Summer School was lonely. Most of his friends were at home, the others at the Hum camp. Summer vacation only lasted about ten weeks and it was still another two weeks before he'd go home. It didn't seem fair that they made him go to Summer School. If you flunked a course, yes, but he didn't flunk, just got a C-minus. It was Mr. Friedman — he did it.

"Hey, kid, whattya you doin' here?" It was a Biggie from one of the halls. Nick had seen him in the dining room where they all ate in the summer. "You're gonna get in trouble hanging out here. They'll think you hopped the wall. Better go down to the playground or the pool."

"Mind your own business. You taking remedial lessons on how to be a housemaster?"

The big kid shook his head in disgust. "Such a smart ass, I'll bet you're here for Summer School."

"Yeah, and what are you doing here instead of being home?"

"I'm here because I'm going to the second session of camp in August." Suddenly the big kid looked funny in a sad kind of way, and Nick found himself feeling sorry for being so nasty. "Actually, I don't have any close family, kid, and there's no one to take me, so here I am and then I'll go to camp." Turning, he walked away.

Nick really felt rotten. He banged the back of his head against the stone base, rose and started for the playground.

◆

The next afternoon, sitting under his Eagle, Nick just didn't feel like reading. He didn't feel like doing anything. He rested his head against the cool, shaded concrete, eyes closed.

"You still here?" It was that same Biggie.

186

Nick felt sorry about what he said yesterday, but didn't know how to say he was sorry. He might make the guy sad again, or he might make him mad. He kept his eyes closed.

"Did Edmund Dantes escape from his prison cell yet?"

"No," said Nick, opening his eyes and looking straight ahead.

"I know what's wrong with you," his voice gentle, but not sissy-like, the Biggie said. "You're lonely." Nick looked up. The kid was probably sixteen, a Junior in Mariner Hall. Probably graduate in a year or so. He looked like an athlete. Not too tall, but with broad shoulders. The muscles in his arm rippled when he rubbed his eyebrow. Dark brown hair, short but not too short. He had a soccer ball under his arm.

"Look, kid, I was put in the Hum on my sixth birthday. I've been here over ten years and there're two things I think a Hummer's gotta learn if he's gonna make it. First is, you learn that everyone's a little lonely here, even in all the crowds on the playground or in the chapel. The first few weeks here, boy, you know that. After a while, after you get to know some other Hummers, you think it'll go away. Then one day, you realize it never will. Sometimes, when you're alone, you wonder about being home with your mom and brothers or sisters and friends and wonder what you'd be doing with them. But it disappears just as quickly and you're busy with everything you have to do here. I'll bet you never heard anyone say they were lonely." He seemed to be staring at the soccer ball in his hands and talking to himself.

"You're in Lafayette, about to go up to the halls? Most guys, by the time they're moving up, have learned to live with aloneness. After a while you get so used to it, it just doesn't bother you. Maybe it gets so deep inside, especially with Hummers who don't see their moms on weekends. You notice it a little when you come back from vacations."

Closing the book, Nick rested it on his knees, and said softly, again not looking at the boy, "Sometimes I feel like I'm starting to feel

187

that way. I like getting letters from home, but I'm not waiting for them every day the way I did in Junior School. Now I write home maybe every few weeks and sometimes I feel bad about that. It's when I'm in bed at night and imagine what it must be like to be at home. Or if I see something …like one of those blue Evening in Paris bottles I saw on Miss Lockwood's table when she called me into her room one time. I felt bad that night thinking of the one on my mom's bureau." Nick stared at the unopened book, then brightened and grinned when he saw the big kid drop the soccer ball between the wings of the Eagle.

"Maybe he'll give it a blessing, so our ball will fly into Northeast High's goalpost this year and we'll be the city's soccer champs again."

"Yeah," Nick said. "That would be great."

Nick thought that would end the conversation, but it didn't. When the boy saw Nick smile, he said, encouragingly, "Look, kid, in the Hum you're surrounded by kids whether it's in class or playing sports or doing homework or chores. Some of them may be buddies, but in the end, every day, it's just you, without any other guys or even your mom. Even if you go home on weekends and see your mom, she can't do anything for you. She gave you up completely when she signed those papers. And they can do anything they want with you. You feel lonely now because you can't go home and all your buddies are gone, too."

The slow pealing of the Westminster chimes began ringing out from Founder's Hall roof. "Gotta go. Game can't start without the ball…or me. I'll tell you the other thing Hummers gotta live with some other time. This is just part of my lecture."

With a short "hang in there" punch in the air towards Nick, he grabbed the ball and raced away. Nick watched him disappear around the corner of Lafayette.

◆

His Eagle above him, his book on his knees, Nick waited after remedial class the next day hoping the Biggie would come by again, but

188

he didn't. He didn't want to feel lonely, but he did. It felt weird because he was going home in a few weeks and would be with his mom and sister and cousins. Just to throw himself on his bed would be great. He should be happy, he told himself. He was promoted; even going to Summer School didn't stop that. He'd go from Seventh Grade to Ninth Grade. And he'd get long pants; even the shortest guy got long pants when they got to the halls. He'd never have to wear dopey knickers again. At least when it got warm, like now, they got shorts. Maybe it was because when he came back from vacation the first week of September, nothing would be the same. Everything he was used to would be gone. It was kind of scary. A new building, lots of new kids, new housemasters and teachers…and going to the high school with all the Biggies, even Seniors. He'd actually be a Biggie.

"Sorry, bud, but you can't stay here." It was a housemaster from one of the halls. "Where should you be?"

"Down at the playground, sir."

"Okay, get moving."

Musical Enlightenment

Music flowed through your life as a Hummer from your first day until your last. On that first full day, you attended a service where hymns were sung or went to the Junior School auditorium where hundreds of kids elatedly sang, often comically acting out with youthful zeal — "I See The Moon," "Down in the Valley," "Comin' Round the Mountain" or "You Are My Sunshine." On your first Friday afternoon, playing with new friends or alone on a bench, immersed in melancholy thoughts of home, you heard a sound that would invade the rest of your life at Girard.

"The Band and the Batty!" someone cried and you followed the throng across the playground to stand on benches or lean against the pipe railings facing the Main Road. Down the ramp from the Armory marched the Band followed by the Battalion in the blue and gray uniforms of West Point Cadets, shouldering M-1 rifles. Each Company was led by a much admired Captain with a shining saber to his shoulder. As the Color Guard passed, some kids saluted; you, like most, stood, hand over your heart, watching in awe, knowing someday you would be in that parade.

After a month or two of Friday afternoon and Saturday morning parades, every little Hummer could whistle or hum America's most famous marches — "Stars and Stripes Forever", "Washington Post," "El Capitan" and the "National Emblem" as well as the Army, Navy and Marine Hymns.

Entering Girard at ages six or seven, newbies lived in House A, B, C, D, E or F in the West End and were introduced to group singing by the governess, who often played music on a record player or radio. On Sunday, West Enders marched up the Main Road joining the entire student body for chapel services. Sitting upright and silent, they tried to understand sermon and anthem. Learning to lean forward, right arm across the pew in front of them, head down, forehead on the back of their hand, they listened to prayers.'

All sixteen hundred orphans, aged six to seventeen, said The Lord's Prayer in unison. Hymnal in hand, the young ones began to memorize the school's religious repertoire: dozens of Christian classics from "Onward Christian Soldiers", and "Fairest Lord Jesus" to "Holy, Holy, Holy," and "For All The Saints." In Junior School, you were taught music by Miss Benner. Along with "I've Been Workin' on the Railroad" and "Blow The Man Down," we listened to recordings of "Peter and the Wolf" and the "Carnival of Animals" and lighter, more melodious works of the Three Bs, along with a childish introduction to the composer and what should be listened for. Radio themes used for The Lone Ranger, The Green Hornet and Sergeant Preston of the Yukon were much requested. Teachers kept an ear out for boys with good soprano voices, sending them to audition with Dr. Banks for the Junior Hundred, the youthful section of the Glee Club.

In the Middle School, at ages ten through thirteen, when living in Good Friends and Lafayette, Miss Frame taught us the basics of music — the types of notes, rests, syllable singing, and we even learned how to gracefully draw the clef sign. Song favorites included "My Grandfather's Clock", "Celito Lindo," "Camptown Races", "Flow Gently, Sweet Afton," "Finiculi, Finicula" and "Aura Lee" with snickering requests for "Massa's in the Cold, Cold Ground."

When, at fourteen, you were promoted to High School, you were allowed to audition for a musical instrument. Unfortunately, the long sign-up lines didn't necessarily signify grateful orphans determined to expand their musical world — if you didn't play in the band, you were relegated to the Battalion with its relentless drilling sessions, tests and inspections.

Auditions weeded out the tone deaf while others, though accepted, were dropped for poor attendance or a frivolous attitude. Rolling sheet music into balls and wielding the clarinet as a baseball bat brought an angry "Get out! You're in the Battalion now, Mister Swahl!"

So entranced with the "Saber Dance," a popular selection the Concert Band played on Saturday nights in the Chapel, I switched to the trumpet. Never did get my hands on that trumpet, and the cornet I did get didn't last long with me, either. Baseball season arrived weeks later and I scribbled "I quit" on the rehearsal sign-in sheet, a mistake I've regretted many times. We had no parent, guardian or mentor to provide mature direction. Our mothers knew little of life at Girard, except what we told them. As you grew older, you were given more responsibility for making choices, and, as you often ruefully learned, you had to live with your decisions.

Though formal music classes ended when you entered High School, you continued to sing and be sung to; music was as constant as the wall surrounding you. Membership in the Glee Club added to your musical experience as you sang "The Hallelujah Chorus", "Jesu, Joy of Man's Desiring," and "Deep River." Friday or Saturday evenings often found everyone in the Chapel enjoying performances by Fred Waring and his Pennsylvanians, the University of Pittsburgh Choir, and local male and female singing groups. Performances by the concert band included favorites such as, "Finlandia," "Scheherazade," the Overtures to "Tannhauser" and "Lohengrin" and Broadway hit tunes.

Morning assemblies in the High School auditorium were often highlighted by twenty minutes of singing from a big blue songbook — "The Lost Chord," "Stout Hearted Men", "When the Foeman Bares His Steel" and "Men of Harlech," rousing versions ending with enthusiastic clapping. Art songs such as Shakespeare's "Who is Sylvia" and the Welsh melody "All Through The Night" were looked on with male disdain and sung reluctantly. Monday morning featured two student disk jockeys bringing us radio station WBMJ — "Wash Away Blue Monday with Jazz." After one or two corny jokes, sure to invoke groans, Bob Furmanski and Bill Flanagan "spun" records by Glenn Miller, and the Dorseys, plus current hits by Les Paul and Mary Ford, Nat King Cole and Guy Mitchell. At the mournful end of "Cry" by Johnnie Ray, played for the first and only time, an outraged Mr. Zarella leapt from his seat, shouting loudly, "That's not music!"

Each hall — Banker, Merchant, Mariner and Bordeaux had a radio, probably donated in the past by a housemaster. They could not be turned on until after classes at four o'clock. About five-thirty, when everyone was washed up for dinner, we listened to The 950 Club, Philadelphia's most popular disc music program, until we had to jump up and race to the dining

192

room. Some kids did have their own radios, tiny white Arvins. As a Senior, I had a record player and a small stack of 45's featuring The Four Aces' "Garden In The Rain," and lots of Dixieland. I learned my first opera aria when I discovered "La Donna Mobile" on the reverse side of Mario Lanza's "Be My Love."

Our musical education in the upper halls included a unique version of yet-to-be-created elevator music: Girard's novel approach — play it outdoors. As we sat on benches or steps or walked with friends, circling our buildings, waiting for the call to lunch, music filled the air above us, broadcast from the roof of Founder's Hall. Rain or shine, every day, instrumental renditions of show tunes from Broadway musicals, "The Blue Danube," "The Merry Widow" and other waltzes and stirring marches showered down on us until we crowded into the Dining Room. And, reminding us of where we should be, Westminister chimes rang out every quarter hour.

On Memorial Day, the Battalion surrounded the statue adjacent to Founder's Hall, honoring Girardians who had fallen at Gettysburg, the First and now, the Second World War. "In Flanders Field" was read, memorial statements made and flowers placed. "Ase's Death" from The "Peer Gynt Suite" was played, the service ending with "Taps."

The National Anthem was sung often, the Chapel organ's majestic swell inspiring us. On many occasions, it immediately swirled into another anthem, one we found easier to sing and with rousing but confusing lyrics, especially for the younger Hummers. Growing older you became familiar with certain words and phrases and sang those; and at the start of the required two years of French (Stephen Girard having been a Frenchman), we finally learned the lyrics of "La Marseillaise" from the suitably named Miss Amelie (Frenchy) Frey.

Hummers endured dance classes, learning to Fox Trot, Waltz and even Samba with another boy. The reward was Coke & Pretzel Dances with girls brought in from other orphanages and Proms when you brought a girl in, taking her home immediately after the Swing Band ended the evening with "Goodnight, Sweetheart."

Your musical involvement at Girard ended on your last day. It also included a formidable musical task graduating classes inevitably failed. You filed in to Elgar's triumphant march, the 2,400-seat Chapel filled with the student body, governesses, housemasters and teachers with mothers, sisters, brothers and other relatives and friends looking down from the balcony,

Youthful speakers spoke briefly, not so the adults. Mounting the stage for your diploma, you joined your fifty or so classmates, faced the crowd and, led by Dr. Banks, sang, with the student body, a robust "Hail Girard." This was followed by a silence of uneasy anticipation. Through all those years, observing each January and June graduation as you moved forward in the Chapel, every Hummer had to wonder whether he could complete "The Farewell Song."

With strong voices we got through the first verse and refrain:

"Sixteen Hundred looking on, we are in the van;
We have run our marathon from child to growing man;
Out beyond the open gates Lights of Promise glow;

You who cheered us when we came, Bless us ere we go.

Farewell. Farewell. Dear temple on the hill;
We'll not forget you till our hearts be still."

Words in the second verse seemed to get caught in your throat, some never surfacing. You recalled astonishing moments in the past, watching even the least liked Hummers you knew struggle to sing, heads lowered, hands covering faces disfigured by crying. The last verse was barely audible; the refrain ending, as it did year after year, an organ solo.

From your first day to this, your last, music had enveloped your life at Girard.

THIRTY-SIX

Nick was in the Yukon, trudging through a blinding snowstorm with Jack London's White Fang, when he heard the chimes announce noon and lunch. During the summer, everyone, except Junior Schoolers, ate meals in one dining room. Seniors and upper classmen sat at certain tables, Lafayette and Good Friends Middle Schoolers at others. By the time Nick got to the dining room, everyone was seated. A housemaster Nick didn't know pointed to the nearest table. But an arm waved at another table. It was the Biggie pointing to an empty seat near him. "Hiding under the Eagle again?" he said as Nick sat down.

"Right," Nick replied. Everyone bowed their heads as a scowling kid at the head of the table hurriedly muttered grace. Nick leaned forward, surreptitiously surveying the table of Biggies, when a huge guy opposite him drew a big laugh as he leaned forward towards Nick and said in a raspy gangster voice, "What's a matta, kid? You're lookin' 'round like this is a South Philly Mafia meeting and you gotta figure out which one a us is gonna wipe you out." Nick felt his face heat up. He smiled back, weakly, and looked at the chapel Biggie.

"Ignore him," the Biggie said. "The only reason he hasn't been kicked out," he tapped the top of his head, "is because his is so big and dense he can head a soccer ball more than fifty feet."

That started an entertaining few minutes of bantering until lunch was served and the table quieted down. At breakfast and lunch, anyone could leave the table whenever they finished their meal. At dinner, everyone waited to be dismissed. By the time Nick ate his rice pudding the table had been abandoned except for a few guys deciding their afternoon activities. The Biggie pushed his chair back and turned to Nick. "I didn't tell you the second requirement to be a Hummer."

"Oh, no. Guess who's gonna give his 'How To Be A Hummer' Lecture?" the huge guy announced to the others.

"I said the first thing is that you're actually alone in this crowded joint. You can talk to your buddies all you want, but in the end you're on your own."

"Right," someone called, moving closer, "remember, the cheese stands alone and so do Hummers."

"C'mon, this is serious, you guys," but the Biggie had an amused look.

"Young man," someone said in a high pitched, professorial voice, "Stephen Girard wants you to be an independent, self-confident, conscientious, hard-working gentleman…able to leap tall buildings."

"Hell no, Harry," another voice interrupted, "…able to leap a ten foot wall's good enough!" Everyone was in the act now.

Clapping his hands loudly, another Biggie declared "Decorum, decorum! Stop this uncontrollable mirth. I want proper decorum or I'll clear the room! That's the daily Girard threat, but you know that by now, kid."

The Biggie Nick knew raised his hand again to stop any further comments. "The second thing a Hummer has to learn about the Hum," he went on, "is that as soon as you get used to things, they change them on you."

"Geezus, MacIntire, you sound like Doggie Haskell," someone said as he rose to leave.

"Doc Haskell will be one of your English teachers," the Biggie said to Nick, who was now relieved to learn his friend's name.

"The old Doc's right, too," the big guy said. "Junior School's easiest, most guys are there for a couple years. Then they ship you over to Good Friends for maybe a year or so."

"Then you spend, maybe, half a year in Lafayette," someone added, "and up to the halls. A year in Banker or Merchant, then a year in Mariner, another in Bordeaux and six months in Allen Hall before you graduate."

"If you graduate," warned several voices.

"Why are you in here anyway?" someone asked.

"He's here for some remedial work," the Biggie said.

"We've all been through that at least once in the past," the big guy added sympathetically. And when Nick added, "It was math plus the U I got for hopping the wall," he was rewarded with appreciative nods and "good Hummer!"

"Lunch is over." A housemaster stood by the table. "This isn't some Bertie Wooster's Drones Club, where you privileged English gentlemen can loll about wasting time and taking up space. Disband now or help out in the kitchen."

Outside, MacIntire started up the steps to Mariner Hall. At the door, he turned, saw Nick and waved. "See ya around, kid." Nick answered with a grin and a wave, "Not for a while, I'm going home this weekend for the rest of the summer."

THIRTY-SEVEN

It was two weeks since Nick had gotten home. Remedial classes and Pleasure Camp were quickly forgotten, although he had to admit it helped him learn about how to approach mathematics and he felt it would help him with classes in September. Now, he just wanted to enjoy August. Sitting on his bike after days of riding up and down his street, South Fulton, he realized how big the Hum was. How far you had to go up the Main Road from the Armory to Founder's Hall. Here you'd be all the way down Market Street, almost to the top of Stegmaier Brewery's hill. And Philadelphia had such wide streets, like Broad Street and the Parkway by the fountain. Fulton Street seemed as narrow as Elfreth's Alley — that street the sign said was the oldest in America that people still lived on. The house his mom rented was a duplex; the Tudor James family lived in the other half. South Fulton began at Market Street, a busy one like Girard Avenue with lots of stores, but it ran just one block past their house and stopped, dead end, at Puritan Lane.

Whenever Nick came home, Aunt Edith brought him a present and it was always his favorite. In the summer it was a big bag of dark red cherries; at Christmas and Easter it was a box of chocolate covered cherries. And she always complimented him on how well dressed he was. He was polite, and thanked her, but he hated his Hum clothes when he was home. His mom said she'd buy him some sport shirts so he didn't have to wear a shirt and tie every day and a pair of shorts he could play in. She said no to long pants because he was starting to "shoot up" and would outgrow them by next summer. So, he wore his knickers when they visited people or went to church or town, and occasionally they caused trouble.

Yesterday Evan Morgans rode his bike right up next to him and started taunting him in front of some other kids. "What weird country did you come from where they wear these funny baggy things?" Then,

198

looking around to make sure everyone was watching, he leaned down, and said, trying to be funny, "I wonder what holds these clown pants up?"

As his hand neared Nick's knee, Nick turned on his seat and punched Evan's shoulder hard. He toppled over with a loud "Ow!" followed by an angry "Ouf!" when his bike landed on him, entangling his legs. Furiously kicking it off, he rose, rubbed his backside and rushed at Nick, who'd already got off his bike and pushed it towards Charlie Hughes to hold. Kids down the street, hearing the street bully yell and seeing him on the ground, came rushing, anticipating a fight.

◆

"I guess one thing you learn at that school with nothing but boys is how to fight," Charlie Hughes called from his porch next door.

"I don't know that I won," Nick replied, rubbing his still red elbow from when Evan had pushed him down, "but he knows I'm not afraid to fight him."

"Well, you got some good punches in. His lip was bleeding. Musta got stuck by a tooth."

"How often do you guys fight at that school?" Meredith Winslow, who'd suddenly appeared by Nick, asked anxiously. Nick looked at Meredith. With a name like that, he wouldn't last long at the Hum, Nick thought, shifting on the seat of the thick-bodied Schwinn. He's sort of a sissy and he'd get a nickname fast. No brothers or sisters, and his mother and father always yelling for him. Always making sure where he is and who he's playing with. Has a real nice house with a big yard, not part of a double block like everyone else, and a yappy little black and white bulldog.

"Not a real lot, Meredith. You just have to make sure other guys know you'll fight back. If they're really big, you can kick, too, but no biting," he added, enjoying the effect. Now Meredith really looked frightened.

"He'll never make fun of your pants again," Jackie Fisher said, joining in.

"Maybe. I wish my mom would just get me one pair of long pants. I hate these knickers."

"Does everybody wear them?"

"No, Biggies don't. But you have to wait until you go up to the halls; that's when you go to high school. Or you have to be real tall — like Richard would probably have long pants already," Nick said, with a pained look. "Nobody notices knickers back at the Hum, 'cus everybody's wearing them. When you go out, though, you know people are looking at you. Sometimes little kids point at you. And bigger kids outside laugh at you, unless you're with some other Hummers. And the school's known by lots of people around Philadelphia. People passing you on street will even say, 'Boy from Girard?' and smile like we're special. That's why, from when you're a little kid, you're told Girard has a special reputation and you better keep it up when you're outside the walls."

"What do girls say?"

"They watch you with their eyes big and whisper to their girlfriends and then they laugh, looking at you. You know they're making fun of you, even here. It's always the knickers."

"But some of the girls around here really like you, like Mary Pularo and Owen Williams' sister. They say you go to school in Philadelphia and you're real smart and act different."

"Who makes you do your homework, like my mom does," Jackie asked.

"At Girard no one ever asks if you did your homework," Nick said to unbelieving eyes, "unless it's a teacher in class when you don't know an answer."

"One good thing about those knicker pants," said Ivor Morgans, who'd inched into the group, "they can't get caught in your bike the way the cuffs on our pants do," the small group amiably agreeing. A year older than Evan, his brother, Ivor was small, wiry and smarter. He'd watched yesterday's fight, silent though everyone else was cheering for Nick, and didn't try to help his brother with his bleeding lip. Ivor never picked on anyone and Nick couldn't remember anyone ever fighting with him. Other kids listened when he spoke, almost as though he were a grown up.

"I know," Nick said, reaching down to scrape some dirt off the thick white front tire with his thumb, "But I still feel like a freak when I'm away from the Hum, even when I'm out on a pass and roaming around the city with some buddies."

The group eyed Nick in awe. "You mean they let you go out in Philadelphia by yourself?"

"We tell 'em we're going out to the park, but I think they know we don't always go there," Nick said, watching Meredith's eyes grow.

"Whattaya do?" Jackie asked.

"We go down to where all the big buildings and movies and stores are."

"You mean like going downtown here to the Square?"

"Yeah, but they call it Center City and some of the buildings must be thirty stories high. Billy Penn's statue's on top of City Hall and he's the highest."

"Geez! Do you walk everywhere and see these things?"

"Mostly, but sometimes we go down into a subway stop and ride the subway."

"What's a subway?"

"It's a train that goes under the streets — but sometimes it comes up out of the ground and goes up in the air on tracks over the streets. Then they call it the 'El' for elevated."

"Wow!" Meredith said, "Where does it go?"

"I don't know. We just get on and go to the end of the ride. People get on and off all the time 'cus there are lots of stations. 'Course they look at us because of our knickers and sometimes smile and ask us about school. We look down on buildings, and houses and people doing things. At the end, everybody gets off and so do we. We go down steps to the street and walk around. We're never sure what we'll see. It's always different. Men building brick walls. Big trucks dumping stuff. Sometimes we watch them digging a big hole where they're going to build a building. Sometimes we go down by the river and watch the barges and the oil tankers go by. We see other kids, but don't talk to them. We try to talk to girls walking by, but mostly they laugh and keep goin.' We buy candy and soda or chocolate milk. Some guys buy ciggies and smoke." The group, stone still, was captivated.

"How do you get back to your school, the...the Hum?"

"We go back to the station, give the lady our money and then you can push the gate open and wait for the train. Once you're on, it's really noisy and rocks back and forth. It's fun to hold onto the straps that hang from the ceiling. Some guys swing around in circles until somebody stares hard at them. When the man announces Girard Avenue, we get off — it's named for the man who started our school. Then we walk back to the Hum."

"God! That's like starting out on an adventure and not knowing where you're going!" Jackie said, excitedly. "Where else do you go?"

"When we go downtown, sometimes we go in the Automat."

"Is that a car?" Meredith asked.

"No," Nick smiled. "It's a restaurant. One wall is full of little windows with food behind them...sandwiches and salads, Jello and tapioca and pumpkin pie. People put money in a slot next to a window that unlocks it, and then open the window. Sometimes I put three nickels in and take out a tuna sandwich like my mom makes. Or you can sit at the counter and order things like soup and hamburgers. That's what we like to do, and plates come out of a hole in the wall on this wide belt that runs past everybody."

"What's on the belt?"

"People tell the lady behind the counter what they want and in a little while plates with soup or macaroni and cheese or a hot dog or a plate with meatloaf, peas and mashed potatoes with gravy comes out on the belt thing."

"Geez!" Charlie exclaimed. "do you ever try to steal something like a muffin or a donut off the belt, and put it in your pocket?"

"No," Nick said, "the lady watches and knows what you ordered, picks it up and puts it in front of you. Besides," he tugged at one of his knickers, "with these darned things lots of people know who we are. Even cops."

"That's too bad."

"Not always, though."

"A kid I know in Seckie Twenty-Seven has a younger brother in Junior School. They go home on weekends and their mom gives them money to ride the trolley back to the Hum and enough to ride back home the next week. And they always get a little extra for a candy bar."

"What's a cop got to do with it?"

"Give 'im a chance to tell us, will ya!" Charlie scowled at Jackie.

"At a store they spend half their trolley money on candy, keepin' enough to get home again. Then they walk fast to get back for dinner. Andy says it's almost thirty blocks to the Hum, so sometimes they hafta run part way."

"Probably eatin' their candy while they run, I'll bet." says Jackie.

"When they get to the Zoo, they're more than halfway and his brother jumps on his back."

"Huh? His feet hurt or somethin'?"

"No."

"No? I don't' understand."

"What he does, Jackie, is walk by the entrance to the Zoo slowly, where there are lots of people. People know by their knickers they're Hummers — from Girard — and come over and ask if everything's all right. Andy said somebody always calls a cop and points at them. The cop comes over and asks Andy if his brother's all right. Andy says he's okay, just tired. The cop, or maybe just some man, will ask why they didn't take the trolley. He tells them he doesn't have enough money, so the man gives them money or the cop stops the next trolley and tells the driver, and they get on and ride for free. It gives them extra candy money."

The Fulton Street gang shrieked with glee when Nick concluded, "Andy says they've been doing it since Easter and they're gonna start doin' it again when summer vacation's over."

THIRTY-EIGHT

"Do any of you know that butter can fly?"

"Yeah, sure, butter flies," someone said insolently, "and cows flop."

"And birds gotta sing," someone threw in.

"Newcomers always get it in the end — their asses kicked by being so smart," Mike Sweeney said, "I'll get to you guys later."

"Why do Hummers always have to prove they're smart alecks," Nick said, to no response.

"Now, as your mature table head, I'm entrusted to teach you some of the finer points of 'messing around.' The secret to successfully flying butter is that you can't do it when you first sit down because the little squares are too hard. But, if you wait too long, it sticks to your knife and won't fly."

"Or," Phil Bartow included, "it lands on the guy sitting across from you. That means some punches and butter stuck up your nose."

Mike Sweeney was educating newcomers Returning from summer vacation, Nick had been promoted to Seventh Grade and moved up from Good Friends to Lafayette. Now thirteen, he was in Section Twenty Seven with only a few guys he knew.

Nick knew what "messing around" meant. In Junior School, it was anything that a governess, housemaster or teacher felt was improper behavior, failing to reflect proper decorum. Not the way proper Girardians acted. He'd paid for it with whacks on the head, hands and backside and hours and hours wasted on the grudge line or time back in a classroom after school was out.

"The consistency's right," Sweeney said, tapping the little yellow square on his butter plate with his finger. "Okay, everybody slide your knife under it all the way.," he said. "Now, hold it level like I'm holding it, not so high that somebody might see it. Put your finger on the tip of the knife. Pull down a little then let go — snap your wrist real hard and then stop fast. That makes the butter fly." Little yellow mounds landed on the white tablecloth or on the luncheon plates in front of the novices.

"Cripes, you guys'll never get it," he said, disgusted. "Instead of flicking it up in the air, you twisted your wrist too far and it came down in front of you. And you," he sneered at Nick, "you didn't even try it!"

"Because I already spread my butter on my bread," Nick shot back at him, "or would you like me to throw the whole slice like some sorta buttered discus?"

"Gotcha, Sweeney," someone said while others chuckled.

"Pretty big mouth for somebody who just landed here, Mister." But Nick could see Sweeney liked his remark and before Sweeney could say anything else, Nick said, "Okay, I'll try it."

"Phil," Sweeney asked, "lean over to that table and get Dave Crowley's butter. He hates butter." Turning back to the table, Bartow handed Nick a coffee saucer with the butter on it. Nick slid the tip of his knife under the butter, then positioned it ready to fly, his thumb pressing down on the knife's end. "So, what do I aim at?"

"You aim at one of the big white light globes hanging down from the ceiling. If you hit it, it's really great because after a while the butter starts to melt."

"And, if you're lucky, it drips down on someone!" Dave Conyers said optimistically.

"Here goes."

Everyone watched the missile sail out in an arc over the dining room. "Where'd it go?" someone questioned. "It didn't hit any lights that I can see," someone replied. "Look, Table Nine, everybody's laughing," Sweeney said. "Wow, you guys, on this kid's first try he hit somebody."

Nick, half standing up with the others to see, slapped his forehead in horror. The back of some kid's head had a lustrous gleam — a sunny yellow splotch on dark brown hair. Hearing nearby laughter, the victim wiped the back of his head and looked at his hand. He half stood up, turned and stared angrily in their direction. He raised his arm and held up his yellow hand as evidence.

When Sweeney cried, "Geezes, if we were the Eagles and he just holds his other arm up, you kicked a field goal and scored three points." Nick couldn't contain himself, exploding with laughter until he noticed how big and mad the guy was, and that his hand, butter oozing out of it, was now clenched in a menacing fist. "C'mon, you guys," Nick pleaded, "pretend you're laughing too, or he'll know it's me!" The mimed mix of exaggerated laughter and fake sorry-about-that faces enraged the kid so much, he stood up and leaned forward in anger.

When Mousie Elman, the housemaster, rose to see what happened, everyone dropped back in his chair and looked down at their plates. "Act normal, you guys, act normal. Don't look away from the table. Look at each other and talk. Pretend you're eating."

"Yeah, yeah, mutter, mutter, mutter." Sidelong glances at each other made them grin even more.

"When we leave the table," Sweeney continued from experience, "stick together. If he's waiting out there, he can't jump us all. Just say we saw it fly over our table and that's all."

That night in bed, Nick relived the scene. The big kid, waiting for them said he knew it was someone at their table and when he found out who it was, "and I will!" he can expect a broken nose.

Darn, Nick thought, in the silence of the dormitory, every time I go to a new building somebody asks me to try something new. Every time I do it, they get a laugh out of it and I get into trouble. In the glow of the red exit light, he made a pledge out loud. "From now on, I am not gonna be the first guy to try stuff."

"Quiet!" he heard from across the dark dormitory. "You'll get stuff — a shoe in your mouth if you don't shuddup!" someone threatened. Nick, putting his hand under his arm made a noise he hoped sounded like a fart and turned on his stomach to go to sleep.

THIRTY-NINE

Nick followed Freeman, Caruso and Ken Mazak into the lavatory. Perspiring, with an array of red bruises from hectic games of doubles in tether ball, they needed to wash up for dinner. As Nick bent over his washbasin to splash cold water on his face, he heard someone say, "Hey, Dale, I heard you seen your mother."

"I did not."

"Yeah, you did. Martin was with you, by Wanamaker's window." Nick saw it was McCann talking to Dale Winton.

Suddenly Winton rushed at McCann, pushing him hard on the chest. McCann cried "Yow!" and fell onto Sam Thomas, who was sitting on the long shoe rack polishing his brogues. Then Winton turned and ran toward the lavatory doorway, a hand to his eyes.

"Move!" he yelled at just entering Bob Nordstrom, whom he shoved out of sight.

"Who did what to that guy?" Nordstrom asked, poking his head around the corner to the puzzled bystanders. "He's crying."

Winton was a little older than Nick and had been in the Hum longer than Nick. He was always right in the middle of whatever was going on — waving his hand to be picked for a baseball or soccer game or with an answer in class. And when he was about to kick the ball or swing the bat, his mouth opened wide and his tongue came out. With his bright red hair flying away from his pale, freckled face, he was funny to see. Chet Van Why said he belonged in a comic book. Even the housemasters laughed, especially if he missed the kick, which often happened. Nick liked him because he just smiled back when others imitated him.

When Nick got in line going into the dining room, he found himself between Groome and Broussard who'd heard about Winton's explosion.

"And he goes everywhere alone, anymore," Groome said over Nick's shoulder. "Doesn't even look at anybody. He bumps into kids in the halls and now doesn't even shove back when they shove him. We're pretty good buddies with him and he won't even talk to us. I finally told him, when you wanna stop being weird, come find us." Broussard hunched his shoulders to emphasize his lack of understanding, as the dinner line began to move forward.

♦

As the crowd was leaving after the meal, Nick caught up with Broussard and gave his sleeve a pull and pointed to an empty bench. Nick sat down but Broussard, watching, gave a shrill whistle that brought Groome over.

"I know what happened to Winton, but ya gotta promise to keep it a secret," Nick said. With a grave look, each nodded yes. They stood in front of him as Nick leaned forward. "Hank Deibel asked me to go down town with him last Saturday. We were on the other side of City Hall when Hank says, 'Look, there's John Martin and Dale Winton. Let's spy on them.'

"So, we followed them. Hank hides behind telephone poles and people, and I run in and out of the store openings, but they don't see us. They stopped at Wanamaker's Department Store and are lookin' in these windows, and Hank says, 'That's the restaurant part.'

" 'I know,' I told him. I was with nutty Ed Rosen once and he snuck along low in front of it and then jumped up high with a funny face, scarin' the people at the tables inside. A cop yelled at him, so he makes a face at the cop — and even the cop smiled."

"So, we sneak up," Nick continued, "getting ready to jump on them and scare them, when Winton turns to Martin, 'I toldja, that's my mom! That's really my mom! And that's my Aunt Neddy!' He moves right up close to the window and Martin's behind him and they watch, real quiet. We were hiding behind a newsstand, but we could see two ladies just standing up, laughing with the waiter, grabbin' big shopping bags.

"So, we get right behind them, ready to yell, when Martin says, 'Hey, Wint, they're probably on the way to the Hum to see you. With presents, too. Go catch 'em and surprise 'em!' Winton nods yes. Then Martin says, 'But make it real fast. It's after five and we're gotta run back to the Hum in time for dinner. Then I see Winton's face change in the glass. His face squeezes up and he yells out loud, 'She's not coming to see me. It's too late to take me out for the afternoon. All the way from Easton and she ain't coming to see me!' He's crying so loud people going by are staring."

"Geez, what happened next?" Groome asked.

"He starts runnin' down the street with Martin after him, calling his name." Nick was silent, pausing to look down at his brogues as though he didn't want to say it. "When he finally stopped running, he musta told Martin his mother didn't love him. Came all that way and didn't come in to see him.

"We stayed right behind them and they never looked back. We could hear him sayin' loud over and over, 'But I love her!' "

Another silent pause. "Martin had his arm over Winton's shoulder till they got close to the Hum. We figure Martin promised Winton he'd never tell anyone."

Broussard furrowed his brow. "McCann's the wise guy that got Winton all upset in the lavatory, how'd he find out?"

" 'Cus Hank remembered looking back when we were coming up Corinthian Ave. McCann and Stribaugh were behind us, waving their arms and laughing at us. Now we know why."

Broussard slapped his head, and sputtered, "They were spyin' on *you* guys!"

"Yeah, those rats must have been spying on us and heard Winton — and McCann told him they knew."

210

In bed that night, Nick couldn't forget what happened to Winton. He was glad it was dark because his eyes got wet. *My mother would never do that.*

When he'd said his prayers, he asked if maybe it had been a mistake and could Dale find out it wasn't his mother. He was trying to think of what he could say to Winton when he fell asleep.

◆

Nick pushed through the crowd leaving the dining room after breakfast, looking for Winton but couldn't find him. When the bell rang at 11:45 for lunch, he raced down the steps, but he wasn't in the lavatory washing up either. Then Nick saw Jim Broussard.

"Jim, have you seen Dale Winton? I'm wondering if we should talk to him.

"Nick, Toogie and I decided we should just ignore it. He'll come around and we'll never let him know we know. That's the best way, the only way in here."

Jim put a hand on his shoulder. "Ya gotta forget it, Nick. Like Mr. Dunkel always says. He went to the Hum a long time ago, and says we gotta learn to cope, 'cus that's what makes us Hummers."

"Yeah, and I know his mom was wrong, but let's look for a chance to get even with McCann, anyway," Nick answered angrily, as he kicked at a stone on the walk.

MERCHANT HALL

(pictured below)

and BANKER HALL

Grades 9 and 10
Ages 14 and 15
1949

FORTY

Dear Mom,

Sorry I haven't written sooner. I really had a good time on vacation. Now that I'm back at the Hum and it's already more than a month since I've been in Merchant Hall, vacation seems a long ago. Almost everyone here is new to me. They're fourteen too, and moved up from different sections in Lafayette, and there are guys here who are already fifteen. In January they'll move up to Mariner Hall and start as the youngest guys there. Most of the kids I got to know in Lafayette Hall went to Banker Hall instead and I'm in Merchant Hall now, so they're enemies. Not real ones, but our teams play against theirs and we want to beat them. We play the older classes in the other halls, where the kids are 16 and 17. Guys say it's not fair, but that's the way it is. We don't have governesses here, just housemasters. Our Senior Housemaster, Mr. Craig, said we'd be here for a year or so and he would ignore us unless we caused trouble or broke rules. It was up to us to do our jobs around the building and be on time everywhere and do our homework. He said to forget you had governesses and mothers. Mess around and he'll make sure you're sorry. Don't do your homework and you won't be here either. I will be fine.

I saw a kid who was in Section 11 with me for a while back in 1944 when I came in. He's in 2-1. He told me about the classes and how you move up in the buildings. It was confusing, so I wrote it out this way and showed it to him. I'm in 1-1, which means a Freshman in the first half of the year. Then I'll be in 1-2, so I'll be a Freshman in the second half of the year.

Banker & Merchant Halls- 14 yr. olds in 1-1
and 1-2 (Freshmen)
15 yr. olds in 2-1 (Sophomores)
Mariner Hall — 15 yr. olds in 2-2 (Sophomores)
16 yr. olds in J-1 (Juniors)
Bordeaux Hall — 16 yr. olds in J-2 (Juniors)
17 yr. olds in S-1 (Seniors)
Allen Hall — 17 year olds in S-2
(6 months — then graduate!)

Nobody gets you up here. The lights just get snapped on at 6:30. You still make your bed and wash up and dress but it's up to you to walk over to the D&S (Dining and Services Building) in time for 7 o'clock breakfast. There are separate dining rooms for each hall. Guys wake up friends so they won't be late. After breakfast, if you haven't been assigned a job cleaning the building (I haven't yet) we go over to the high school and study until 8:30. Then there's a twenty-minute assembly for all grades. After a prayer we sing. Or they have some sort of demonstration. The fencing team demonstrated this morning. I think of home when we sing the Welsh songs.

After Assembly we go to class. School keeps getting harder and everyone has to take French because of Stephen Girard. We're starting to learn the French National Anthem. We get lots of homework and assignments that require going to the Library after class. If you don't know an answer or seem slow in answering, the teacher gets mad and tells you to come back in after school is over at 4 o'clock. At night everybody goes back to big study hall rooms in the high school from 7 to 9:15, except Friday night when they show a movie in the high school auditorium or there's a slide show or

214

lecture in the Chapel. No talking in study and they don't like it if you ask to go to the bathroom. On Saturdays, we do whatever we want to until bedtime. On Sunday nights, we go back to the high school again to study. One kid said he thinks that's how we can skip 8th grade, by so much homework and studying. They said when you get to Mariner and Bordeaux Halls, if you have really good grades, you can study in your hall living rooms instead of going back to the high school.

"Hey, Nick, whatcha doin'— writin' home?"

"Yeah, Sabs, telling my mother what the Hum's like in Merchant Hall."

"Did you tell her about your first month in the Batty? And," he said with a friendly smirk, "all about your rifle trick?"

"Of course not...and my legs still hurt." The incident flashed through Nick's mind.

"At ease," Colonel Rabola had ordered, then added, "you've been pretty good so far, so fall out and take a break. You new recruits, from Banker and Merchant Halls, will spend two hours practicing basic drill routines. Better get it right, because you'll join the company you've been assigned to and your Captain will make life difficult for you."

As everyone drifted off into little groups, Nick recognized some guys he used to know in Lafayette and went over to them. They were watching Digger O'Connell, a tall, skinny kid, tossing his rifle in the air and catching it again in a circular movement. "That's really great, Digger. Where'd you learn to do that?"

"I saw it in a war movie when I was home one Saturday."

"Nick, you try it," Digger said, "it's not as hard as it seems."

"Yeah, Nick," others praised him, "you were always pretty good at tether ball, you can do it." Watching confidently, Nick saw Digger twist his rifle in slow motion. "Put your hand under the butt, toss it up so it goes in a circle, and drop your left hand ready to catch the butt again and quick shift it to your right when it comes around." Moving away a bit, Nick gave his rifle a hard shove, up and to the left, lowering his left hand to catch it when it came around. But it didn't. It flew past his shoulder and landed on the wooden floor with a loud metallic clatter, instantly ending all conversations. His friends stood silently, aghast; Nick, frozen, looked over at the rifle.

"That boy!" Colonel Rabola roared. "Pick up your rifle! If there is one thing that you should never allow to happen, it's to lose control of your weapon…it is not a toy!" Nick felt hundreds of eyes on him. Should he speak, apologize? No, he knew not to — Hummers didn't. They took their punishment no matter what.

"Now, hold your rifle out in front of you. Horizontally! Now begin to squat — stop there. Now, walk to that wall and return to me!" The armory was quiet except for Nick's feet, duck-like, stomping, left then right, across the basketball floor. Above, on the circular track, runners stopped and draped themselves over the railing to watch. Slowly, wincing, he made his crab-like way to the Colonel.

"This is what happens to anyone who loses control of his weapon!" With that, he turned away, ignoring Nick and called out over his shoulder, "Drill dismissed," dispersing the recruits to their new company lockers.

"You were lucky it was Colonel Rabola," Jerry Magee said to Nick, as they were hanging up their uniforms. "They say Company B's Commander, some Senior named Moz Bagramian, gives the saber treatment to guys who screw up. Not just for what you did, but even for walking out of step when they pass Colonel Hamilton during the inspections behind Founder's Hall. The kid bends over, holding his rifle straight out and that rat makes his Sergeant Major whack the kid hard on his ass five times with the broad side of his saber. It must really sting."

"Don't expect any more rifle tricks from me, Sabs, I'm gonna take the tests as soon as I can and become at least a Lieutenant someday."

"Sure you are and I'll be the Cadet Major." Looking at his watch, Sabol said, "It's getting close to dinner time, goin' over?"

"Not yet, I'll be there but I want to write some more, see you later."

I have to stop now, Mom. I played step ball and need to take a quick shower. We take showers whenever we want to now, they're not supervised the way they were. Most guys take them before dinner; some take them after dinner, but you're supposed to take a shower every night.

Back again — it's 7 p.m. Had ham slices with pineapple and rice that was kinda hard and lima beans that were too soft — but really good peach pie. I miss your lamb stew with potatoes in it.

This is such a long letter, Nick thought. It's almost like an assignment.

*The biggest change is that we are now in the Army —
the Girard Army. If you play a musical instrument you have
to be in the Band — except for things like the violin and
cello, then you're in the Concert Band. Everyone else is in the
Battalion. We have blue and gray uniforms copied after the
cadets at West Point, and M-1 rifles, but they can't shoot.
All the freshmen from Banker and Merchant have drill
lessons together. A real Colonel has been teaching us to stand
at attention, do right, left and about face and march together.
We know how to present arms and take our weapon apart
and put it back together. And all your brass has to be kept
shined or you get demerits. From now on until we graduate,
every Friday afternoon, after school, we put on our uniforms
and drill, and once a month, on Saturday morning after
Chapel, we march up the Main Road to the field behind
Founder's Hall for an inspection. The band goes before us
playing marches. I remember how much I liked hearing them
when I was back in Section 11.*

*You're right when you said they keep us so busy we
don't have time to be lonely, but I miss you and Janet,
especially when I come back here after being home on vacation.
Someday I will come home for good.*

*I will close now. Write soon. Kiss Janet for me. I still
pray for you every night in bed. No one makes us do that
anymore.*

Love, Nicholas

*P.S. I just heard that we are going to get our 3-year
Typhoid shots this week.*

FORTY-ONE

"I hate this! I hate this!"

"Shut up, Nick! She'll hear you!"

"I don't care. I hate this. Toizer said it too!"

"So, do I!" Leo Troy hissed back, "You think I like dancing with you?"

"Hey, this just comes with being a Biggie," John Martin called, shuffling by with Art Felberbaum. "Ya didn't complain about giving up knickers for long pants when you moved up from Lafayette, so live with it."

"Pretend you're Groucho Marx," Felberbaum smirked, dipping and rocking his shoulders like a wave-tossed boat and getting a punch on the shoulder from Martin.

Nick's right hand was on Troy's shoulder. He kept his left arm, encircling his partner, moving away from Troy's movement so he wouldn't actually "hug" him. His fingers spread out, claw-like, lightly pressing on the small of Troy's back. "I hate this," he muttered again to himself.

Suddenly Miss Magee stood before them. "You are making a travesty of a beautiful fox trot. Don't lumber like that, move with the rhythm." She grabbed at him. "Get your right elbow down before you put someone's eye out." A chorus of laughter drowned out Perry Como's "You Do Something To Me."

"You're making your partner sway while he's — while she's trying to dance. Put your arm up right against him snug, not that tight. Dance with a girl like that and she'll get sea sick." More laughter. "Yeah, Nick, and she'll puke on your Sunday suit!"

"Quiet, Mr. Wakerics."

She signaled to Mr. Keenan, the dance instructor, who lifted the arm on the small record player. "We're not getting any support from this class. If it continues, I'll schedule remedial dancing classes —

after school hours." A group groan was heard. Miss Magee was the Social Director of the High School. Tall, thin, graceful but not very attractive, she reminded Nick of the old, unmarried ladies who taught some of the Sunday School classes at church. Everyone liked Mr. Keenan. When he taught and she wasn't around, he didn't expect them to be perfect. Being a guy, he probably understood how they felt; it was painful watching guys dance with guys, though Nick had to admit it was funny, too. Ernie Podagrosi, the class giant, was dancing with his chin resting on the head of Andy Bressi, entertaining everyone by hanging his tongue out while Bill Flanagan, the toughest guy, grimaced into space inches over white-haired little Ronnie Davis' shoulder. Each 45 record seemed to last longer, everyone moving sluggishly, avoiding eye contact.

The lively version of "Goodnight, Sweetheart" finally ended and Miss Magee said sternly, "Time for a break…for all of us. Mr. Keenan and I will return in about fifteen minutes." As they left, Ed Ransteadt dropped his hand from Chink Cernicki's shoulder and yelled from the far corner of the room, "You know what this looks like — a drugged zombie dance." No one laughed. The group strode wearily to the benches lining the walls of the gym. Nick sat down next to Marty Maloupian, who never stopped talking, in class, in the dining room, even while he was goalie, playing soccer.

"Cripes, this is torture. It didn't start so bad. Y'know, learning to stand up when a lady comes in. And that introduction stuff — who says what to whom first because of their sex or age."

"Yeah," Dar Klinger, who'd squeezed in between them added, "and don't lean against a wall or a desk or anything — or hang your leg over the arm of a chair if you're with a girl. And if one of your hands isn't using any silverware, it should be out of sight on your lap. Geez! All these manners Hummers are supposed to know. They're always sayin' Girardians have a reputation to uphold."

"Hey, Dar," Nick said, fake poking him with his elbow, "remember to always walk on the outside with a girl like in the olden days so when somebody throws garbage or wash water out from an upstairs window towards the curb, you get hit."

"No way, I want her to get hit so I can be a good Hummer and clean her up."

"Feel her up, you mean," Chip Carter said.

"And when dining," Charlie Wakerics joined them with a silly sing-song voice, imitating Miss Magee, "no slurping, that's only acceptable in Japan. Cut everything into mouth-sized pieces, lower your spoon into your soup and very gently lift it in an arc away from you over the plate so it drips there and bring it back, gracefully, to your mouth. Never, never lean forward to it!" Lunging at Nick, Wakerics jabbed him in the chest with his finger, declaring with a deep voice, "Sire, remember, you may stab an enemy with your sword, but never, never, never — intoning higher with each never — spear your food with your fork." Jumping back, he inserted his weapon in an imaginary scabbard, as guys down the bench, leaned out, enjoying the game.

"Remember when we practiced pushing a chair in for a lady? Crazy Zerby shoved Boswell into the table so fast 'n so hard his face turned red and he went 'Ulp!' and stuck his tongue out?"

"That was fun last semester compared to this. Now it's slide, step, close. I thought we were finished with dancing last semester," Furmanski whined.

"That was square dancin' then, not real dancing like grown ups do. You got to put your arm around girls an' grab their sweaty little hands and swing them around."

"You're the one with the sweaty hands, probably dirty fingernails, too."

"Yeah," Furmanski countered, "you kept doin' it wrong so's you could crash into the girls."

"Where'd they get these girls anyway?"

"Miss Magee said they come from different schools like the Hum. Orphan girls from the Ellis School and the Burd School out in West Philly, where somebody's sisters, Julia and Lauren, go. When we get to go to Proms, they bring in girls from Girls High and Central High for Girls. And Little Flower, in case we're Catholic. And when you get to be a Junior, you can bring in your own girl, if you have one."

"Right. Hey, Nick, are you gonna get a taxi and go to Wilkes-Barre for a coal miner's daughter?"

"Sure, as soon you bring in a Wall Rat."

"Imagine Podagrosi coming on the dance floor with Black Gert?"

The door opened and in came Miss Magee carrying an easel. On it was a big white poster board with black paper cutouts glued on it. "Everyone up. We're now going to learn the most genteel dance of all, the waltz."

◆

"Can I have more gravy on this bread?" Nick passed his plate down to Charlie Mangione, who was table head this week. As it came back, Bob Sterling, held his fork over the gravy sodden slice.

"There may be a slight carrying charge."

"Yeah, and I'll give you a charge that'll have them carrying you out," Nick replied, kicking his foot up under the table, missing Sterling's leg but making everyone's dishes shake. Having created a satisfactory response, Sterling passed the plate on.

"How'd it go today, Fred Astaire?"

"Screw you, Cohen," Nick answered.

"All Cohen knows is the Hora," Barr said, "I think it's a dance for Jewish hookers."

Ignoring him, Cohen said, "I heard you guys were so bad that she's adding more lessons. You'll never get out of there."

"It was that crazy Ken Mazak," Dale Heffner grumbled, "he never knows when to stop. Kept falling down backwards and dragging

222

Log Richan with him and sayin' 'Miss Magee, I can't do this boxy step. The squares are too hard — I can hardly make the triangles with my feet.' "

"He was funny," Dale said, "until she said, 'Go down to Mr. Davis' office and tell him exactly...exactly what you just said.' Then, she's talking with Mr. Keenan, an' Mazak holds the gym door open and makes a fancy bow, swishing his grubby cap in the air like he's the Scarlet Pimpernel or something. Sarky Surgeoner tells him, 'Get ready for more bowing, wise guy. Old man Davis ain't gonna waltz on your ass with his paddle. You'll be hoppin' around the room dancin' with pain.' That's when Mazak stops smiling and closes the door and Miss Magee says, and she was mad, 'Everyone go now, but I'll see all of you right here tomorrow after class and...Thursday and Friday, too.' "

Nick, batting bacon bits off the lima beans with his knife, then tapping on them with his finger to eat one by one, said resolutely, "I guess we really should learn to dance; gotta keep remembering what Jim O'Neill says, 'It's the only way we can legally get our hands on a female body.' "

Thanksgiving Dinner

Holidays like Christmas, Easter, Fourth of July and New Year's Day were celebrated by most Hummers with their families because they were home on vacation. But those that occurred during the school year were non-holidays, barely noted. In February, when we were young, we were encouraged to make and send a Valentine home to our mothers. You certainly didn't send one to another guy, unless it was insulting and delivered secretively and anonymously. But hanging around to see the reaction could be deadly if you couldn't enjoy it with an innocent face. Mother's Day brought the inevitable haranguing for us to send a thankful card or letter home. No big fuss was made for Washington and Lincoln's Birthdays. A few reflective words would be said at Chapel services about the qualities of these men and how we might emulate them.

Thanksgiving was one of those non-holidays. We got up, did our chores, attended a religious assembly, went to class, studied and played after school with frequent discourses by governesses, housemasters and teachers about our being grateful. What made Thanksgiving special was lunch, although it was actually a dinner. A much anticipated meal of turkey and gravy with ice cream for dessert. It even made lukewarm, squishy peas acceptable.

The Thanksgiving dinner I remember most vividly was one I should forget. Moist turkey slices were heaped on a low stack of white bread slowly turning dark brown as gravy soaked its way into it. Crowded to the edge of the plate was a curved volcano of mashed potatoes, its crater also filled with gravy. I can't recall what I did or said, but the Senior who was the table head apparently didn't like it for the dinner plate passed down to me, to the obvious joy of certain others, was still shiny clean and empty.

The table head was an Italian kid, Dan DeLullo, captain of the wrestling team, with the body of an orangutan and a temper to match. I was a definitely unimposing, skinny, little Freshman. So I sat back in my chair watching others send their plates back for seconds and even thirds. There was no joy in staring daggers at them as they accepted bowls of vanilla ice cream hidden under fresh strawberries; they would only flash a non-sympathetic glance at me before attacking it. So my Thanksgiving Dinner was spent stoically stirring my glass of water with my fork until the meal was over and everyone rose to leave. There were still a few slices of bread on the serving plate, but I didn't swipe one as I went by. A real Hummer wouldn't stoop to that and give the table head satisfaction.

Several years later, as a new table head, I was able to hold up for everyone to see a deep, broad bowl of lime Jello laced with fruit cocktail. I scored it down the middle with my knife, indicating what was theirs (the nine serfs) and what was mine, though I soon learned nobody can eat that much Jello. As a table head I also discovered life was much more agreeable and less menacing when you tended to share more fairly.

FORTY-TWO

"What a stupid joke!"

"Then why'd you laugh?" They had passed in front of Mariner Hall on their way from Merchant Hall to the D&S building for dinner, groaning at Dack Popdan's joke, when Frank Newman, in front of them, turned and held up his hand, silently stopping them. On the right, a man was hurriedly approaching along a walk from the Main Road. Crossing in front of the group, he smiled and nodded thanks at their courtesy. Then he stopped abruptly and turned back to them.

"You." He pointed at Nick. "When was the last time you pressed those trousers?" Nick looked down at his dark gray pants, then furtively looked side to side at Newman's and Popdan's. Theirs had creases, though they weren't really sharp. Nick's had none; they were curved. "Lincoln was a very tall man," the man said, confounding everyone.

"Huh, Sir?" someone asked.

"And he wore a very tall, black stovepipe hat." He gestured, making a circle with his hands. "Completely round...like the pipes that run up from pot-bellied stoves." Curious onlookers, who had formed a semi-circle around the man, burst into sarcastic laughter when he said loudly, "You look as though you're wearing two of his stovepipe hats, without the tops, of course, on your legs." Turning, he winked at the crowd, and then just as abruptly, hurried away.

"You must be a new twerp from Lafayette that just landed at Banker or Merchant. That, stupid Freshman, was the principal of the High School. It's a good thing he didn't ask your name."

"You were lucky he was in a hurry," someone called out as the group disbanded.

"I didn't know we were supposed to press our pants," Nick said to Newman. "That's 'cus we didn't have them in Lafayette — ya can't press knickers!"

"Go see Shermie," Bernie Weir said, "he'll show you what to do, if he's not too busy. He's on the second floor in the D&S. When I got my long pants after I got here, the Jacob Reed tailor who measured me said I should press them and doin' it once a week would probably be enough."

◆

The pressing room was long, warm and damp. Four rows of wide ironing boards were bolted to the floor, not like the one his mom folded up and put in the closet. Nick, ignored by everyone concentrating on their handiwork, went down a side aisle until he found an unused board near the end. He hung his coat on a wall hook, then leaned against the wall and watched. Some were Seniors from Allen Hall he recognized from seeing them play on varsity teams. Other must have been Juniors and Sophomores and the kids his age were probably from Banker and Merchant. They were talking and laughing as they worked, but never looked up. On the broad end of each ironing board, a black, triangle-shaped form held a dull metal iron, bigger than his mother's. It was heavy and cumbersome, he could feel the heat through the leather covered handle when he lifted it.

A kid, older, probably a Junior from Bordeaux Hall, brushed by, stopping at the empty board next to Nick. After hanging up his coat, he yanked out his belt, and his pants abruptly fell to the floor. Stepping out of them and curling his belt over his coat, he hurriedly placed the pants on the board, folded one leg back and smoothed the other out flat. Reaching under the ironing board he pulled out a large canvas-like piece of material. Nick watched him go to a utility tub where he soaked it and then twisted the water out of it. Returning, he put it over the pants and rapidly ran the iron, steam loudly escaping from it, up and down the leg. Turning it over, he pressed that side using the same technique. Nick had to smile when the kid pulled them on, pushed through the belt, grabbed up his coat and, whacking his bottom, griped about "how hot these damned things are" as he sauntered out like a bow-legged cowboy.

Nick watched as coats, pants and ties were being pressed, with the greatest care given to Band and Battalion uniforms. Some brought polish and rags and shined the brass buttons and buckle, too, sitting on a long bench against one wall. At the end of that wall was a rack with black suits hanging from it. Al Toizer told him they were funeral suits. Hummers who had to go to a funeral came in, got their size suit and a white shirt and black tie. When they returned they changed back into their regular clothes.

A man at the back of the room, probably Mr. Sherman, was using one of two big pressing machines. Nordstrom told Nick when Mr. Sherman wasn't too busy and saw some kid he knew who really took care of his clothes and pressed them a lot, he'd do them for him on the big machine because it did such a good job and lasted so long.

Pulling off his pants, Nick pressed them and, waiting for them to cool down, ironed the wrinkles out of the back of his coat and the lapels. Then, as he'd seen some others do, he bent down so his chin was touching the edge of the ironing board, drew his tie onto the board and ironed it, careful to keep the hot iron away from his nose. Hanging the damp cloth under the board, he dressed and left, feeling good about having learned to do something for himself, the way Hummers are supposed to. When I go home for Christmas, he thought, I'll surprise Mom and show her how I can iron things.

Walking by Merchant and Mariner Halls

FORTY-THREE

Slamming the Merchant Hall door behind him, Nick raced to the living room where the Philadelphia Inquirer and Evening Bulletin were still hanging on the wall rack. Guys who ran the baseball lottery always tore out the sports page to prove which bettors won and lost. Quickly flipping the Bulletin's pages, he found the article Sam Thomas mentioned at the dinner table.

"Hey, Nick, I see your coal town finally made the big time. Some kinda strike with a picture of women holdin' signs an' all. Better clip it out and hang it in your locker."

Nick creased the page, carefully tore it down part way and ripped it across to get a ragged edged copy of the entire article. Tucking it in his breast pocket, he headed for study hour at the High School, just getting there as the door closed at 7 o'clock. Seated, he started to read it, but Mr. Shuster waved at him, shaking his head no. Disheartened, Nick put it back in his coat. At 9:15 dismissal, he rushed out again to a bench near a street light. The women's signs read: *Fair Wages For Productive Workers.* Nick recognized the long concrete building in the background, the silk mill where his mother worked. The article said the women were on strike because the company wanted them to work a longer day with no increase in their pay. It quoted the manager as saying the owners might close the mill and move it elsewhere if they couldn't improve the profits.

Nick remembered how strikes occurred in the summer when he was home. In Junior School and Good Friends they frightened him. Older, he became angry, as he was now. How often did he see his mother rubbing her hands with Vaseline where the silk threads cut her fingers and palms? She spent eight hours walking up and down an aisle of spinning frames retying constant thread breaks and separating and retying snags. She got mad, too, but was never violent and he was shocked the first time he heard her call the managers "snakes" because they were so indifferent to the workers.

One summer strike, to shame the management, the women brought their children to the mill. He could feel her rough hand holding his as they stood with her fellow workers in a show of solidarity. To his surprise, some of the women were mad at his mother. One shouted at her, "See what you and your big mouth started?" Nick was proud of her when she shouted back, "But you're striking, too. You know I'm right!" The harsh words brought tears to her eyes, but all he could do was hug her. Nick was so mad at them. She was alone. She had no husband who was working and making money. Most of them did. It was so unfair.

At breakfast, he was chided for not joining in the sarcastic conversation contest. He felt weak, tied with invisible ropes, and he couldn't get loose to help her. And he felt sad, too, because there was nothing he really could do. The only relief he could find was that all strikes ended, but then his mom might not have a job. The owners knew how to get even. He couldn't get that thought out of his mind, like a new vocabulary word he'd memorized that kept returning and returning. Should he write to her and say he saw it in the paper? No, he couldn't. If she knew he knew, it would upset her more.

Every day that week, Nick raced to the newspaper rack after his last class at 4 o'clock. Once he was late for swimming practice and Coach Severy yelled at him. Another day, he had to report to class after school because Dr. Dunlap said he was daydreaming. Nick continued to scour both papers until, on Friday, he found the report in the Financial Section. A two-inch blurb, as Mr. Bonekemper at the Print Shop would call it.

Wilkes-Barre Strike Settled

After an all night session, management of Sheridan Mills and negotiators agreed to a wage settlement. Ratification by approximately 170 workers is expected Monday evening.

231

He sank back in the leather wing chair. He'd felt so tired this week. Rereading the article, he felt better, a lot better. She hadn't lost her job before, why should she lose it now? That was probably what would happen. He felt strong again: that weak feeling was gone, and he had an idea — he'd write home. Tell lots of good things: he'd signed up to help with the Dramatic Club and that his grades were pretty good and how he enjoyed singing "Joshua Fit The Battle of Jericho" in the Glee Club last Sunday and he'd ask how things were at work. He hadn't written for several weeks, so she'd be sure to write back quickly. Exhilarated, he sprang from the chair and, checking his pen in his pocket, headed upstairs for the stationary in his locker.

FORTY-FOUR

"What a nifty Sunday!" Walt Uebele exclaimed, the sun shining on his round face. "Look at that sky, bright blue and not a single cloud."

"It'd be a perfect Fall day if we didn't hafta go back to the Hum. We coulda stayed in the park until it got dark," John Martin said.

"We still have some time," Nick looked up from his watch, "It's only four o'clock. Let's stop at the Dugout. I want to get some Mounds to take back."

"Well, at least we're legal," Uebele said, "but I was lucky to get my pass, though. These female teachers...Mr. Brewster asked Miss Dandois to join our table for lunch on Friday. She said, looking straight at me, she would but preferred not to eat at a table where food was passed by someone with dirty fingernails. So, I excused myself and ran to the water fountain in the hall. Scraped them with the fork I grabbed when I went by the waiter's table. Held out my clean nails to Mr. Brewster when I went back in, and he remembered today and wrote me a pass out."

The trio stopped at Martin's brick row house on Brown Street, a few blocks from the campus. He unlocked the door and went in while they waited. "My mom's not home," he said, coming out, "but we can have these." Walking along, they passed the pretzel bag back and forth and drank from a bottle of Pepsi.

"Where'd all that sun go?" Uebele complained, after they dropped the bag and bottle over a fence into someone's trash can. "How come it's black, like at night?"

"Solar eclipse?" Nick asked and smiled sardonically at Martin.

"There's your eclipse," Martin thumbed toward his right. They were walking in the enormous shadow of a thirty-foot high stone wall, one that ran a full block along Brown Street, then down Corinthian Avenue, then along Fairmont Avenue with the ugly, intimidating main entrance, and then back up Twenty Second Street to Brown. It was the Eastern State Penitentiary.

"Holy cripes, I didn't know you lived so close to the penitentiary," Uebele said. "Isn't that scary?"

"Yeah," Martin said, "my mom doesn't like it. Nobody around here likes it. They're afraid somebody'll escape and hide in their yard or break into their house. We tease my mother because every time she walks by here, she looks up, expecting to see guys climbing down, ready to kill anyone who sees them." The other two laughed, with polite "Yeah's."

When they got to Corinthian Avenue, they turned left, away from the towering wall with the silhouette of a man with a rifle in the corner turret, and started up the three blocks to the school's entrance. "Let's go to Woarman's instead of the Dugout."

"Good idea," Uebele quickly replied, "we can have a quick smoke before we go back. That okay with you Nick?"

"I've been by it but never went in 'cus I'm not a big time smoker."

"No lectures, please." Uebele was checking the contents of a crumpled Camels pack. "Let's turn on Poplar and then down that little cattycorner alley."

Looks like a regular drug store, Nick thought as they pushed through the glass door. On the left was a soda fountain with a line of stools, two occupied by a man in a white tee shirt and a woman with gray hair. The mirrored wall was covered with menu item prices and ice cream and soda signs. A skinny kid, bored, leaned against the counter, empty glass in hand, waiting for a shiny metal container to stop shaking. The right side of the room was lined with racks displaying easy to reach cigarettes, White Owl and Philly cigars, candy, razor blades, shaving cream jars and brushes. High shelving along the back wall offered lipsticks, perfumes, deodorants, skin creams and hair dyes.

Following the other two into the back room, Nick was astonished and jabbed Martin in the back. "This place looks like something out of a gangster movie." Martin, always the actor, jumped to one side, gestured with a pretend gun in hand, his face twisted in a sneer. "We don't like that talk around here. Bang! You're dead!" Acknowledging the clapping and gruff retorts from those nearby, he dropped into a chair that was kicked out for him, cowboy style. Uebele was already seated between Al Toizer and Jim Broussard, waiting for a hand in their card game.

Rough looking round tables and cheap wood chairs packed the room with little space for movement. All the tables were filled with at least two or three smokers, some tables tightly crowded with six or seven. And there were quite a few girls. Two ceiling fans sucked up the gray puffs from the smokers below, scattering it to the far sides of the room. Rubbing his eyes in a hopefully unnoticed gesture, Nick told himself not to remark on the slowly swirling ceiling haze. This would make a really interesting place to describe in an article for the Girard Magazine, Nick thought, before reconsidering; I'd have to hop the wall forever before any of these guys got to me.

"Yo, Nick, c'mere," Dack Popdan called from the far corner. Martin was already occupied at a table, so Nick squeezed his way over to Popdan, who was pulling another chair up. "This is Lenny Karas and this is Jim Stanford. They're both in Mariner Hall. Nick's in Merchant, a class behind me. We knew each other in Section Eleven, a long time ago."

"Cigarette?" Stanford offered.

"No, don't smoke."

"What're you doing here?"

"Just came in with John Martin."

"Know anybody else here?"

"Lots of Hummers I recognize but don't know. Just some guys in my class, Ernie Podagrosi and Toizer and Eckard and Furmanski.

And there's Sam Thomas. The others must be Sophmores, like you, and Juniors and Seniors."

"Right, most everybody here's in Mariner, Bordeaux or Allen. And a few twerps sometimes come in from Good Friends and Lafayette, but they don't stay long."

"Where do all these girls come from?"

"From the neighborhood," Stanford replied, "most go to Dobbins High School, some from Central. The Hallahan girls are all Catholic, so they see the guys when they go to the Gesu Church on Sundays before Chapel. Sometimes, though," he looked up at the ceiling and crossed himself, "we come in here for a smoke instead."

"Nick," Popdan said, "I think Ernie wants to see you."

Three girls at Ernie's table watched him approach. Ernie was talking to them, but looking at Nick. Two were dirty blondes, as his mother would describe them, and the other had dark, shiny hair. "Nick, I want you to meet the three most beautiful girls in the world." The blondes looked at each other and smiled, used to his amusing exaggerations. The brunette, showing uneven white teeth, rolled her eyes at Nick. Just as Ernie was about to introduce them, Nick felt a hand on his shoulder. "We gotta go, Ernie," Martin explained. "I promised Smokey Stover I'd meet him at five o'clock and give him five bucks I owe him." He looked down at Nick. "That's why we stopped at my house."

A few minutes later they were headed up Girard Avenue a few blocks from the school entrance. "Where's Walt?" Nick asked.

"He was talking to some girl and waved me off. Thanks for walking me back, Smokey was really a good guy to lend me…" His words were lost in a sound behind them that kept growing louder. Looking back, they saw a stream of Hummers running towards them. A baby began crying as the first ones swerved around a woman pushing a carriage. Breathing hard, arms swinging, they raced forward. Nick stepped back as one sprinted past him. One tripped just as he neared an oncoming couple. He rolled hard on the sidewalk in front of them, then jumped up and tore off. The frightened couple turned, the old man holding up a fist and cursing.

Then the beeping began; car and truck drivers, fearing an accident, as frantic runners began angling across the street through traffic. Nick grabbed a porch railing and swung up on the step to avoid a sure collision, but Martin was forced off the curb where he just kept his balance and yelled, "Hey, you bastards, what're you doing?" Enraged, he grabbed one of the smaller ones by the arm as he came by and swung him against a tree trunk. "What the hell's happenin', buddy?"

The kid knew John was mad and didn't try to get away. After a few deep breaths he found his voice, "Somebody in one a the halls heard one housie tell another one he was going to have a Check Up in a little while. The kid called Woarman's to tell his friend and we're all tryna get back in time to check in. I already got a U and a VO this semester; one more and I'll be going to school back in Clarks Summit." With that, the kid ran off, now last, trailing the disappearing delinquents.

"Probably hopped the wall to get a smoke," Martin decided.

As they approached the high open gates, Nick pointed down Girard Avenue. "Look, you can see all those guys down there jumping up and pulling themselves over the wall." Martin's unexpected burst of laughter surprised Nick. "What's so funny?"

"That looks like the opposite of what people around here are scared of," Martin declared, "convicts jumping off a wall to freedom. But everybody going by must be confused." He grinned again. "Why would a gang of orphans, already free, climb their prison wall to get back in?"

The Lodge man, looking out the window, wondered what those two kids did that made them laugh so hard.

Yellow Squares

We didn't realize in Junior School that Girard had a unique double curriculum. In Seventh Grade, before moving to the High School at Ninth Grade you began a "tour" of vocational courses. There was no Eighth Grade, which is why most of us graduated at 16 or 17. We spent the mornings in class and the afternoons at one of the trades — foundry, drafting, electricity, carpentry, sheet metal, pattern making, printing, automotive repair or the commercial course teaching typing and stenography. And you didn't just drop by and see if you were-interested, attendance was compulsory. You learned the basics of each trade and were tested and graded. At the end of your Sophomore year, having completed the four you selected, you made your choice of one as your vocation.

Then, as a Junior and Senior you spent a half day at your trade and the other half studying English, French (required), German, Spanish, General Science, Biology, Mathematics, History and Public Speaking. Stephen Girard, the founder, wanted us to have a good education along with a trade to fall back on.

I chose Printing and by the end of the first semester was capable of setting type, locking it up and helping print the Girard News, the Girard Magazine (fiction), and The Corinthian, the Senior Yearbook, as well as some other basic educational materials. The instructors, Mr. Daffin and Mr. Bonekemper, personally printed important administrative documents and forms when we weren't around, locking them in their office.

But there were times when the ink was still wet on the printed matter and it would be stacked loosely on a shelf outside their glassed-in office. Whoever spied stacks of little yellow squares drying, excitedly and silently signaled the rest of us. Suddenly there was a "yelp" in the back of the room and Mr. Daffin would hurry there hoping to save the linotype machine. Almost simultaneously, a loud metallic sound arose from the other side of the room — falling lead type clattering on the wooden floor. Mr. Bonekemper, a slight, mild-mannered man, continuously tormented by the printing gang, broke into a frenzied race to the scene of the accident. Meanwhile, a body would sidle along the long rectangular makeup table, reach up to peel a few yellow squares off a stack and rise up slowly a distance away. His grin of success meant sure grief for anyone we chose to torture.

On the Main Road after our Printing Class was over, we shared the squares. There weren't many; we only wanted a few, maybe five or six, because taking more than a few off the pile might give us away. We each got one; the thief got any extras; a rare moment of agreement. It was a joyful stroll as we animatedly decided who should be sentenced to suffer.

Imagine enjoying breakfast, laughing, arguing, criticizing, and taunting others when a hand appears over your shoulder: it puts a little yellow square on your butter plate. A little yellow square is a Dental Appointment Pass. The table is silent as everyone watches. You know what it is, ignoring it for a while, finally picking it up. Maybe the monitor made a mistake and it's not your name; but it is. You are hereby ordered to appear at 10:30 tomorrow morning at Dr. Mervine's dental chair. Breakfast is ruined. The day is ruined. And tomorrow's worse. At least it could have been French, not the Library or Swimming you missed. What rotten luck!

And you didn't get sympathy, just the opposite. "Better eat up now, it's your last supper!" "Man, those drills hurt so much, especially when they press down an' ya kin see the smoke risin' and smell burnt teeth."

"He's got such a big mouth now, imagine, guys, what it'll look like at lunch tomorrow!" "Kin I have your meat tomorrow night 'cause it's gonna hurt to chew!" They kept it up and kept it up. How could you feel more miserable?

That was the joy of possessing a blank dental pass, using it to torment an enemy — some wise guy who perhaps came up with a rotten rhyme to your name. Or purposely tripped you on the stairs, saying coyly, sorry, it was an accident. Or was stuck-up, thought they were a big shot and so smart. Finding a victim was never a problem.

You casually checked at the next meal to see who'd been selected by the housemaster to pass out the official dental appointments that week. Then

239

you'd fill out the pass for the next day, find that legal distributor, explain the situation and give it to him, making sure, of course, that it wasn't one of his friends. They enjoyed being in on the game and never got into trouble, planning to say they were just passing out what they were given if questioned. It was important to be at the table or an adjoining table when the gift was delivered. And you'd tell guys you could trust so they could enjoy watching the victim get his deserved grief. It was a satisfying event we enjoyed together, watching his first response on seeing it. You put your enemy in a dark mood that lasted the rest of the day, into the night and the morning of the impending pain, and made breakfast a table wide persecution festival.

One reason we did it so often was that there was never a repercussion. Nobody who had it pulled on them ever made a big deal of it afterward. We figured when they were waiting on the bench with other heavyhearted orphans and the nurse held up a yellow square and announced — "This is wrong, you're not supposed to be here." — their relief was so great the thought that it was more than just a mistake never entered their minds. They never knew and we certainly never told them.

Since Junior School, governesses, housemasters and teachers were eternally preaching that you should take full advantage of all the opportunities at Girard, you now began to realize how enjoyable and rewarding that could be.

MARINER HALL

Grades 10 and 11
Ages 15 and 16

1950

FORTY-FIVE

"Nick, go buy a bottle of that stuff for us so we can be invisible when we hop the wall."

"The only thing that'll be invisible will be your money, Jigs."

"I know, I know, I was just kidding. What's occult mean anyway?"

"It means crazy, weird stuff," Ed Rosen said, "like everything in the window. Potions to make you stronger and charms to hang 'round your neck and ward off evil spirits...those cards'll tell your future. Those books are about black magic. How you can put a curse on Caswell McGregor. Or how to make your enemies bow down to you."

"Look at that rag doll with needles in it," Nick said, "I wonder if they'd make one that would look like..." A loud whistle turned all three away from Harry's Occult Shop window.

"Hummers — over there." Across Arch Street, Tony Cline yelled and pointed down the street. "C'mon, the show's gonna start in a few minutes." Nick, Jigs Schepisi and Rosen, picking their way through the passing traffic, caught up with the others as they crossed Eleventh Street. Nick could see the marquee projecting out over the sidewalk; colored lights blinked out "TROCADERO." It looked like a movie house, like the Big F on Girard Ave.

"You been here before, Tony?"

"Hell, yeah. Everybody comes here. Sometimes it looks like the whole Senior class is here."

"It's a long line, hope we can get in in time," Harry Grasser said. Nick counted eleven Hummers, including himself at the end of the line; fourteen-year-olds from Banker and Merchant and his gang, mostly fifteen, from Mariner Hall. In front of them were a couple of men who looked shabby, not neatly dressed like the men at the Hum, and younger ones alone or with friends, laughing and poking each other with their elbows as they looked at the posters in one of the big

242

windows. The window nearest them had a life-sized cutout of a woman with bright red hair smiling as she kicked one leg up in the air, her arms held out as though she were welcoming you to a big bear hug. Nick never imagined breasts could stand out so straight, each ending in a sparkling red circle with a little silver bell hanging down.

The line began to move forward. "When you put your fifty cents in the window," Tony said, "don't wait for a ticket, just keep moving and go in the door. That way she doesn't have to bother about whether you're too young; you're supposed to be eighteen to get in." Nick held up two quarters. "Why does it say a dollar and a half up there?"

"Because that's for the seats downstairs, but we're up in the balcony."

Pushing through the door after paying, Nick followed the others down the dimly lit lobby, as they stepped around shiny spots in the muddy red carpeting. A fat man with his thumbs stuck behind bright red suspenders, leaning against a red wall, except for white specks where the plaster was missing, smiled strangely at Nick, and asked, "Playing Hop Scotch, kid?" Nick ignored him and started up the brown wooden steps.

The Hummers were the only ones in the balcony. Some were already seated, leaning forward, arms and chins resting on the skinny black railing that ran along the curved front row. Nick followed Tony into the second row where Schepisi, Rosen and Grasser were already lighting up cigarettes. Down below Nick could see customers scattered throughout the seats.

"Look'it that." someone called. Several guys stood up and looked down. There was a commotion below with laughter, then cursing. "What happened?" Rosen asked.

"Butterfingers Toizer dropped his pack of cigarettes. It hit some guy on his bald head. And everyone sitting behind him musta laughed and made him mad," Reds Eckard said, "so he looks up here and shakes his fist, then he throws the pack on the seat beside him and points at it . . .and looks up with a mean smile, like sayin', 'Come on down and see if you can get it back.' " Toizer stood up by the railing, his back to the stage and, holding up both hands to catch everyone's attention, said, "Hey, guys, whoever goes down and gets it — I'll split the pack with them...and it's almost full. I mean it," he shouted over the snide "Sure you will" responses and even he had to laugh when somebody said, "C'mon, guys, who's going down for Al and get his unlucky strikes?" Toizer countered with, "When the lights go out, just crawl down behind his seat and grab it. You'll be safe, he won't chase you in the dark."

Then the lights started to go down and the orchestra, maybe five musicians in the little hollow area down front, began blasting out a brassy buildup. A beautiful young girl with upswept blond hair opened the curtain and stepped out in a ball gown with a skimpy top that just held in her colossal breasts. Some of the Hummers whistled. As the music swelled, she gracefully threw an arm toward one side of the stage as a voice boomed out, "And now, America's Funny Man, direct from Atlantic City, Billy — Cheese 'n Crackers — Hagan!"

The audience clapped and whistled when a skinny, little guy swaggered out in bright, baggy, mismatched clothes. On seeing the girl, he staggered toward the audience holding his heart, then rushed at the supposedly frightened maiden and, with a Red Skelton trip, tumbled and slid headfirst under her long gown. The music stopped. Looking at the audience the blonde's smile turns to surprise, then she screams, hops over Billy and escapes behind the curtain. He rises slowly, turns to the audience, a satisfied look on his face, and says something they roar about that Nick didn't understand. "He looks like an Irish Charlie Chaplin," was Nick's only comment to Rosen, sitting beside him.

After about fifteen minutes of hopping around, making faces and jokes, some of which seemed stupidly obvious to Nick, someone yelled from the audience, "Bring on the girls!" Immediately, five girls wearing thin red straps crossing their nipples and providing legal cover below, danced out, forming a line behind Cheese 'n Crackers who, discovering them, changes his dance routine so he can try to paw them. The balcony group howls in mirth as the chorus line dances in circles around him, teasing him, just out of reach.

Rosen called out his opinion as always, "Coordinated they're not, but they sure are sexy," rolling his eyes like Groucho Marx. As the music ends in a loud flourish, the girls, throwing kisses, dance off, the comedian chasing them, with a big wave at the audience as the room dims to black. After a few seconds a spotlight, hard on the eyes, erupts above them, wildly circling the stage and walls and coming to rest on a bare leg piercing the red curtain, igniting raucous cheers and foot stomping.

Tony instructed, with a sophisticated tone, "Here comes the best part, Nick."

◆

"Well, what'd ya think of the Troc?" Rosen asked, but before Nick could answer, someone called out, "Walk fast but don't look back." The group, now eighteen strong, had raced down Arch Street, then up Eleventh.

Two blocks later, at Spring Garden Street, another order, "Now just walk regular, but still don't look back," and "We can start talkin' now." When Gene Halpern grabbed the street sign and swung around it in a circle, a Senior barked from the back of the group, "Stop that, we don't need any attention from the cops."

"That was fun," Nick recalled, still exhilarated by the last hour's excitement, "especially the fight." It all started when Harry Grasser, the first one down the steps after the program ended, yelled up, "Fight!" They rushed down, two steps at a time, and looking in at the big auditorium saw the bald man, standing in front of his seat holding the pack of cigarettes and cursing at someone under the balcony. A small box, hurled from under the balcony, hit him on the shoulder and

245

exploded; more began arriving, enveloping him in clouds of white. He stood in what looked like snow squall but was greasy, buttered popcorn. When someone behind him laughed, he turned and pushed the man so hard he disappeared over his seat and onto the floor. The rest of the audience seemed to be standing on their seats for a better view, some goading him on, others having pulled up loose, rickety chairs, holding them above their heads threatening to join in the action by throwing them. Several strangers started down the aisle toward the bald man, while, at the other end of his aisle, apparent defenders were coming to help him.

The popcorn brigade came out from under the balcony, and Nick's mouth formed an oval in surprise — they were upperclassmen Hummers.

"Stop it! Stop it!" the announcer raged repeatedly. "The police will be here any minute and we're going to prosecute every one of you to the fullest extent of the law."

Two shafts of light slashed through the dimmed room as exit doors on both sides of the room, up near the stage, were swung open and customers began streaming out. Tony was waving at the Seniors. "This way," he thumbed toward the front doors, "this way!" When they reached him, he pointed to the balcony steps, and said emphatically, "I've been through this before. We need to sit here."

As they crowded onto the steps, the four front doors opened and a squad of policemen, waving billy clubs, hurried past them. "Now," Tony said, "let's get out of here."

Scrambling out the front door they almost collided with policemen who were turning down the narrow alley next to the building to catch the exit door escapees.

Safely away, the group slowed down. Nick and Tony walked behind the Seniors, listening to them compare the attributes of the performers. Starting up Girard Avenue towards the Hum, Rosen entertained everyone by declaring himself Billy "Cheese 'n Crackers"

Hagan, dancing around fireplugs, ogling some girls who quickly crossed the street, and even retelling some of the jokes, after which he made raspberry sounds, like the orchestra.

◆

Grace over, Drew MacMullan asked Nick, "How was your virgin visit to the Troc? I heard there was a fight." He got several "So's?" the taken-for-granted expectation that a full explanation would be forthcoming. Knowing how others would tell their "tales" at their tables, he responded, making the fight and the flight as graphic as possible and even adding a few humorous extras, like the girls, in costume, running out the front door with them, and Martin pulling one of the thin red straps loose and everybody getting a great close up. "Sure, sure," said the non-believers, after which Jerry Magee asked, "Who'd you see?"

"Georgia Southern." That required Nick to provide a detailed narration about the twirling of the red cape, the peeling of the long red gloves, and his estimation of the width of the round pasties on her enormous breasts, plus some other new additions to his vocabulary; and how she swung her hips and smiled devilishly, encouraging dirty comments from the audience. When he described how she made her huge breasts swing simultaneously in opposite circles, the silver bells on the red pasties flashing like airplane propellers, his listeners were silent in awe.

"Boy," he said, completing his recitation, "I wish I could use those cantilevered projections for my Physics project in Bo Dennis' class." Then he began to awkwardly move his chest in circles to the delight of the others, and pretended not to notice the disapproving look from Miss McCracken at a distant table.

"Are you going to go back to the Troc, Nick?" Andy Bressi asked.

"Of course he is," Charlie Merkel said adamantly, "you can't be a Hummer if you don't go to the Troc!"

FORTY-SIX

Standing alone by a window in the front room of Mariner Hall, looking out on the Main Road was an odd thing for Irv Rostoff to do, Nick thought. Everyone had headed down to the playground and Nick was just coming off waiting on tables. Noticing a suitcase by the hall doorway, he said, "Irv, what's up? You hopping the wall again and this time for good?"

"Yeah, but this time I don't have to hop the wall." His voice, usually vibrant, sounded listless. Nick moved next to him, and leaning forward, pretending to study the plain, pale plaster wall. He looked over expecting a smile, but saw a tear. "What's wrong? You sick or something?" Irv rubbed his hand over his cheek, then his eye with a fist. "My mom's coming for me. She's taking me out of the Hum."

"Why would she want to do that?" Nick put a hand on his shoulder and shook him gently. "In about two years you'll graduate." Still staring blankly out the window, Irv said, "Remember, I told you she got married to some guy last summer. Larry's a nice guy. She met him at the Budd Company where she works."

"So, that's good."

"Well, she must've called the office and talked to them and Mr. Campbell told me to call home. When I did she was all excited. Said they were sending Larry to Detroit and we were going to move there."

"What did you say?"

"I said that was great and then she said now we could all be together, with my sister and all." Taking a deep breath, he went on, his voice starting to quaver. "I told her I didn't want to go. That I loved her but wanted to stay here. She said she knew that and sounded like she was going to cry, but she couldn't live with me so far away and not coming home on weekends." He turned and looked at Nick, eyes watering. "I don't want to go. I'm a Hummer. I like it here at the Hum.

All the guys I know, like you." Nick tried to say something good. "But you're a good athlete, Irv, you'll do fine."

"Sure, they probably don't even know what soccer is."

A horn beeped several times. "There they are." He grabbed his suitcase and Nick followed him out into the hall. As he pushed open the front door, he looked back. "I'll write to you. Please, Nick, will you write to me? Promise?"

"I will, honest, I promise" Nick sat on the steps and watched Irv's new father lock the suitcase in the trunk, then Irv was in the car and they were gone. Not even a chance to wave goodbye, Nick thought, lowering his arm.

As soon as Nick propped the envelope against his bread and butter plate, an arm swept by his shoulder and grabbed the envelope. "What the…?" Nick cried angrily. "Just want to sniff it, big boy," Dar Klinger said with simulated tenderness as he threw his arms out gracefully, waving the envelope, entertaining everyone waiting for dinner to be served. "I love the ingratiating perfume girls spray on love letters."

"Ingratiating?" came one reply.

"You and your vocab cards," came another.

"Does it smell good, Dar?"

"No," was the disappointed answer. "No," Dar sniffed the envelope once again. "No sexy aroma. I only smell glue."

"No wonder, his girlfriend prob'ly eats Elmer's glue," Conradi said. Deibel snatched it from Klinger's hand and read it. "It's from Ostroff. It's from Flint, Michigan." Then he passed it to Nick who opened it. "What's he say, Nick?" Hank asked.

"He says he doesn't like it there. School's not hard but he doesn't have any friends. They make fun of the way he talks. He says they talk funny. And nobody ever heard of soccer, except kids who live where his mom doesn't want him to go. She said they're all foreigners.

He went over and played with them once but some kids from his school saw him and now they call him a foreigner, too."

Nick turned the page over. "Wants to know how the varsity's doing. Are they still undefeated? And who got caught hopping the wall or got any U's or VO's? Have we been to the Troc lately and who was there? And where's our class stand in the basketball league. Did we beat Bordeaux and how many points did Mangione score."

"You'll be a real buddy to write him back," Jack Pace said.

"Yeah, that's great," Ronnie Davis, always the littlest Hummer anywhere, said.

"No, it isn't, it's cruel."

"What?" was the disbelieving response.

"What I mean," Conradi said deliberately, unlike his normally vehement declarations, "is that the more Nick writes to Ostroff, the more he's going to remember what it's like in the Hum, and make him want to be here with us...well, with some a you guys. He ain't here anymore, he ain't gonna be here, and he's gotta get along where he is. So it's not really helpin' him."

Nick slid the letter in the envelope and pushed it down in his coat pocket. He'd felt so good about what he was going to do. Now he hoped Irv wouldn't write again. He knew he wouldn't write back.

FORTY-SEVEN

It was Nick's fifteenth birthday, March thirteenth, and he hoped nobody would know.

After rushing out of the dining room to the Mariner Hall office and grabbing his mail before the crowd got there, he searched out somewhere his friends wouldn't think of finding him. Crossing the wide walkway that separated the two buildings, he sat on an empty Merchant Hall bench and opened the envelopes. The birthday card from his mother had a five-dollar bill in it and a note saying how sorry she was that he was so far away and that someday he would be home on his birthday and they would celebrate it with a big party. Another card held a dollar for "big brother" from Janet, and others from Nannie and Aunt Elvira, each with two dollars. In the next day or two he knew he'd get his present from Aunt Edith; a slim package wrapped in an inside-out brown Acme shopping bag. Her gift was always the same and one he never shared, not since she began sending them when he was in Junior School. Cella's Chocolate Covered Cherries. One at a time, over weeks, on solitary walks, he'd slowly let one melt in his mouth, steering clear of anyone who might want to talk to him.

"Yo, Nick," someone called from the Mariner Hall steps. "Whattaya doin' over there? Fraternizing with those Merchant jerks?" That detonated an exchange of retorts and curses from others drifting over from the dining room.

"Ya wanta know what another word for mariner is?" someone called from one side of the broad slate common between the buildings. "Sea Dogs — you Mariners are dogs all right, paddling around in a sea of stupidity."

"Yeah," someone threw in, "check it out in Roget, if you know what that is." Then a round set of admiring "Right, right, you said it," and "They never heard of it, those stupid soph-morons."

251

"Come over here just halfway," one voice threatened, "you freshmen bastards and we'll synonym your..." A shrill whistle instantly quelled the clamor, all heads turning in its direction. Nick, who rose and started across the area at the first outcry, saw Mr. Cunningham standing on Mariner's steps, whistle still in his mouth, daring anyone else to call out.

He knows it's not serious, Nick thought, just good-natured fooling around. Whether it's baseball, soccer, snowball fights or just taunting each other, Hummers have loyalty to the building they're in. In Junior School, everyone felt their section was the best of the West Wing and that "our" West Wing was better than the East Wing and their six sections. Same thing between sections in Good Friends and Lafayette, and again in Banker or Merchant; and now we're in Mariner. I guess in Bordeaux and Allen, it'll be the same. What's weird is that everybody is loyal to the building they're in but make fun of them when they move. Doc Wolf said it was just Hummers learning to live with constant change.

"Look!" Gentry pointed at Nick as he approached the instigators. "Those aren't letters, they're cards, birthday cards." With that, Henry Gentry, Chet Van Why, Bernie Weir and Leo Troy surrounded him and took turns punching him on both shoulders, hard but not too hard. "One, two, three..." counting loudly in unison to fifteen. "And one for Good Luck." This was a hard punch.

"Will you guys knock that off and quiet down!" Beaky Cunningham, the housemaster on duty, walked past with a few boys. Scowling at them, he said, "I know you were the ones who started the ruckus. Next time I'll find some chores that'll keep you busy on Saturday and make you happy to go to bed right after dinner."

"Forget him, guys," Nick said quietly, waving the envelopes at them. "Let's go up to the Student Center before it closes — the drinks are on me."

"And the pretzel rods, too," Van Why declared.

Something bright wakened Nick. It was the full moon, scattering patches of light through the tall windows as clouds swept past them. Its brilliant fingers crossed the covered forms of Andy Bressi and Ronnie Davis, ending its clutching grasp on his bed. It was the same light that was shining through his bedroom window at home and maybe onto his own bed. His birthday was almost over now, March thirteenth, but he didn't feel sad. He'd forgotten what birthdays felt like. The only Hummers who had birthday celebrations were guys who lived nearby or those who lived far away and had birthdays during summer, Easter or Christmas vacations. The only times he thought about a real one was the twinge of resentment he felt, which he finally admitted to himself, when someone who went home on weekends came back and gathered friends to sit on a distant bench listening to the birthday boy describe his party while they unceremoniously fingered loose chunks of birthday cake from a white box. After Lafayette, though, it was considered babyish and stopped.

Bob Furmanski told him kids who entered the Hum at six, or, like him, at seven, and were at the West End for their birthdays got a box of chocolates from the alumni association. They took a few and had to share the rest with others. In Junior School, Miss Saunders always made a point of announcing to everyone when it was someone's birthday and took candy from the storage closet and passed it out.

"Kids, when they got packages may have picked out a few goodies, but the rest went into the storage closet. At different times, when she thought the sections behaved very well, she brought out goodies and passed them around. Birthdays," he went on, "really stopped when you got to Good Friends."

Nick knew that. From then on, no one knew when you had a birthday, but getting more than one card in the mail or a package signaled friends and that got you punches on the arm. They stopped when he opened the box and passed out the cookies or hard candies.

But the little box of cherries he put under his arm inside his coat — no one got those.

In Lafayette, he recalled, all March birthday boys like himself crowded onto a trolley car with Mr. Dawson and headed for the Sportsman's Show at the Convention Center. They watched a man standing in an artificial pond whirling a thin line back and forth trying to land the bug on the end of it in a floating bucket. They laughed seeing burly men spinning on huge logs tumble into the water. After hot dogs and sodas, they lined up for the trolley ride home. Down the street Nick could see the University of Pennsylvania's Archeological Museum where they had spent the day in Fifth Grade.

Someone might use gift money to buy friends candy. Or on a May or June weekend, coming back, hot and sweaty from climbing mini-cliffs in Fairmount Park, they'd stop at the Zoo entrance, and he'd treat everyone to snow cones. Holding a metal ball with a crescent shaped hole in it, the snow cone man would scrape along the top of a big block of ice and empty the shaved ice into a thin white paper cone. Nick liked to edge his way around the man's wooden cart until the sun, gleaming through the tall glass bottles — orange, yellow, green, red and purple — colored him. He thought about the time when he asked his friends, "Do I look like a Multi-Blue Boy from Miss North's art class?" striking dumb poses. "You look like one of those crazy clowns by Pablo whatshisname," Al Smith answered. They watched silently as the man trickled syrup over the ice. Nick always chose purple, grape. He remembered snow cones didn't last long on hot days. The ice began melting and the syrup began leaking out of the bottom of the cone. Holding it in front of his nose, he could skillfully alternate between syrup dripping on his tongue and quick bites of the ice.

Nick tried to picture his last birthday at home — he must have been seven – but couldn't. Time to go to sleep, anyway, he decided. Birthdays aren't important in the Hum, and mine's over.

A Little Usury

When I was in Merchant Hall, like Biggies, I looked forward to the weekends. Friday night usually meant a movie in the High School auditorium. Saturday, if there wasn't a morning Battalion inspection behind Founder's Hall, you were on your own with lots of free time. Sundays meant Chapel and, again, freedom as long as you turned up for dinner, followed by study hours in the high school. Then I noticed how, first thing on Saturday mornings, some Hummers would search out a friend, usually a classmate they anxiously conversed with, then, looking unhappy, dashed off to find another friend. They were always kids who lived not far from the Hum — South Philly or the Great Northeast or Overbrook or in the suburbs — Collingdale, Media, Willow Grove, West Chester, even over in Jersey. They were allowed to go home as long as they were not detained, made to stay on campus because of some transgression committed during the week, and they had to return by 6 p.m. for dinner.

Before they returned late Sunday afternoon, their mothers gave them spending money for the week including trolley, bus or subway carfare for next week's trip home. However, after buying candy, sodas, pitching pennies too vigorously, losing dimes on players who didn't get a total of three hits in the illegal Baseball Lottery or buying a pack of cigarettes before coming through the gates, on the following Friday night they found they didn't have enough carfare to get home.

Financially distraught, they went from room to room before breakfast searching for a friend who would be sympathetic to their predicament. They'd borrow money from that friend, but that only lasted a week or two until the generous pal tired of it. They "tapped" another friend, for a few weeks, and, inevitably, their borrowing reputation ended all potential money sources.

If the impecunious didn't turn up at home they knew their mothers would phone — and then they were in real trouble because that meant the housemaster or governess had been "bothered." I was happy that I lived so far *away I didn't have to go home every weekend, though I felt sure my mother would understand how I meant it.*

My limited investment in tall pretzel rods and Frank's Black Cherry Wishniak soda and an occasional fling with the Baseball Lottery always left me with funds in my pocket. And I had a fairly consistent method of earning money. As Junior Schoolers, we were frequently ordered to our desks, and in the silent section room, wrote letters home. We were directed by our governess to write nice things, not bad things other boys did to you, or how you were punished or whether you had a cough or cold. "Your mothers have enough to worry about without your adding to it. Send them a letter that will make them happy and proud of you."

My mother, perhaps unintentionally, taught me that communicating could be very profitable. Every third or fourth letter I got from her included a dollar. So, I happily wrote letters almost weekly, telling her all sorts of things (nice) that happened. I described the Halloween Bonfire, a trip to the Zoo, what I saw in Fairmount Park the week before or some funny things kids did. Later, my letters concerned schoolwork and reviews of events such as Founder's Day or a concert by Fred Waring and The Pennsylvanians. I never mentioned any dances or girls. Writing home may have been a good creative exercise for me, but that was not the intent.

One Saturday morning I was approached by a kid I didn't know. Turned down by friends, he was now asking everyone in sight, could he borrow a quarter — please! I put my hand in my pocket just to check that my wallet was still there and suddenly two others appeared behind him. One wanted a quarter, the other sixty five cents."

I didn't really want to get involved with kids I didn't know, so I decided on a financial arrangement I was sure they'd turn down. And one-time only, too. Never again.

For a quarter they had to give me 35 cents that night. For a dollar, I wanted a dollar and a quarter back. They were furious. Their faces said, Are you crazy? I knew they wouldn't gang up on me, I was a class or two ahead of them, and bigger than they were — and they needed the money.

256

Several of my classmates, watching from not far away, began to berate me. "For Christ's sake, Rinko, you're screwing these poor guys!"

"I'd pay you back by throwin' it all at you in pennies!"

"Yeah, take the money now and stone the bastard tonight!"

I just smiled sweetly at my good fortune as I put my wallet back in my pocket.

That night as we gathered outside the D&S Building for dinner, I saw two of them talking with friends. They broke from the group and approached. As surreptitiously as possible, they handed me their payments. Scowling, but silent, they turned away to rejoin their friends, whose sneers were accompanied by obscene gestures. I gave them a hey-that's-the-way-it-goes look, and, pleased with my quick windfall, joined the mob as it crowded in for dinner.

Sunday morning after Chapel, I was searching the first floor rooms looking for guys who might want an outside right for a pick-up soccer game when I heard, "Hey, Rinko, kin I get a dollar from you?" Another kid I didn't know, but I'd seen him around. Geez, I thought, stuff sure gets around fast in the Hum. I handed him a dollar. "Thanks," he said quietly. "See you tonight with a dollar twenty five," I added.

From then on I was in the loan business. I still wrote to my mother, but not as often. Every Saturday and Sunday morning before Chapel, kids from Banker and Merchant searched me out. I'd plop myself down in one of the old red leather wing chairs in the living room and wait for them. Sometimes there were five or six in a line, not saying a word while I recorded each transaction in a little notepad. Friends and enemies would make a point of passing by just to insult me. I told them they should've listened when Dr. Odgers read stuff in the Chapel. They would have learned about the ancient people who took their talents — that's what they called money then — and buried them in the dirt. For playing it safe they got yelled at, so even the Bible says you're supposed to put your money to work.

Unfortunately, we had just finished reading and discussing at great length The Merchant of Venice and that's how I got my nickname, Lew the

257

Jew, and it came with lots of wisecracks about pounds of flesh and the quality of mercy. At first I took it personally, resulting in pushing fights; then I either ignored them or responded with a threat: don't ever come looking for me if you ever need money. Sorry to say, none of them ever did.

◆

Final exams took place at the end of the semester and you were either promoted or you vanished. Most kids were promoted but more than a few disappeared. Poor grades or bad behavior got them kicked out. Guys going into tenth grade moved from Banker and Merchant Halls to Mariner Hall as Sophomores when they returned from summer vacation. I did, too, and restarted my weekend enterprise, but fewer and fewer customers turned up. I guessed they matured as they aged and didn't need me anymore. It ended one Saturday afternoon when I came upon some friends talking about someone who was just kicked out and was headed for the entrance gates with his mom.

"Knobby Welch?" I exclaimed. "He owes me money from this morning!" I scrambled down Mariner Hall's steps and started toward the open gates when I saw them. He had his head down, carrying a suitcase. She had her head down too, clutching a white handkerchief in her hand. I sat on a bench and watched them go through the gates.

Forget it, I decided. I'd already made good money on him in the past. I rose from the bench and headed back to the building, no longer in the loan business.

FORTY-EIGHT

"Time's up. Send up your tests." The only sound was the waving of papers as they were passed over, shoulder to shoulder, to the front desks. Dr. Haskell stood and gathered them from the outstretched hands. "Last week I gave you these ten words. Now, we'll find out if you can spell them and define them," he said, carefully sliding the sheets into his thick briefcase. "You," he suddenly said – "chicanery!"

As Nick rose, he thought, I am sooo glad I didn't go to the park yesterday and worked on these with Bob Kase. "Chicanery, c-h-i-c-a-n-e-r-y, noun. Trickery, especially in legal proceedings."

"Good, now use it in a sentence."

He and Bob made it a game by coming up with crazy examples.

"Well, let's hear it."

"Sir, Doctor Haskell, Charlie Mangione thinks Mister Newman should be put in jail. He committed an act of chicanery when he convinced Mister Barr to buy his share of the Liberty Bell." Barr turned in his seat, a pained look on his face, and cried out, "Newman, you didn't own it?" The class laughed. Dr. Haskell smiled and waved his hand for quiet.

"Let's try someone else. How about you, Mister Uebele?" Walt Uebele rose and looked tentatively at Dr. Haskell. "Antediluvian."

"Can I try emolument, Dr. Haskell?"

"You can, Mr. Uebele, but in your case it's going to cost you." Even with that, Walt seemed relieved, Nick thought. He was okay until he was supposed to use it in a sentence. Then, Dom Tremonte, waving his hand, popped up. "Sir, Dr. Haskell, why should we learn words like emolument and antediluvian when no one ever uses them?"

"Yeah," Barr jumped in. "People talk about their salary or pay and they just call anything really old like those words, old-fashioned."

259

Dr. Haskell smiled. He was Nick's favorite teacher. Everyone liked him because he had a sense of humor, smiled a lot and he said he wanted to scratch everyone's imaginations. You could say things in his class you wouldn't think of in most classes. As long as they were pertinent, he said, he would entertain all questions.

"Mister Barr, you finally asked a good question." Barr looked around the room, reveling in his achievement and accepting the expected smirks and sneers.

"I said at the beginning of the semester we were going to begin a crusade to enlarge your vocabulary. Now, why would I choose words like chicanery, or emolument, or travesty, or obdurate?" Going to the blackboard, he drew a large triangle with the chalk. Then he made a line of what looked like waves running across the triangle, about a third of the way down from the top.

"Your vocabulary," he sat on the edge of his desk and pointed at the blackboard, "is like an iceberg. Just as we see only the tip of the iceberg, but know there's an enormous amount of it down below, out of sight, so our tip of the vocabulary iceberg consists of the same words we use over and over, day after day. There's nothing particularly wrong with that. We don't want to use language that people don't understand. You're right, Mister Tremonte, we don't say, I've received my emolument, we say I've been paid.

Pointing to the iceberg drawing, he said, "You can use this unseen intelligence mass in two ways. By knowing the meaning of words, you can read with greater understanding and increase your knowledge. And when you use the right word, one that expresses yourself or describes a situation effectively, it impresses others. They think you know even more than you may, which will be a tremendous advantage for some of you. And for words that are not customarily used, like patina or malleable, you are learning them so that, when you come across them, whether it's in a book or the newspaper, you understand what the author is saying or describing. You can picture things in your mind accurately. So, get ready for ten new words later this week."

He returned to his desk, sat down and said, "Now, let's turn to 'Lines Written Above Tintern Abbey.' Mister Wakerics, tell me what elements caused Wordsworth to be considered a Romantic poet."

High School

The Library

The Armory

FORTY-NINE

"Hey, Nick, where ya going?" Nick saw Todd Ross, Ray Smyth and some kid called Beansey, all from Mariner Hall. They were farther down on Corinthian Avenue than Nick and on the other side. "We're goin' to Gimbels and see what we can lift. C'mon." Beansey loved to tease passersby, making them turn and stare.

Nick cupped his mouth, "No, I'm meeting some guys down at Woarman's." It wasn't true, but he couldn't say it. He went with the guys a lot — all over Fairmount Park and Center City, watching people, what they were doing, listening to them talk and making fun of them. Sometimes bums on benches in Rittenhouse Square, with squinty eyes and what Ernie called a squashed voice, would call out, "Any you kids got a smoke?" Ernie and John Martin always gave them a cigarette. He always threw his hands in the air and said, "Sorry, don't smoke."

Today Nick just wanted to be alone. Even though cars and trucks were driving by, people walking and talking, sirens screaming somewhere — as long as there weren't kids everywhere you looked, Nick felt he was in another world. Being alone like this was like escaping the Hum without hopping the wall. No one was giving directions; no class assignments or chores having to be done right then; no place to be at a certain time. He was free and could decide what to do and when to do it.

When he felt this way he liked to wander the streets in what old Doc Haskell would call "floating lazily down your cerebral stream." Daydreaming in class, though, brought quick retribution, as Nick well knew: "Well, now that you joined our world again, Mister, why don't you stop back after classes today and check out the world of Alexander Pope. You might learn something from his wise couplets."

Nick turned left off Corinthian Avenue onto a street that looked like all the rest. Brick row homes with broad marble steps to the front door and concrete ones leading down to an area with trashcans and the basement door. Trees were planted every so often near the edge of the sidewalk, tall, skinny Ginkgo trees with triangular leaves. Dr. Presson said it was difficult to tell the male trees from the females and most streets had both. In the fall the female trees dropped berries that rotted and smelled like rancid butter. Kids called them "stinko" trees. People kept sweeping them up. Nick liked the bright yellow, fan-shaped leaves and put a few in one of his letters for his sister, Janet.

"Hey! Hey you!" Nick was startled by a loud voice. He looked around but didn't see anyone. "Down here, handsome." Nick looked down. A girl stood at the basement doorway of a row home, hand on her hip. "C'mere, c'mere," she curled her hand and motioned. He approached the steps. She motioned again. Slowly, eyes on her, he started down, one hand sliding on the railing.

She met him at the bottom and stood, hands clasped in front of her, an inquisitive look on her face. She started with his brogues, paused at his vest and tie, glanced up at his pompadour and then looked him full in the face. Head still, her pale blue eyes moved deliberately from feature to feature scrutinizing his chin, his mouth, his nose, his eyebrows and finally returning to his eyes.

"Satisfied, Sherlock?" he asked in as sarcastic a tone as he could muster. She leaned forward, her nose almost touching his, and, as though inspection time was over, one eyebrow rose and one cheek dimpled in her smile. "Yup," she announced. Nick laughed, his head rocked back. She laughed, too, as she stepped back. Not a little bell tinkle like some of the girls in his church class at home. It was almost like the guys' back at the Hum with a sort of smartass sound to it. "What's your name?"

"Nick," he replied. She nodded her head in agreeable acceptance and smiled back at him. "What's yours?"

"I'm Eleanor," she dramatically curtsied, "after the President's wife. When I was small everybody called me Ellie. I hate Ellie. Sounds

264

like some dopey girl on a farm somewhere milkin' cows and shovelin' shit." Nick was taken aback, but tried not to show it. "So, I changed it to Lenore, kind of a short cut. My sister said I'm tryna' be a Main Liner. I shut her up fast. I told her, 'Want me to tell Mom and Dad what you're doin' with the guys downstairs while they're over at Aunt Monika's?" She paused.

"So," Nick said, quietly. "You're Lenore."

"Yes," she pursed her lips, "I like the way you say it." Nick felt his face begin to burn. "Geez!" she exploded, "My friends would die laughing if they ever seen anybody blush over me." She poked his shoulder. "C'mon, let's go in." Nick moved around her and held the door open. "A girl I know said you guys from that place are something. I hope you don't use manners when you fight. Even the girls don't 'round here."

A narrow hall led to a large room with a washer, dryer and shelves stacked with boxes and folded clothing on one side. On the other side was a couch in front of a long, low table, some folding chairs and a small television set on an end table with a record player and a stack of 45s. Behind it, a tan paneled wall was covered with framed photographs.

"Your coat, sir?" She draped it over a folding chair. "Soda? orange or black cherry?"

"Black cherry, thanks." She turned and ran up the stairs. Nick wandered over to the wall. Wedding photos, a couple in front of a car, little girls in white dresses holding bibles, girls and guys sitting on the beach. One caught his eye. Lenore in a restaurant, smiling in the center of a group of girls holding up wineglasses. A folded card propped up against a bouquet of flowers read: Lenore's 17th – May 2, 1950. Seventeen -- he was two years younger than Lenore!

Before he had time to react, she came hurrying down the steps. "Here, Nicholas," she emphasized his full name. "Sit there." He took the bottle and sat back on the couch. She sat down in a folding chair opposite him, crossed her ankles and watched him. She was unlike any girl he'd ever met. You didn't have to try to talk to her. She knew what she wanted to say, not like most of the girls they brought in to dances at the Hum. They spent so much time giggling together.

Lenore had never heard of Wilkes-Barre. He had never heard of Dobbins High School. She had two sisters and a brother, all older.

"Do you have a boyfriend?"

"Lots," she said with a nonchalant wave of long blond hair. Curled at the bottom, it swirled around her neck. "But they don't pick me — I pick them. And I decide how far to go. Pow!" she made a fist. "Even the Taney Street Rams don't bother me. My brother taught me how to fight. And," she added, "I bite, too," showing her teeth. "But I can't imagine fighting with you." She stood up. "Well," her eyebrow went up again, "maybe some wrestling."

Sliding the chair closer toward his knee, she sat down, took his soda and set it beside hers. She then leaned forward and looked impishly at him, knowing he was studying her this time. Wide eyebrows, darker than her blonde hair, arched over blue eyes. Her face was heart shaped, with a cleft chin and her skin, with a little peach fuzz under her nose, shone as though she spent lots of time outdoors.

As he looked at her lips, wide and light red, he felt her hand on the back of his head. It was warm. She smiled; not with her mouth, with her eyes. She was enjoying whatever was going to happen already, Nick thought. Then her lips moved to his, soft and warm. He felt a warm glow invade him, his face, then his chest, and then below. Her smooth cheek moved over his in a slow circle. He could smell flowers. Her lips were holding his ear lobe, her tongue was moving back and forth over it. She took his hand and slipped it through an opening in her blouse, pressing it to a lightly covered breast.

A door opened above them and a voice said, "Lenore, are you down there?" Lenore pulled back, her eyes wide, a finger to her lips. "Yes, Mom, I'm down here."

266

"What are you doing?"

"Doin' some homework." With a devilish smile, she leaned forward and gently rubbed Nick's nose with hers.

"I'm home from work, but I've got to go to the store. I'll be back to test you in a while."

Lenore rose and whispered, her hand on his shoulder. "I gotta go upstairs so she doesn't come down. Don't move." Nick was glad. He knew he couldn't stand up right then. Maybe she'd laugh at him and he'd die.

He could hear voices and stood up. After a few minutes she came down the stairs. "When she goes, you'll be safe to go." She hugged him, her arms around his shoulders, her face rocking gently on his neck. "I don't want you to go, but you'd better," she murmured.

When they heard a door slam, she went down the hall, opened the basement door and went out; returning, she waved him to come. "Give her a minute to go down the street, then go up and look. She'll go left. If she's talking to some neighbor, like old lady Kleinhurst, even far down, wait, she might look back."

As he squeezed to the right to get by her, she leaned against him and laughed, her hand furrowing his hair. "You're such a doll. Ya gotta come back. I never got close to a boy like you before." With that she gave him a quick kiss on the lips and then pushed him out the door.

FIFTY

Standing in the Mariner Hall phone booth, Nick was disgruntled. This was the third time he'd called; twice before dinner and now, after dinner, there was still no answer. He knew he was taking a risk that somebody else in the family might answer; if they did he'd have to fake a wrong number. In about twenty minutes everybody had to leave for the Chapel for a slide show lecture by some guy about Africa. He'd met Lenore almost two months ago and on Saturdays she'd meet him a few blocks from her house and they'd decide what to do. They might go to a movie at the Big F or walk to Boathouse Row by the Art Museum, sit on a bench and watch the scullers on the Schuylkill River or sit by the Calder fountain at Logan Square across from the main library. They did a lot of walking and talking. Sundays she was at big family dinners at home or at relatives.

"Hello?"

"Great, someone finally answered the phone!"

"Well, if you're gonna act grouchy, I'm sorry I answered."

"No, no. Wait. I'm sorry. I just needed to talk to you. I can't make it this weekend."

"What? Why not?"

"Because I got in trouble and I can't get a pass out until next weekend."

"You know next weekend I have to go to my cousin's in Jersey. What'd you do that was so bad?" Now, she seems grouchy, he thought, so I'd better not tease her.

"Bob Sterling and Joe Camperson started picking on me in the lavatory. Just foolin' but kept it up and kept it up. Finally, I shoved Camperson and he shoved me into Sterling and we began wrestling. Somehow we got over to one of the windows and fell against it and broke it."

"What!"

"And Stubby Craig, the housemaster, walked in right then."

"For supposedly being so well educated, you and your Hummers sure act dopey sometimes."

"I know and I'm sorry and…whoa!"

"Whoa?"

"The phone booth's starting to move."

"How can that be?"

"It's tilting. It's going to go down on the floor!"

"You'll get killed if it falls on you," Lenore shrieked, "you'll get cut when the glass in the door breaks. Yell, call for help!"

"I can't — I mean I can, but it won't help. That's what they want me to do."

Standing under the stairs at the back of Mariner Hall, the booth had three wooden sides and a folding door with glass windows. Nick was on the built-in triangular seat when the booth started moving. He could hear laughter and mumbling outside but couldn't see anyone. An arm and hand across part of the glass door kept it from flying open. As Nick began to lean forward, he said to Lenore, "It's a joke. It happens all the time. Some jerks are lowering the booth so the glass door's on the floor and I can't get out."

"No!"

"Hold on." He let the receiver swing loose. Kneeling on the floor Nick pressed himself against one wall, clutching the edge of the seat. The booth continued its descent until the pranksters gently rested the glass door on the floor. Success brought cheers and loud thumps as they celebrated by kicking the wooden sides to further agitate their victim.

The angle now pitched him so he landed face down on the glass door. Rising a few inches he groaned and turned over; the uneven surface of the raised molding around the windows and the depressed glass panes made lying there painful. His sudden burst of "Damn you guys! I'll find out who you are," was drowned out by more jeering and a series of even harder kicks.

"Lenore," he yelled up at the speaker, "I'm all right. It's just a joke." Stretching, he caught the swinging receiver and held it close enough to his ear to hear "...worried about you and it's just a joke. Well, enjoy the joke — and enjoy your weekend inside. You can spend the rest of your life inside those walls as far as I'm concerned!" and the phone went dead.

◆

"How many windows do we still have to go?"

"Maybe eight or ten more," Nick answered Sterling.

He and Bob spent all Saturday afternoon working off the broken window, cleaning every window in the building. Camperson was wiping down every chair on the first floor with a damp cloth, after mopping all three stairwell landings. Now, they were sitting with dozens of others on the back steps of the hall waiting to go to dinner, when Hank Wyzykowski joined them. "Nick, heard Bell of Pennsylvania screwed up your love life."

"Naw," he said, inspecting the start of a blister on his thumb, "it was really my fault, but some wise guys made it worse." He looked up at Wyzykowski. "I'll bet Newman, Surgeoner and Nordstrom were in on it."

Hank's grin confirmed it. "Newman and Nordstrom make a lot of phone calls, trying to make time with girls they meet at the Big F. Next time I see one of them on the phone I'll get some guys and get even."

"I'll help," Sterling said eagerly. "How'd you get out of the booth, anyway?"

"Farmer Jones was on duty and heard the racket. Those guys ran out the back door, and he called some guys on their way to the Chapel to come back. They raised it slowly so I wouldn't fall against the glass door. I told Mr. Jones I didn't know who did it. But ya can't be nice around here. When I said, 'Thanks, guys,' one of them was big mouth Constantine Begos. 'Oh, you're quite welcome,' he says in his snide way, 'we're always glad to pick up a fallen Hummer,' n'even Farmer Jones laughed at that."

"Aw, forget him. We'll keep an eye out for who's using the phone," Sterling said. "It'll be easy to get guys to help us, but first let's go to dinner. I'll even eat liver tonight."

FIFTY-ONE

"Like they say in the romance magazines my sister reads, was it good for you?" He was looking up at the ceiling but didn't really seem to be seeing. She reached over and turned his head until he faced her. "Yes," then, moving his hand up from under the cover to gently cup a breast, his thumb caressing the nipple, he said, just audibly, "It was great."

A moment of quiet as though she was pondering something, then, returning his smile, asked just as quietly, "Was it your first?" He turned again to stare at the ceiling. "Yes."

They lay quiet for a while, listening to each other's breathing, until she sat up, threw out an arm as though she was announcing to the room, "That's exactly what I like about him!" she said vehemently. "He's the most different boy I ever met. After a question like that, most guys wouldn't admit it was their first time." She clenched her fist and waved it at the ceiling. "They'd get mad instead and say — 'so how many guys have you been with?' Of course," she looked over at him and raised one eyebrow which she knew always amused him, "they'd known I wasn't a virgin." He didn't respond immediately; another pause, another ceiling stare.

"Everything went so fast...and when I saw how beautiful you were, I couldn't think of anything except to get as close to you as I could."

"No," she laughed, "you didn't hesitate and you were good for the first time."

"Oh?" he made no attempt to suddenly sound experienced. His hand behind her head, he gently drew her face to his, wanting to study it just as she had scrutinized his when they first met. She looked back at him, into his eyes, with a go ahead, do it expression. Tracing one eyebrow, then the other with a finger, he kissed each eye closed. She smiled and he touched the dimple on her cheek; the smile faded and it disappeared. He had just started across the red curve of her lower lip when both eyes opened extra wide and she bit him on the finger.

"Hey!" It didn't hurt as much as it surprised him. "What the...?"

As though she had been reading his thoughts, she declared firmly, "I am no angel, Nick. I haven't been one. And don't try to look at me and make me one. Sooner or later you'll be disappointed."

Taking his finger, she kissed it, ran it across her closed lips, and put his hand on her breast, over her heart. "I'm a realist, my dad says. He says it's good because I don't sit around dreaming or waiting for things to come to me; I decide what I want and go after it." She put a hand on his heart. "Just as I took you, Nick."

She was startled when he looked away, but then felt he was in one of his reflective moods. "Funny," he questioned himself aloud, "in all the books we read at school, especially the poetry, whenever love turns up it seems so sappy, so fake, like the writer is trying to make it fascinating or overpowering. We all make fun of it." Turning back to her, he said, "I never liked anyone before like I like you. It feels so good to hold you against me, to kiss you everywhere, to just be with you." He lay back and held his arms out. "I love you, Lenore. I'm glad you want me." She put her head on his shoulder and closed her eyes.

Head back, he pictured Lenore in a gown coming through the gates with him to the Battalion Ball. With Founder's Hall all lit up and the guys in their military uniforms dancing with girls in beautiful dresses, he thought she'd feel like they were in a movie.

Seeing that she was asleep, he reached out, lifting his French textbook off the table. The pages swung open when he held it up with one hand and he began to read about the approach of Bastille Day.

Later, he noticed the time on the wall clock and nudged her. She'd been asleep for almost an hour. "Lenore, better get up. It's almost four. When's your mom coming home?" She's a deep sleeper he thought, not good if you're a Hummer.

She barely lifted her head, slowly yawned and then opened her eyes — fully awake with a mischievous grin. "We've got 'til five thirty." Shoving the textbook off the bed, she slid a leg between his, turned his head so she could bite his earlobe, and then whispered enticingly, "You do have homework to do…and teacher's going to help you do it right now."

Battalion at Founder's Hall steps

Battalion Prom

FIFTY-TWO

"What a building," Rita exclaimed, "I've seen Founder's Hall from outside the gates, but to walk along these huge columns, you really feel small. I never saw the door open before, and Mr. Girard's statue."

"Nick said they only do it today, Founder's Day, when they celebrate his birthday, and alumni come back and families come in," Lenore explained. "The first time Nick brought me to a dance here, I felt we were in one of those old English movie ballrooms with the marble floors and tall windows and the gigantic chandelier."

"My mom says these orphans must be doing pretty well," Gloria added. Then a deep voice announced from behind a column they were approaching, "I'm sorry, my dears, but the orphans don't live in buildings like this."

"That's Nick!" Lenore shouted, "trying to act like some kind of spirit or something. Come out, you spook, so we can see you." She waved her friends to circle around one side while she started round the other. "Ha! This ain't a ghost!" she cried, finding Nick atop the column base, feet splayed on the circular molding, arms hugging the huge marble shaft, "It's alive."

Grabbing one of Nick's ankles, she pulled it. "Whoa!" He began to fall backwards. "He's gonna hit the steps, grab him!" Lenore pulled Gloria next to her, Rita joining them. "Oohf." Nick's back slammed down on their upraised hands; forcing them a few steps lower and then, steadying themselves, they shoved him upright to land on his feet beside the column base. "That was great," he whined, shaking his head from side to side in exasperation. "Sorree," was Lenore's disdainful reply, pushing out her lower lip in an exaggerated pout. Nick laughed with the girls and shook his head at them in a does-anybody-ever-know-what-this-girl's-gonna-do-next look to which Rita replied, "We're used to Lenore's performances — we love them."

Ignoring them, Lenore gave him a motherly kiss on the forehead, took his hand and said, "Saving you made me hungry. Where's that ice cream you promised?"

"This is a beautiful staircase," Rita's voice echoed as they started up the wide steps that curved along the wall to the second floor of Founder's Hall, "but look how they shaped these steps, every one dips down in a curve, from one side to the other. It makes it hard to walk up, and it ruined the marble, too."

"They didn't make them that way," Nick answered, "they were perfect in 1848, when the school opened."

"This is 1950," Lenore said, "so, boys like you have been running up and down these steps for...um, let me think," she pursed her lips, "for one hundred and two years. No wonder they're worn down like that." Nick glanced back and gave her an approving look. Seconds later she whacked his bottom and then made a disapproving face at him. Entering the Student Center, Nick saw Don Loder and Bob Englehardt behind the counters. Loder waved them over. Nick introduced the girls to Don and that drew Bob over immediately.

Nick was pleased that the conversation was going along so well with a minimum of sarcasm, when Bob asked Lenore, obviously Nick's date since she was holding his hand, "Did he tell you he was just elected treasurer of our class?"

"No, of course not. I have to pry things out of him, good and bad, like when he climbed over the wall to leave flowers on the trash can for my birthday. He knows I'm the youngest and I take the garbage out."

"Enough," Nick said. "Now, let's find that ice cream — and you want to see Mariner Hall." Nick paid, but they wouldn't take his money for the girls.

"You two go on," Don said, "Bob and I would like to discuss an upcoming dance with certain new acquaintances." The girls, unwrapping ice cream sandwiches, coyly agreed. Bob, all saccharine smile, said, "Our break is coming up shortly, and we'll be glad to bring your guests over to you, Nicholas." Lenore was surprised by Nick's burst of laughter. "God, Hummers actually acting like considerate Girardians!"

♦

They sat with the crowd on the back steps of Founder's Hall watching the soccer game. As they finished their ice cream, Lenore said, "I didn't really know what you meant about being in the Battalion until I saw the band come up the main road with your army behind it."

"Well, I wouldn't call it an army," Nick said, "four companies of a couple hundred guys."

"When I called out to you," she continued, "and of course you ignored me, a little old man next to me said you were a Lieutenant. And another kid who started talking to me said he knew you. He said you'd probably be the Captain of Company D next year." She looked at him but got no response. "And it's really nice to see all these graduates return, old guys and lots of young guys, shaking hands and talking together about their times in your Hum. Some went over and talked to the little kids watching the parade from the Junior School playground. Lots of mothers come in, too, and families...even girls."

Lenore, with a deft nod of her head, said, "Thanks for letting me bring Rita and Gloria. They couldn't believe how big the Chapel is and how those enormous doors were made so even little kids could open them."

"Yes, press the lever handles and they open hydraulically. First building ever built with it and that was back in 1933. It's some place," Nick admitted. "Once, when I was home, I went to some of a buddy's high school classes. They don't seem too hard, and I realize how different the Hum is. Our library is one whole building, two floors. They don't even have one teacher they call Doctor. And they don't know what a Battalion is. They couldn't believe we had study halls in

278

the morning and at night. They couldn't believe we have such a different life."

"Would you change it? Leave if you could?"

"Maybe when I was small, now it's too late. I'm used to it. We gripe a lot, but everyone feels loyal to it; underneath, I guess we really like it."

As they approached the steps to Mariner Hall, Lenore could see Merchant Hall just down from it and, beyond it, Banker Hall. "These buildings all look so old and they're all the same."

"They are, even Bordeaux Hall, on the other side of Founder's Hall. They were all built long ago in the eighteen hundreds, and then they added things like electric lights and inside toilets. Allen Hall, where you live for the last six months before you graduate, has separate rooms, not dorms. You choose and room with two to six buddies, classmates."

"These steps are worn down a little," Lenore said, "and chipped too after all these years. Look, there's a space between those steps; you could get the tip of your shoe caught in it."

"Never saw it happen. Most guys run up and down them and usually jump off them. Actually, there was a time when you might see a wisp of smoke rising from these steps."

"Silly, stones can't burn."

"They didn't. Some guys poked a hole in the concrete wall in the basement and found a space under the steps shaped like the inside of a pyramid. They hung a big poster over the hole and stood on a chair to climb in."

"Wasn't it dark?"

"No, probably some guys who were taking electric shop, stole wire and ran it along the wall to a small lamp. Probably stole that from somewhere, too."

"What'd they do there?"

"They smoked, of course, and drank beer."

"You and your buddies drank and smoked. I don't believe it, not you, Mister Perfect." Two guys sitting on a bench across the way jumped up, raising their hands in shock when they saw Nick slap Lenore across the face; it was a mock slap stopping at her cheek and didn't change her questioning look. The two sat down and kept staring.

"You actually smoked and drank beer?"

"I don't smoke, my dear, but I do enjoy a cold Schmidt's of Philadelphia on occasion."

Lenore rolled her eyes at his pseudo sophistication. "Where'd you guys get beer, anyway? You're too young."

"At the Eighteen Fifteen Bar. You wait until a rummy comes out and give him money plus fifty cents to keep and he goes back in buys a few quarts for us."

"You Hummers. Do they still use this hideout?"

"Not any more. A Housemaster noticed the wire, followed it, uncovered the hole and had it cemented over. But Ernie, Reds and Paul Guida created what they called their personal smoking room, like the old guys in England had for after dinner."

"How'd they do that?

"Back in Merchant Hall there was a little room on the second floor where they once stored suitcases or something. They noticed four screws on the wall holding in — I guess some sort of access panel. Inside they found a tiny room they couldn't even stand up in. They pulled the panel back in, wrapped a piece of string around a straightened out paperclip, stuck it in a shoe polish can and lit it. But the smoke was so oily it was still hard to see. It was their secret smoking lounge . . until they lost it."

"What happened?"

One of them kicked over the can and the floor caught on fire.

"No! What'd they do?"

"They put it out with the only liquid they had."

Nick smiled as he pinched his nose, "and Ernie said it smelled so bad, they couldn't go back there anymore!"

"You Hummers are so — "

"Resourceful," Nick said.

"That's not the word I had in mind! Let's just drop the subject."

Some kid, coming out, held the door open, gave Lenore a once over as she squeezed past him into the hallway, with an approving look at Nick. "Turn right," Nick said.

The living room was large with one wall lined with windows. It was furnished with end tables with lamps and a number of Windsor chairs. "This is great." Lenore settled back in one of the large overstuffed club chairs, much to the enjoyment of surprised occupants of the room. "Really comfortable, and all leather too," she rubbed her hand along the burgundy arm.

"Would you like to relax with today's Philadelphia Bulletin?" Someone rustled the paper he was reading. She smiled, shook her head as she rose and followed Nick around the attentive viewers to the far end of the room where there was a second doorway. Across the hall was another doorway.

"That's another living room." In the hall, they passed the housemaster's empty office and a stairway. "That goes down to the lavatories and toilets. I don't think you need to see that."

"This tile floor is so shiny. Who does that?"

"We're all assigned different jobs. With all these guys running in and out, it's a mess. But it was just polished. The whole building's cleaned up so it looks good for today. The rooms at this end of the building are the same size as the two living rooms. That one," Nick pointed to the left, "with all the chairs is the TV room."

Looking in the other room, she saw boys at a pool table, others watching. As they approached the rear entrance doors, passing by a second stairwell, Nick turned to her and, clasping his hand over her eyes, said, "I want you to do something, sight unseen, and then apologize to me."

"What," she exclaimed, "I don't understand? And . . ." clearly bothered, shaking her head side to side, but not dislodging his hand, "and I'm not going to apologize if this is some sort of trick with your buddies."

"It's not," he reassured her, "just let me lead you somewhere...now step up a little." Then he pressed down on her shoulders. "Sit."

She held on to the small wooden seat under her until he abruptly replaced his hand with one of hers.

"Your participation will only take a minute." She sat stiffly upright, "And you think I'm gonna apologize?" she muttered before pressing her lips into a defiant line. A door closed next to her and then she heard Nick's voice, a distance away. "This is where you got mad at me." Then the room she was in suddenly tilted forward.

"Hey!" She threw one hand forward and touched a wall. When it began to lean she felt she might slide off the seat, she uncovered her eyes and put her other hand forward and found herself, head down, pressing against a brown wall. "Stop! Stop, Nick!" The room slowly dropped back until it was level. To her right was a phone on the wall, to her left, through two folding glass doors, was Nick, grinning mischievously, the way he said she always did to him. She was in the phone booth.

He opened the door, but she stayed right where she was, not looking at him, studying the wood paneling. He remained silent, waiting for her reaction. Finally, as though having made a decision, she rose and faced him. His face was blank, not sure what to expect. Stepping out of the booth, she threw her arms around his shoulders, kissed him hard, and, shaking her head side to side, said, plaintively repentant, "Okay, okay, I apologize."

Rita and Gloria turned up Parrish Street after thanking Nick for their day at Girard with hugs and subtle smiles to Lenore conveying successful prom arrangements. Lenore and Nick started down Corinthian Avenue, then turned on various streets to make the trip home as long as possible.

"Those little boys are so cute in their knickers and coats with shirts and ties and vests, holding their caps on when they run. Do they dress that way every day?"

"Every day, from their first day here, and they hate those knickers and coats made of tweed. It's scratchy on your skin; you'll see them picking at them all the time. Bob Hennessey told me he had a Sunday suit — pale blue tweed, coat and knickers and lived in a tough neighborhood in Southwest Philly. Got to be a good fighter because when he went home kids picked on him every time and he had to fight back." Hand in hand, they paused at the alley that ran off Wallace Street. "I really like your school now that I've seen it; and Founder's Hall is amazing. I wish my folks could see it sometime."

"Well, you'll see it again next month…at the Prom."

"I know," she squeezed his hand, "I can't wait. How late can you stay out?"

"Have to be in bed by midnight, but they don't check carefully. If I'm not there, somebody'll stuff my bed. I do it for guys all the time. Just have to sneak in and be quiet. Not wake anybody up."

"Lucky us. My mom's going to a wedding, someone at work. She's making my dad go. I'll tell them I'm going to Kathy Donato's, that I'm borrowing her dress and staying there.

"Devious, devious," Nick said, sliding his arm around her waist and pulling her to him. "Some author we read said, 'don't trust a conniver,' and now I love one."

She pulled her long blond hair over her eye like Veronica Lake, "Aaand I'll get Aidan Luna, a guy I know, to buy me some champagne.

283

We'll have champagne and shrimp and then we'll celebrate in our own special way. And you won't even have to sneak into the house." She started for the street corner, "I'll see you in a few minutes when I unlock the cellar door."

Nick learned to go down the back alley on Saturday afternoons, strolling under the kitchen extensions as though he was a new kid living somewhere down the line of row homes. His tie was stuffed in his coat pocket, which he slung over his shoulder, the two top buttons on his shirt opened. No Hummer ever looks like this, he thought.

Pulling up one of the metal cellar doors, he backed down the steps. She laughed when he'd first grumbled, "When I lower that door, I feel like I'm in a submarine, the light over the door is so dim."

"You're lucky," she said, "I thought about putting the light out and starting the washer and dryer to really spook you."

"Whatta friend."

"Hey, sometimes I'm not your friend. But," her eyes looked soft, "right now I am." Gripping him around the shoulders, she kissed him. "I'll never do anything to hurt you, unless you call me a Wall Rat."

"That I'll never do. The housemasters call them that. They're really nice girls. That's their most effective way to communicate in a social emergency," he explained. Rubbing the tip of her nose over his, Eskimo-fashion, she said, "I don't want you for an education, I want you for entertainment!" Putting his hands on her shoulders, he pushed her away. "I want you to go over my vocab cards with me before you think of entertainment, sly one." Her look was scornful when he said, "But first I want to look up and add a new word...vixen."

284

Chores

I don't think there was ever a time, child to youth, when a Hummer didn't have an assignment to accomplish, beyond the eternal ones of schoolwork, proper behavior and good manners. Some guys took longer than others to learn that complaining about chores didn't do any good and performing in a slow and slovenly manner meant a repeat effort and might even result in some additional tasks to rectify your attitude. Eventually you matured enough to realize the best thing was to get it done as quickly as possible and get out of there. You could still enjoy complaining as long as you kept it to yourself and your buddies.

In Junior School, the governess might assign you to be the temporary shoe or towel monitor. Every boy had two pairs of shoes with the second pair stored in little bins at the back of the section room. Brogues were for every day and oxfords for Sunday Chapel and special events. You were expected to use the daubers, polish and brushes in the washroom to keep them presentable; no matter that you wore brogues all day, every day, in classes and playing. She occasionally asked everyone at their desks to raise their legs so she could inspect them and you were reprimanded if yours were not shined, and punished if they needed repair. They were to be given to the shoe monitor if the soles or heels were worn. You could wear the oxfords only until the brogues were returned. Many a heel was lost as you played baseball or soccer or just chased someone around the macadam playground. Painful hobbling from being shinned, tripped or recovering from an inept slide into a base was acceptable; limping because a heel was missing was not tolerated.

The shoe monitor, after stuffing a paper with your name on it into one shoe, tied the laces together and added them to his pile. How Dickensian he looked headed up the Main Road to the shoe shop with pairs of mini-brogues swinging wildly over his shoulder on the end of a long pole. Monitors were often paid with Hum Muds or given candy from the goody cache in a locked closet.

In the lower grades you might also be sent to the Dining Room early. Eight, nine and 10-year-olds set the tables with plates, glasses and silverware, rolled up linen napkins and stuck them in shiny nickel rings, and cleared the tables afterwards. The only domestic help aside from the dietitian and cooks were seamstresses and workers in the bakery, laundry and shoe shop. Boys also loaded dishes, glasses and silverware onto wooden racks, sent them through the dishwasher, and dried them when they came out. Waiters were not paid, but those who helped around the kitchen often left with a treat from food preparations for the next meal, perhaps an apple or an orange.

My favorite chore, which I got to do only a few times, was to dispense sugar. Another kid, hugging a deep stainless steel pot, worked his way around each table, plopping a ladle of hot cereal — creamy yellow goop or dark brown tweed-like stuff, in each bowl. You followed, dumping a spoonful of sugar; sometimes brown sugar with raisins mixed in, on top.

When you came to the chair of a buddy, you tapped the kid on the shoulder. He waited until you put two or three spoonfuls of sugar in the empty bowl before he filled it with cereal; then you added the legal spoonful on top. There was always a nervous dietitian roaming about the room, so it had to be a covert act, making the whole ruse all the sweeter. Someone you disliked might find his breakfast salted from the purloined shaker in your pocket. This morning crew rejoined their various sections to await the breakfast call, keeping quiet about any devious services except to share them with the beneficiaries and alert them to observing the victims. With job assignments varying every day, it was impossible to track down the perpetrators.

Working in dining rooms and kitchens continued through Good Friends and Lafayette and in each of the Halls until graduation. Though I never received any payment, others recalled, as adults, they were paid twenty cents an hour for scrubbing pots and pans and running the dish and glass washers.

Sometimes, when Junior School playground time ended and the twelve ragged columns of boys lined up before being dismissed to wash up for dinner, the housemaster ordered everyone to do an about face, spread out, and pick up

286

every piece of paper or any large stone somebody could trip over. "When you get to the end of the playground, turn around and walk, and I mean walk, back!"

During some playground recesses in Junior School, we were issued long handled brushes with sturdy bristles and spent the hour sweeping up leaves and dirt around the building and on the steps, sidewalks and curbs along our side of the Main Road. Beginning in Good Friends and thereafter, you and your class might also be assigned to sweep the pigeon dirt off the multitude of steps on all four sides of Founders Hall. And the coming of Fall meant hours sweeping up the leaves on the Main Road and loading them into wooden pushcarts with two big wheels.

Supervised showers took place every night before bedtime for Hummers aged six to thirteen. At fourteen, moving up from Lafayette to the halls, you were personally responsible for taking a shower before going to bed, although most guys, hot and sweaty from playing a sport, took theirs before dinner. You might skip one occasionally, but anyone who exuded a malodorous aroma was soon harassed and then threatened. Ignored warnings resulted in the scrub brush treatment; the "stinker" was dragged into the shower room, stripped, and underwent group purification that left him pink and in pain. It rarely happened twice.

Everyone entered a formalized work program from Good Friends on. First thing in the morning, after breakfast ended at 7:30, you either worked or studied. Anyone without a job or not wielding a pass to the Infirmary went straight to school to study until the 8:15 morning assembly began. After completing their tasks, workers were free until Assembly.

Each building and surrounding grounds had to be cleaned every day. All the Biggie halls, were similar in design: a long, narrow center hall, two living rooms, a TV room, a recreation room, two upper floors of dormitories, a shower room and a basement with lavatories and toilets, plus stairs at both ends of the buildings, broad walks and lawns, and shrubs.

The most traveled feature, the tiled main hallway running down the center of the first floor, was not only swept daily but scrubbed, polished and

287

buffed once a week, extra liquid applications occasionally turning it into an indoor skating rink.

Everyone also had to serve as a waiter twice a semester in two one-week stints. In the minds of a few impatient diners, you were there to fulfill their every demand, outdoing other waiters by successfully returning with second servings of raisin bread or extra servings of liver (for the gravy) or whatever they thought they didn't get enough of. Should either of your two tables become unhappy with your performance, you could expect to be cursed or promised physical impairment, and the most irate might turn over their plates and butter them. This forced you to slide the plate across the linen tablecloth to the table's edge where you could finally grasp its rim. Securing even five bread and butter plates could take quite a while and your antagonist's shoulders were often used to thwart your effort.

Waiters ate after each meal, so those who cleared their tables quickly got to the Waiter's Table first and feasted as they pleased. Arriving last meant a meager selection, if anything other than milk and bread were left. Most meals did not turn out this badly because you reminded anyone considering a slowdown that someday they might have to wait on you! Assignment as a waiter, from Good Friends to Bordeaux Hall, provided years of practical experience in blending the arts of diplomacy, prevarication and intimidation, generally in that order.

My most memorable assignment occurred when I was fifteen. After breakfast, I made my way to the Television Room on the first floor of Mariner Hall. Closing the doors at each end of the room, I shoved the thirty or so Windsor chairs to one side of the room and swept. Then shoved them to the other side and completed sweeping, after which I lined them up, theatre style, in rows in front of the television set with an aisle running along the wall. Adjusting the rabbit ears, I got a slightly snowy Philadelphia station, WPTZ, on the Dumont black and white television set. A burly disk jockey at a desk played the latest Perry Como or Patti Page hit and banged away on a set of chimes while calling out the time, though it was continually shown on the bottom of the screen. He accompanied his zany jokes, preposterous *observations and serious-turned-silly poems with a variety of comical expressions. He was hilariously absurd and, mid-way through the semester, I mailed a postcard to join his Morning Club. When the heavy duty paper card came in the mail, I treasured it. The reverse side defined the outrageous rules and supposed membership benefits. The front side named me an official member of EEFMS — the Early Eyeball Fraternal Marching Society. It featured a black and white photograph of our leader: thick, black eyebrows hanging over humorously squinting eyes, and under a wide, bristling moustache, a torpedo-like cigar protruded from the corner of his mouth at a swashbuckling angle as he smiled out at me. He had personally signed his name, Ernie Kovacs.*

A Housemaster, at some point, walked through the building to make sure the work was completed satisfactorily. While most guys, chores finished, took off, I usually slumped in a chair a few feet in front of the Dumont grinning at Ernie until it was time for Assembly.

What might have been bothersome chores to boys outside the walls became habitual, everyday activities to a Hummer. You never thought twice about making your bed, brushing your teeth before breakfast, polishing your shoes, taking showers, pressing your pants, or having to attend assembly or chapel services every day where you listened to the prayers and sang the hymns. Like every other Hummer, you just did it.

289

FIFTY-THREE

It was three weeks since Founder's Day and that was the last time he'd seen Lenore. She probably wondered what happened to him, but she said she'd never call Mariner Hall or ask him what else he was doing. He'd be embarrassed to tell her. He and Flanagan had been wrestling in the lavatory. Just fooling around, they weren't mad, it was just a game. Then some guys who were watching soaked washcloths and threw them. So he and Flanagan threw them back, and then a real fight started, guys flipping towels at each other; targeting faces, too. Then Doc Dulebon walked in. Nick liked him, though he was teased a lot behind his back. Literate, well spoken and courteous, tall and skinny, kind of like the history book pictures of Abe Lincoln. He had a doctorate from Penn so his nickname was Doc Doodlebomb for the horse that came in last on Spike Jones' record. Unfortunately, it was right when he and Flanagan, now near the door, had their towels twisted and ready to strike. He jabbed his finger towards the two of them, and they lowered their arms. That took care of passes out any day for the next two weeks for all six Hummers. Nick didn't get to see Lenore and he certainly wouldn't call. He felt he was gambling on who might answer the phone. Flanagan, who lived in Philly, didn't get to go home.

Nick could only see Lenore on Saturday and sometimes on Sundays. When she told him she had field hockey and dramatic club rehearsals during the week, his comment, "Oh, big surprise — a rough and tumble sport and endless theatrics," got him a punch in the stomach that actually hurt.

Although he thought of her often, especially at night in bed, he did need lots of time to spend on class preparation; it seemed to be increasing and more difficult each semester. After two or three guys didn't have answers, right or wrong, in French class, Dr. Wolcott jumped on the whole class. "When will you boys learn? We have to compress your education because we don't have Eighth Grade *plus* you have your trade to learn along with academics. You have a lot of work to do if you're going to graduate, and it's all up to you. Grow up. Nobody's going to nag you. Stop the whining and study."

Nick enjoyed going down to the Print Shop in the Mechanical School every afternoon and learning to set type and run the printing press and the linotype machine. And sports took a lot of time, too. There was the inter-mural league between classes plus competition among the halls, each with their own colors and pennants. Mariner was blue and white. The only chance he had to be with Lenore was on weekends when the varsity and JV team were scheduled to play other schools, and there were only pickup games. He knew he wasn't great, but good enough to play baseball, basketball and soccer on class teams. Everyone who'd seen Lenore razzed him for any screwup he made. "Yo, lover boy, thinkin' of that hot babe, are you?"

It was only three weeks until the Prom and he wanted to know what color dress she was wearing so he could get the right corsage. He still wrote home a couple times a month; short letters, and his mom still included a dollar or two in some of her letters. He also made some money working in the kitchen scrubbing pots; it was nice to be paid with money, not Hum Muds, now that he was older.

One afternoon when he had been at her basement door, about to leave, a letter slipped out of his breast pocket. Noting the Wilkes-Barre address, when she handed it to him, Lenore had asked, "Did you tell your mother about me?" When he said, "No," her eyebrows pinched and she looked stern. "If I tell her, she'll start asking questions in every letter, more and more. And expect answers. How can I describe you to her when I'm still trying to figure you out?"

Before she could reply, he asked, "Are you going to tell your family about me? They don't even know I exist." She raised her chin and gazed up at the sky, then looked sullenly at him but didn't say a word, just closed the door. He never brought it up again.

FIFTY-FOUR

Faces across Caswell McGregor's classroom were apprehensive as they waited for the day's English class to begin. For most Hummers, fear of Mr. McGregor began long before they were assigned to his class. Among the enlightening lore passed down from upperclassmen about the nefarious high school teaching tricks, such as having to learn to type on Remingtons with blank keys and a full range of teacher idiosyncrasies, none were more menacing than those of Mr. McGregor's temper and violent reactions. Now Nick found himself in McGregor's class.

Suddenly the door burst open, and Don Barr rushed in, throwing himself behind his desktop on the front row. As the door slowly closed, a voice, fading down the hall was heard. "Barr, ya sonofabitch, I'll kick the shit outta you one a these days!"

As quiet laughter filled the room, Nick leaned out in the aisle around Podagrosi to see Barr, small and wiry with a sheaf of unkempt black hair and big brown eyes beloved by female teachers, smiling sheepishly at Mr. McGregor, who didn't smile back, just shook his head at Barr's habitual tardiness.

"Mistah Bahr," McGregor spoke slowly with stretched out words, each syllable seemed to weigh what was coming behind it before making itself known. He spoke often of his old school, "Hahvahd." Jim O'Neill said he sounded like Charles Laughton playing Henry the Eighth in the movies.

"Ah'm going to take a few minutes before we consider Milton to teach you how to curse effectively." The room was silent. Eyes widened. Doodling pencils stopped.

"The most effective method of cursing, to me, is when someone doesn't even use a curse word." Knotted eyebrows everywhere.

"I call it creative cursing and consider it an intellectual sporting event. The winners are the stahs — the playahs with an excellent lexicon to which they add imagination…one of the many attributes we're trying to impaht to you indentured orphaaans." He leaned forward across his desk. "Mistah Newman, you look puzzled. If you wanted to curse Mr. Bahr…well, perhaps we shouldn't get into that right now, aftah awahl."

"Aw, let 'em, Mr. McGregor," Norm Cohen called out. Everyone laughed. Barr smiled. McGregor reconsidered. "Losers in the sport, Mistah Newman, would probably say — Bahr, you pissy little bahstard." The oxygen level dropped with the audible sound of in-drawn breath. "Or, as we just heard - you sonofabitch — followed by some scatological activity dealing with your body functions or elimination products."

He looked straight at Nick. "How ordinary, how trite and how ineffective. Better to consider your adversary — his physical appearance, his method of movement, his amusing athletic attempts." Low chuckles. "His grades, his eating habits and whatever you know about his personal life from his girlfriends to his hometown." His eyes swept the room, surveying the faces weighing his remarks.

A hand shot up near the back of the class. "Sir, may I try out a curse on someone?" Amid more laughter, several other hands shot up. "Who is the object of your innovative fabrication, Mistah Mahtin?"

"Don Loder, Sir." All eyes turned to Loder who was staring at Martin disdainfully. Slowly raising his hand, Loder said dryly, "You know I manage the student store, Mr. McGregor, and he arrived as I locked the door. He was late and expected me to open up just for him. You know the rules."

"Well, Mistah Mahtin, I'm pleased you didn't revert to violence, as well as being wrong. Now let's see if you can get even by utilizing your vocabulary."

"Well…" Martin paused, looking distant, then said, "Got it, Sir. See how he's pear-shaped, skinny on top and big on the bottom, that's why he waddles like a duck. He couldn't catch a thief at the school store with his feet flapping like that. That's why his nickname is Duck Loder." The class was silently amused, waiting to see what happened next.

Nick decided to take a chance and called out, "Sure he could, Martin, they'd be laughing so hard they couldn't run fast, and he'd catch them." Quiet laughter; even Mr. McGregor showed a scant smile, while Loder stared at his desktop.

Seeing no response, Martin went on. "He can't help being pear-shaped, Sir. He closes the store to customers, so he can stuff his mouth with free maltyballs."

"I'll stuff your mouth," Loder exploded, "and every other opening!" The sudden uproar of delight quickly ended.

"Okay, mission accomplished, Mistah Mahtin, now apologize. It's just a game." Martin responded in a sing song tone. "I'm sorry, Don, you know how I really feel about you." Loder didn't look at Martin, but the cloying sound brought a clenched fist raised above his opened book.

"Can we try one more, Mr. McGregor?"

"Just one more, Mistah Smith." Al Smith was one of the smartest kids in class. Always got top grades. Standing up, Smith played the game by casually reviewing everyone with a look of superiority. He stopped when he got to Lou Lorenzo, eliciting some "Uh-ohs."

"Lorenzo, you are the epitome of all the insipid, oblivious South Philly characters you idolize. You're cursed with growing up there and don't even know it. The girls all end up like those chunky women at the Italian Market…like your future wife," he searched his mind, "Angelina Corpelini." Smith got the laughs he expected.

Lorenzo, not moving, seemed relaxed in his chair, hands behind his head, eyes straight ahead.

"And your kids, all eight of them, are going to look like giant bocce balls from gobbling up nothing but spaghetti with red g-r-a-v-y. The rabble from South Philly," Smith acknowledged to Mr. McGregor with mock sadness, "don't even know how to spell sauce!" Lorenzo sat up straight in his chair.

"And here in the Hum, you prance around just like the rest of them — struttin' like a Mummer. But the only possible reason South Philly guys walk that way, going forwards and then backwards, and swaying side to side at the same time, is because they're always sluggin' down Dago Red wine."

Nick saw Reds Eckard and Ray Corsini, sitting on both sides of Lorenzo, grab him as he erupted, whispering "Lou, he's just teasing," and "It's a game," as they pushed him down in his seat. "You sonofabitch!" he yelled at Smith. Smith smiled and turned away from him, "See, Mr. McGregor, they're too dumb to learn." Reds and Ray, hands poised, were waiting for the next outburst, but it didn't come. Lou sat staring at his hands.

"Class," McGregor said, "that proves, and I hope Mr. Lorenzo learns, that the same old, overused S-O-B's and mother-whatevahs have little effect on enemies when compared to that of a creative curse."

"Now, let's turn to someone with a real curse, Milton and his blindness. If you use a modicum of the intense interest you've shown in the past few minutes, we'll have a productive class." He leaned back in his chair, his hands clasped behind his head. It was a deceptive pose to anyone looking in the small classroom door window — a relaxed teacher educating in a calm, even enjoyable, learning atmosphere. Far from it; tension grew with every question. When Charlie Mangione stood up and recited the Ode to Blindness correctly, Mr. McGregor waved him down approvingly. Nick got through the opening passage of Coleridge's Xanadu with a barely acceptable nod; but when Jock McKnight lost his way reciting some Longfellow lines, McGregor

295

stopped him. "You'd better review that, Mistah McKnight," which meant Jock had better turn up after his last class of the day, take a seat and silently study.

Class was almost over when Don Barr could not get beyond the first sentence of Portia's "quality of mercy" speech, a past assignment. McGregor sprang forward in his chair, bringing his right arm around and hurling a blackboard eraser full force. Glancing off Barr's shoulder, it skipped across Bernie Weir's desk, hit the wall with a soft thud and a white cloud and fell to the floor.

"You harebrained Tahr Baby." McGregor shouted. Squelched laughter enlivened the tension. "I want you in that corner," he pointed to the farthest desk in the back of the room, "for the rest of this week, scribbling as fast as you can, over and over, you know what!"

It was always scary at first, the surprise of it, then entertaining — when you weren't the target. At the bell, Barr rose and followed the standard procedure. Nick hadn't felt McGregor's rancor yet, but he knew when any missile — chalk, pencil, an eraser or even a book landed, the ammunition was to be retrieved when class broke, and placed on McGregor's desk, never making eye contact.

Don Barr didn't escape the new name, and was immediately subjected to a Hummer's favorite game, taunting, for the rest of the semester. Of all of them, Nick liked Sid Sterling's best:

"Hey, Tar Baby, old Uncle McRemus' been lookin' for you. You better hop your cottontail ass over to his briar patch real quick!"

FIFTY-FIVE

Nick was puzzled, not angry. He'd been waiting almost an hour on Girard Avenue across from the Big F — the Fairmount Theater. Lenore was supposed to be here at 1:30. They could talk about the prom and go to the movie. He wasn't angry because she was never late. Whatever she said she did. There had to be a reason. He decided to walk back to her house, the way they always walked, at least to the corner of her street.

As he made his way along the streets, he recalled last Monday night when housemaster Stubby Craig was the study hour proctor. Everyone had just settled down for the nightly study period when Mr. Craig said, "Kaplan, Kaplan, will you open two or three windows. Maybe a breeze will keep some of our scholars awake."

The large high school windows on one side of the room overlooked the entrance circle, the lodge buildings, the big wrought iron entry gates, and the wall running along Girard Avenue. The only sounds were pages being turned and pencils scribbling, when a high pitched voice carried up to the windows. "Reds! Reds!" Heads went up followed by amused murmurs. "Reds," the voice continued, "meet me Wednesday after school in front of the big F."

Then another feminine voice was heard. "Johnny…Johnny Martin!" Everyone near Martin watched him, head down, eyes glazed, trying to disappear. "Can't be there tomorrow, but I'll be at the Dugout on Thursday about five."

The sounds of chortles were heard throughout the room until Mr. Craig slapped his hand on a desk. "Quiet down, room! Eckard, Martin. You should both know better than to associate with Wall Rats. Nothing good's going to come of it." Someone threw an eraser and hit Reds on the head, but he was thoroughly engrossed in his Physical Science book.

Reds, John and Ernie Podagrosi were going with a trio of girls known on campus as Flopsy, Mopsy and Cottontail — but not to their faces.

Then a third voice was heard. "Nick, Nick! I don't know what happened because you never turned up. I'll wait for you at the Fairmount on Saturday at one-thirty. If there's a problem, we can talk about it. See you then, doll." Probably fifty kids in this room, and I'm the only Nick. Mr. Shuster, who'd stopped by to chat with Mr. Craig, looked at Nick and shook his head. Mr. Craig stood up, crossed his arms and looked at Nick. "I am surprised at you. I really am." Then he paused and emphasized the word. "Doll?" This time he ignored the laughter.

And so it was not a quiet week in Nick's life. "Nick, pass the goddamned — whoops, excuse me, doll, please pass the bread when you get a chance."

"Nicky, you cutie, does my pompadour look high enough to you?"

"Hey, guys, there goes Mariner Hall's famous doll baby. Let's all blow 'im a kiss."

Sometimes it made him laugh, but he punched Mike Sweeney hard on the shoulder when, entertaining everyone as they were crowding into the dining room, he yelled, "Yo, Doll, meet me in the lavatory after lunch. I'll show you mine if you show me yours."

Nick smiled at it now. What do you expect from Hummers. And Lenore had never called at the wall before. He'd talk to her about that. She just didn't know what happened to him, why he had to stay after Dr. Wolf's Social Studies class.

Instead of going down the back alley, he decided to walk slowly down the street on the other side, across from Lenore's house. She might look out and maybe see him. He had her phone number, but he stopped calling. He wasn't sure he could sound like he'd called a wrong number. And if he got her, she might be standing near her parents or

298

sister. No one knew of Nick, yet, so he was safe walking slowly down the street.

He stopped and looked across at her house. It looked different. Hurrying across the street, he stood in front of it. It looked different because the homes on either side had white curtains in the windows. There were no curtains in the windows — Lenore's house seemed to stare back at him. He put his hand to his mouth. His mouth was dry. He tried to swallow but couldn't, and he could feel his heart in his chest. Looking down the steps he saw the two trash cans were overflowing, lids balanced on top and lots of Acme shopping bags stacked next to them with torn pant legs, dishcloths and apron strings hanging out.

"If you're lookin' for that family," an old man was leaning out of a door next door, "you're too late, boy." Nick shivered. Now he felt cold, as though someone slipped a snowball down his back.

"They moved away Tuesday. A real surprise to everyone. The father shows up with a big truck and some buddies and they started loading stuff. When the kids got home, they hadda jump in the truck right then and go. He waved goodbye and yelled he got a job outsida' Chicago." Nick looked at the old man. "Nah," the old man read Nick's mind, "no address, prob'ly don't have one."

Nick wanted to stay there until the basement door opened and Lenore came out, smiling at him. He wanted her to hug him. He wanted to feel her warmth, to kiss her gently, his hand in her soft hair. But she didn't come out. And she wouldn't. He didn't want to look at the house. Slowly he walked back to Corinthian Ave, turning down, away from the Hum. After a while he noticed a wall on his right, low with grass growing back to a second tall wall. It was the Eastern State Penitentiary. At the corner, on top of the high stone wall, in a room with little glass windows he thought he could see the silhouette of a guard.

Nick pulled himself up on the low wall and sat there looking down at the broken sidewalk. Then he brightened. He couldn't find her, but she could find him. Just put his name and Girard College, Philadelphia, on the envelope and it'd be delivered. Then he remembered what she told him once when she thought he might be getting too serious about her.

"I love you too, Nick, but remember what I said. I'm a realist. I take things as they come and don't look back." When she saw how sad he looked, she hugged him tightly, pressing her cheek against his.

"You and I, Nick dear," she said, "we don't just live blocks apart, we live worlds apart...and someday you'll have to face it."

He felt her brush her face with the back of her hand before she stepped back with wet eyes and a weak smile. Holding hands, they ended the silent walk home with a simple kiss.

He would never see her again. Head down, face in his hands, he quietly sobbed.

The Wall

Ask a Hummer what was the single, most influential, significant and enduring structure throughout his life at Girard, and his first response, and mine, too, would be Founder's Hall. That enormous edifice (it can't just be called a hall or a building) would be the expected answer. As children we were bewitched by it — how high it was, how thick the columns and how much fun it was to race around the entire building on the endless rows of steps. Founder's Hall's uniqueness was indelibly etched in our third grade minds when, in the introduction to the Greeks and Romans, we turned a page in our history book and discovered our Founder's Hall was the Parthenon, overlooking the Acropolis.

As you grew older, you enjoyed the amazement of others when they first saw it, especially on a Spring prom dance night when you escorted a girl through the gates and she stood, mouth open, overcome by its size and grandeur, lights accenting the tremendous Corinthian columns and Stephen Girard's statue.

But it's generally believed that Stephen Girard would not have been pleased. He was fond of things plain, admiring the frugal ways and unpretentious homes of the Quakers. He might have appreciated the economy and efficiency of the five austere halls: Banker, Merchant, Mariner, Bordeaux and Allen, and the Infirmary and even those Gothic monstrosities, Good Friends, Lafayette and the Middle School, but he would have not have approved of Founder's Hall. A majestic creation, it was certainly not appropriate for a school for poor orphans. It's said the architect, recently home from a visit to Greece, and with some powerful individuals in Philadelphia's politics, were responsible for its creation. The magnificent Chapel, constructed much later, Girard would have appreciated because of its use in fostering the students' integrity, loyalty, productive labor and upright citizenship founded on strong moral character. The Library would have pleased him too, reflecting his lifelong interest in self-education.

Looking back now, sixty years later, I believe what affected us even more than the imposing Founder's Hall was the Wall. Ten feet high, sixteen inches thick, running a mile and a quarter around the 43-acre campus, it surrounded us and silently affected our lives.

As a six to ten-year-old West Ender or Junior Schooler, the Wall was where your world ended. It was a daily reminder to a small boy, far from home, that he was a prisoner. Though only ten feet high, it was as intimidating as the thirty -foot high wall he'd seen on a class trip down Corinthian Avenue, passing, a few blocks south of the school, the Eastern State Penitentiary. To truly unhappy children who continued to find it difficult to cope with the routine and rules at Girard, only the armed guards were missing on the Hum Wall.

It also became the focus of your punishment when you stood on the grudge line for some infraction. Whether talking when quiet was ordered, fighting with someone, running in the hall or moving too slowly, you stood arm's length away from other transgressors on either side of you. Sometimes the line was short; other times it was long. Erect and silent, you studied the Wall, three feet in front of you, while listening to the excited sounds of play behind you. Such close contact with the Wall, for half an hour to an hour, or more, reinforced feelings of imprisonment.

Just as I was undergoing transformation, willingly or not, by Girard, my attitude toward the Wall was also changing. From seeming insurmountable in Junior School, ten feet was not that high to "smart aleck" eleven to thirteen-year olds. When a baseball or soccer ball sailed over it, unintentionally or not, there was a rush to the Wall. With a well-placed foot and a leap, you could grasp the smooth top stone ledge; then, by swinging a leg up or getting a rump-push from below, you sat riding it. In a few seconds you were up there, calling to a passerby to Please toss the ball back, adding a gracious thank you as you caught it. You were sitting at the edge of the world.

When we found the Wall could be conquered with some athleticism, a new horizon appeared for those Hummers who felt the challenge to get around some of the endless rules and regulations without getting caught.

Since those in Good Friends and Lafayette could get passes out on weekends, but not after school on week days, what was more exhilarating than furtively "hopping the Wall?" Executed after class, you could smoke openly under the Fairmount movie marquee and chat, so cleverly, with girls who were passing by — an hour of freedom; a game made even more zestful by eluding capture upon the return. And you had the admiring glances of the less adventurous at the table as you described your latest feat.

In high school, from Banker to Bordeaux Halls, "hopping the Wall" continued though there was not as much spare time with Study Hall during the week and Sunday night from 7 to 9:15 and bed at 10 p.m. If a Bordeaux or Allen Hall party was planned for after lights out, though, a beer excursion was vital as soon as Study Hall ended.

The Wall offered a few select locations for "hopping" where you were least likely to be seen. In Good Friends and Lafayette, it was the far side of the playground toilets. A long, low building built against the Wall, the far end could not be seen by playground housemasters if they were involved with kids by Good Friends, the closest building. Another good location was the Wall by the bakery behind the Infirmary. No one ever looked out from the windows at the back of the Infirmary; they were too busy tending sick Hummers. And the bakery was only busy in the early morning when bread was made or delivered. It was a remote, rarely trafficked location, ideal for a quick run, a foot pressed on the wall and a leap to the ledge.

Curiously, another great "hop the Wall" location was adjacent to the Lodge, at the school's entrance. There were two lodges, but I never recall seeing the second one used. Since traffic came in through the gate and had to turn right to go around the circle, it was more convenient for the lodge men to admit them from that location. After the Lodge men locked the gates and left for the day, and study hall was over, J-2 Juniors in Bordeaux Hall, about to become Seniors, and Seniors in Allen Hall, used this route to go out for a late night smoke at Woarman's Drug Store or to get the locals to buy them a few quarts of Schmidt's of Philadelphia or Ortleib's Premium. Meanwhile, someone called the pizza shop on Ridge Avenue, and it all came together in a "shush, *be quiet" party in someone's room or in a far, dark corner of a playground. Empties were artfully positioned on the lawn behind the president's house, so unrefined outsiders would be blamed for tossing them over the Wall.*

There were actually two Walls, according to where you were when you viewed it. Standing inside, the Wall may have signified confinement; your view from the outside was completely different.

As Junior Schoolers, walking in a long column of twos up Broad Street from where they had watched the Annual December 2nd Toy Day Parade around City Hall, the first sight of the Wall drew cheers, exhilarating some very tired boys. For Hummers from Good Friends and Lafayette, after a Saturday afternoon of hide and seek outside the Art Museum and a foot soaking in the Calder Fountain, the Wall came in sight promising rest and dinner.

As the weekend dinner hour approached, streets leading to the campus were flooded with boys, streaming in from all directions, relieved to finally reach the Wall because it meant they would get back in time for dinner and elude punishment.

Anyone in the Upper Halls who felt the Hum and its Wall were an urban Alcatraz, changed their minds when, returning to the campus, suddenly coming upon four or five gang members of the Taney Street Rams or the Green Street Counts. If you had an equal number, hopefully more, you'd stand and fight; otherwise, you turned and ran. More than one Hummer, caught alone, came back bruised and bloody, energizing the toughest Seniors and Juniors to go out and get even with the gangs, some members of which were in their twenties. Your only chance was to abruptly break away and out race them to the gates or the Wall with one attempt to successfully scale it — proving the value of having learned previously to "hop the Wall." If time allowed, you could even turn and sneer at them before dropping to the safe side.

So the Wall, high, threatening and confining when you were little, became a surmountable challenge as one grew older; a tool for temporary (though illegal) liberty and adventures, no longer intimidating you. Looking back over the years, you might now recognize it as a stalwart protector of the safe, comfortable life we lived.

Looking down at the Wall from the third floor of Good Friends, Lafayette or the Middle School, it seemed less significant. Traffic beyond it, cars, trucks and trolley cars stormed up and down one of the city's busiest arteries, Girard Avenue — braking, beeping, dinging and screeching along. Far off the undulating howl of a fire truck or police car could be heard.

Across the street, at the Lankenau Hospital, ambulances shrieked their way into the emergency entrance. The sidewalks were crowded with men, women, boys and girls, walking dogs, pushing carriages, talking, calling, waiting at trolley stops, alone or with others. The Wall seemed to be a silent sentry, holding out this frenetic, though wondrous, world.

The campus at Girard has changed over the years, as it must. The West End has been dismantled and rebuilt. Good Friends, Lafayette and the Middle School are all gone, as is Banker Hall. The remaining buildings needed updating to meet today's ordinances. Though Founder's Hall still stands, Stephen Girard would scorn the grandeur of it. The one physical element of his vision that remains, that he would be pleased with, is the Wall. Standing now in the outside world, I believe if you put your hand on those ugly, craggy stones you can sense his hand on the other side; his Wall is still providing protection for his adopted children.

BORDEAUX HALL
Grades 11 and 12
Ages 16 and 17

ALLEN HALL
Graduating Seniors
Ages 17 to 18
1951—1952

Oops, Printer error!

FIFTY-SIX

Bang! Bang! Bang! Dormitory locker doors were yanked open, slamming against others. "This is like the Sooners in Oklahoma," someone yelled, " 'cept we're grabbing free lockers instead of land."

Nick was glad to see Newman, Furmanski and Swartz at lockers on the other side of the dorm. Amused older, S-1 Seniors watched from their beds at the near violent encounters over ownership.

Throwing his books on a bed, he quickly found an empty locker. From his pockets he took his Christmas gifts and set them on the shelf: a leather wallet; black dress gloves; and two boxes of chocolate covered cherries. After hanging up his prized present, a burgundy corduroy jacket he could wear after class now that he was a J-1 Junior in Bordeaux Hall, he stacked his books on the locker bottom with space for his shoes, and locked the door. He covered the bed with his coat to claim ownership.

As he started downstairs, he found Newman and Swartz waiting for him in the hallway.

"Do you think Maggie Magee will be at the dance this month," Swartz said. "Remember dancing lessons when we all had to stay a certain distance from the girl, well she's still at it. At the Fall Prom, when Rex Bierko danced by, she pulled that half ruler out of her purse and rushed after him — poked him in the gut with it, and he jumped back and almost pulled the girl down."

"The 6-inch rule!" Nick exclaimed. "That's enough to make everybody a Puritan...and then she usually goes over to the sponsors, 'Mr. and Mrs. Maillardet that night, and spends time with them but really making sure we all know she's there."

"They make us look like little kids, don't they?" Newman scowled. "No wonder some guys go stag and pretend they'll dance, but never do."

"When Beakey Cunningham and his wife sponsor our dances and just a few guys turn up, they get upset. That's why he calls our class…" Everyone chorused slowly, imitating the housemaster, "You're a bunch of social lunkheads."

"What happened to that wild blonde you went with last year? I talked to her one time when you had to run back up to your locker. She was really something."

"She moved away, Frank."

"Oh, that's too bad. So that's why you were so grumpy last semester."

"Well, he got a new one this summer," Swartz said. Nordstrom told me guys were clapping and whistling for the heavy hugs and kisses before the bus pulled out from the station. She was pinned up inside his locker door at Mariner, signed, 'Love, Dana.' A brunette this time, and another looker, too."

"And," Nick said, "she's National Honor Society and all-state cellist. Don't you serfs know I specialize in brains *and* beauty?" He turned away from the jeers with an enjoyable condescending wave.

"If you're gonna do your vocab card alliterations, smart ass, add fascinating and formidable to that blonde," Newman called after him, "and I'd be glad to take on the challenge of that laudable lass."

Walking away, Nick raised his hand forming a you-got-it-right circle with his thumb and his finger.

◆

Deciding to check out his new hall, Bordeaux, Nick started with the living rooms and game room on the first floor. He moved through the first one, around some newspaper readers and a tense card game sure to end in a fight. The game room was filled with amusing kibitzers around the pool table, but the TV room was dark. In the other unlit, almost empty living room, he went to a far corner. In a leather club chair by a window, one leg thrown over the leather arm, Nick gazed out at the gray clouds drifting in the dim winter light.

308

He only got to see Dana twice to exchange gifts on Christmas Eve and to say goodbye. The two weeks went by so fast, buying and decorating the tree, church services and family get-togethers. He knew how much his family wanted him to be with them all the time. Aunts and uncles came to see him, asking questions and making a fuss over him, something he had gotten used to. His cousins continued to ask about what life was like at the Hum. He did have some money but he could only buy small gifts. When Doc Haskell pointed out just before Christmas how thoughtful words were more valuable than things bought, and lasted a lot longer in the receiver's memory and heart, he probably said it because he knew Hummers didn't have much money. Nick decided to make sure he said, in a quiet moment when no others were around, how much he appreciated something someone did or said. When he saw how pleased they were, he wished he could thank Doc Haskell.

On New Year's Eve he had just enough time to get out for a private goodbye with Dana on her porch, the house was crowded with family. They talked about the coming summer when she'd work to get more money for college and he'd try to get a part time job, too, though her classes ended long before Girard's. Then it would be just a year before he came home for good. After hugs and kisses at the dark end of the porch, he turned to wave at her silhouette before starting down Rees Street, a cobblestone alley, like streets in old Philadelphia.

At home, everyone raised a toast and sang Auld Lang Syne with the index finger on their right hand wrapped with a two dollar bill. Rolled toward them to guarantee good luck in the New Year, it was one of many funny Welsh traditions he now enjoyed and didn't think stupid.

Head back, eyes closed, he thought of Dana and Lenore; how different they were. They would hate each other, but in a lady-like fashion. Well, he smiled, maybe not Lenore. Dana was smart in school; but Lenore got good grades, too. Dana was always modest, but not in a phony way. She was comfortable to be with, cleverly humorous and articulate, something public speaking classes had taught him to admire.

If Lenore was less scholarly, she had an understanding of the world beyond what he knew, sheltered behind the Hum's walls or roaming about the city, an observant tourist. As enjoyably predictable as Dana was, Lenore was unpredictable. That made her fun to be with, and, he now knew, too memorable. Sometimes at night, he dreamt of her and it became a movie — holding hands as they walked up Founder's Hall steps to a Prom and remembering how Mike Light asked her to dance with him. Knowing Mike was the best dancer in the class, Nick insisted on it and how she arched an eyebrow at him with a teasing "See, maybe you shouldn't have" as they danced by and other guys began circling to cut in.

He cupped his hand, as though he could slide it again under the small of her smooth, warm back.

Unlike his life and Dana's, structured and even, Lenore's was one of continued turbulence with her family. But there was nothing he could do about that. He wished he could stop a scene that recurred with every dream — an unusually quiet walk home from a boisterous gathering of Hummers and their girls at Woarman's back room, his arm around her waist. She pulled his arm tighter to her as they approached her street and, looking straight ahead, said in a somber tone he'd never heard before, "You are the only constant in my life."

A bright light in the living room suddenly flickered on and off, startling Nick. A man leaned in the doorway at the far end of the room. "Anyone new to Bordeaux Hall, you're wanted in the television room right now to learn our rules."

A High School class

Soccer practice

FIFTY-SEVEN

"Look, those benches are empty, quick, let's grab 'em."

Jim Broussard, Rex Bierko, Norm Cohen and Nick picked their way around everyone sitting on the steps, passed occupied benches and crossed over the Main Road to the Library opposite Bordeaux Hall. Slouching on two facing benches by the Library entrance, they reviewed last year's game when the soccer team beat Northeast High for the City Championship and the chances for this year's team, still undefeated after good wins over Swarthmore College and the West Chester and Drexel University JVs. They listened intently as Cohen, inside right, discussed strategy about the upcoming game with Episcopal Academy this last weekend in November.

Pushing out the Library doors, Sam Brodie stopped at the bench and sat on the concrete arm next to Broussard. When Norm paused to ponder a question, Sam jumped in, to annoyed glares.

"Did you guys see what Miss Erchinger posted on the bulletin board?"

"She's probably looking for more book worms to restack the shelves again," Jim said.

"No, it's an old Girard News"

"How old?"

"November 1945."

"Cripes, that's not old. It's '51 now, that's only six years ago."

"Doesn't matter. I'm gonna use the material for my talk in Public Speaking this week, so don't any of you steal it."

"What's it about, anyway?" Rex asked

"It's about religion."

"Religion. Why would you want to talk about that?"

Taking a little notebook from his breast pocket and opening it, Sam said, "We started in the West End and Junior School praying before lights out plus grace at every meal and prayers at Chapel and Sunday Vespers.

"From then on," Sam continued, "you had grace at three meals a day, a prayer before every weekday assembly plus two or three prayers at Sunday Chapel. Now, if you take out a week at Easter, two weeks at Christmas and ten weeks in the summer, every year you spent about thirty nine weeks in the Hum."

"Some of us even had to say prayers when we got out of bed in the morning at West End," Rex added.

"I calculated it and figure the average Hummer . . ."

"That's you, Sammy boy."

"…listened to a grace or prayer over six thousand times, and that doesn't include singing hymns or listening to the Glee Club anthems."

"Wouldja' call that getting religion by osmosis?"

"Geez," Jim exclaimed, with an exaggerated genuflect, "I thought I was just another Catholic. By now I must be a saint. Wait'll I tell my mother."

"Yeah, then I must be the only Saint Rex in the world…and I sure won't forgive you guys!"

Jim jabbed a thumb at Nick. "We'd better treat you-know-who right if we want gifts under the tree from him."

"Too late," Nick joined the game, "I've been recording your smoking, drinking, and making out in the Big F balcony all year."

"Bags of coal from a coal-cracker, that's perfect. And if you're right, Sam, I'm the most memorable of all these saints."

"Hail, Saint Cohen!" Rex suddenly shouted and the others copied him, arms above their heads, bringing them down in mock praise.

"What are you loudmouths going on about?" Beaky Cunningham was on his way from the Library.

313

"Sir, Norm says we have to bow down to him because he thinks he's the first Saint Cohen."

The housemaster looked puzzled for a second, and then said, "Ah, the News article. Actually," he smiled, "the only way you'll become saints is if we paddle the devil out of you." That brought laughs followed by good natured jeers. "Thanks a lot, Mr. Cunningham."

"Yeah, we know everyone here is tryin' hard to save us."

"We're even better than the article said, Mr. Cunningham," Nick called after him. "Sambo here says we'll have a total of over six thousand religious, 'um, exposures by the time we graduate."

Before they could change the topic back to soccer, a bell rang and a hungry swarm evacuated Bordeaux Hall, heading for dinner at the Dining & Service building.

"Actually," Brodie said, "I'm holier than you guys, 'cus I've been going to the Church of the Gesu every Sunday before Chapel since I was in Junior School. And anyone not confirmed has to go into another room after Mass and get Catechism lessons from a Jesuit priest."

"I stopped going last semester, Sambo, and I sometimes see you down at Woarman's smoking, too."

"You guys make me glad I'm a Protestant and don't have to get up so early," Nick proclaimed.

"Well, it's not all bad. Lots of guys I know go just to see the girls from Hallahan and Little Flower who know Hummers are going to be there," Jim added. "Hey, there's Ricky Bauer. He's Jewish 'n came in when I did. Rick, walk over to dinner with us." Ricky joined the group, curious because they normally didn't include him with them. "Do you guys really go to synagogue every Friday night?"

"Naw, I went twice a week on Tuesday and Thursday afternoons by myself after class for lessons. Took the trolley and subway. Didn't see any other Hummer Jews." He nodded toward

314

Norm who didn't look at Ricky but genuflected stoically to the amusement of all. "Was gone from four to six," Ricky went on. "Didn't even get into trouble when I came into the dining room late."

"I wondered why some guys at your table clapped for you."

"They called me the Bar Mitzvah Boy."

"Geez, you must hate it in here, all our prayin' and hymns, forcin' ya to become a Christian."

"Doesn't bother me. I like Hum services better. There were some pretty good speakers. I learned a lot of things a Jewish kid on the outside would never know. And there's lots more singing in the Hum."

"Then Norm, here, can't be a saint. He's never been Bar Mitzvahed. You're our Saint Rickey."

"Nah, can't be that, I was never Bar Mitzvahed either, but I am an extraordinary Jew."

"Why?"

Looking away from them, he put his fingers to his lips and whistled. "Hey, Toizer, wait for me." As he started off, he turned back and called, "I'm one of the few Jews in the world who can sing all the verses of "Adeste Fideles" and "Onward Christian Soldiers" from memory."

FIFTY-EIGHT

After eight years, the Chapel was still Nick's favorite place in the Hum. He admired Founder's Hall; it was so impressive, so different from any other buildings he saw roaming the city. He'd come across smaller versions of that Greek style, especially the bank building down by the waterfront. Dr. Wolf explained how that bank, the Bank of the United States, had been chartered for 20 years by the Federal government who decided then to get out of banking and dissolve the charter. Stephen Girard bought the building and opened his own bank, so Nick felt it was special to Hummers.

The Chapel was the quietest place in the Hum. Founder's Hall echoed with the shrill sounds of Hummers calling across the steps and running up and down the marble staircases. The Chapel was always hushed, even filled with over a thousand kids on Sunday morning. He recalled how Lenore had gasped and was silenced by its size and beauty when she saw it.

Where Founder's Hall was spectacular outside, the Chapel was magnificent inside. During the day, golden beams of light poured down from the tall windows, through the gold-leafed designs on the glass. At night Nick remembered "oohing" with the others in Junior School at Christmas. First the ceiling above quickly dimmed to dark, then the colored lights on the two Christmas trees up front came on. And then the concealed lamps in the ceiling began slowly lighting, spreading a golden dawn across the wide, gilded ceiling until the enormous room was bright again.

Sunday chapel service was just about over. Nick joined the others, leaning forward to rest his arm atop the pew in front of him, his forehead on the back of his hand. After the slow, rhythmic rumble of The Lord's Prayer ended, they would stand, sing all the verses of a final hymn and quietly file out. Normally, he was up in the choir loft with the Glee Club, but a sore throat he'd caught coming from swimming practice with a wet head did his voice in, so he sat with his Bordeaux Hall classmates, up front, just behind the graduating Senior class.

At breakfast that morning they turned Nick's raspy voice into a game. He expected it. Hummers love challenges that call for humorous denigration. In Junior School you began learning the art of throwing sarcastic darts. The winner this morning was Jim O'Neill, who said Nick was either Heckle or Jeckle, the cartoon blackbirds, because of his grackle cackle. He did promise to tell Dr. Banks why Nick didn't turn up this morning.

Watching the youngsters in the choir, the Junior Hundred, reminded Nick of Miss Ranck, who taught Music as well as Third Grade. She asked him if he'd like to join the Junior Hundred. Her prospects were always accepted by Dr. Banks, and Nick remembered how proud he was when Miss Stacks, the organist, took him aside and explained what was expected of him.

He recalled that the joy of being in the Junior Hundred was that it made you special. On Thursday nights, when everyone in Junior School was about to start up the stairs to shower, you and a few others went off, joining a ragged trail of boys from other sections up the Main Road, behind bigger kids from Good Friends and Lafayette whose voices hadn't cracked yet. It was an education sitting in the choir loft observing the Biggies, Juniors and Seniors, and overhearing their remarks, curses and telling of tales.

"Hey, you little twerps," they called, "Stop listening to us!" But Nick learned many things, most of which he could not write to his mother.

Dick Conradi counted once and said there were only eighty-three kids in the Junior Hundred. A few made it to Lafayette; that's where Nick's voice cracked during one rehearsal. Hands immediately flew up and pointed at Nick with the gratification of discovery. Afterwards, Miss Stacks told him this happened to everyone. Dr. Banks came over, thanked Nick for his years of singing and loyalty in turning up week after week, and invited him to come back in a year or two.

Dr. Banks explained to the Junior Hundred one night that this was one of the country's finest organs. The pipe loft, forty feet high, contained six thousand, five hundred and eighty seven pipes ranging in size from smaller than a pencil to over three stories high, and the organ resounded through the perforated ceiling, so that it rained down on everyone from above. Nick wrote what he could remember in a letter because Uncle Bill was the organist at their home church. Dr. Banks was a kindly man, small, balding and always smiling, liked by everyone, so few pranks were pulled on him.

Everyone streamed back to their buildings when rehearsals were over at nine thirty on Thursday nights. As soon as the Junior Schoolers entered the basement door by the playground, someone would give the expected scream, exploding a rush down the long, black corridor lit only by the scary red glow of the EXIT signs. Nick narrated the weekly event to Janet's ten-year old friends last summer as though it were a spontaneous request from Mr. Andrews, the public speaking teacher.

"Tell us again," several asked; he did, ending a more dramatic version with, "Our clattering brogues resounded behind us off the tile walls, convincing us a fiendish ghoul was about to catch up and greedily suck the blood out of our necks." Janet's girlfriends listened again with wide-eyed enjoyment. "We scrambled up the stairs, slowing to the proper pace as we neared the dormitory level. We didn't take showers, just moved past the sleepers, undressed in the dark and pulled the covers tightly around our necks to protect them and fell asleep."

The choir had an anthem rehearsal each Sunday before the service began. After breakfast, while everyone in their good suits and oxfords went to their sections to await the march to the Chapel, the Junior Hundred members raced off to join the Glee Club. Sometimes during the service a friend in his section or class would wave discretely at him; he would never wave back, but nodded his head. His mother

318

wrote how happy she was after he described the special trips they made on buses to sing at the Cultural Olympics and the Academy of Music. Music was important in the family. Along with his Uncle Bill as organist, his grandfather was a chorister at the church and sang with the city's Orpheus Club. His mom and two aunts sang at the church, on the radio and at the prison at Christmas.

Sunday Chapel services ended with a hymn and a final prayer and everyone quietly moved toward the exit doors. Al Smith caught his eye and motioned as though gripping a bat handle, asking if Nick wanted to play that afternoon. While some left in what Nick thought was a solemn spirit, having weighed what the speaker said; others burst out of the Chapel, focused only on a day of freedom.

Education at Girard

Near the end of a vacation, a neighborhood buddy asked if I wanted to go with him to his high school. Curious about what an "outsider's" school was like, I went. What I found amazed me: their teachers were so young and lively with few gray heads among the top administrators. I genteelly answered the many questions about Girard asked by some attractive female teachers. And, in classes, I was curiously stared at or smiled at by many good-looking girls — how could I ever again be satisfied parsing dull sentences amid clod-like Hummers in Doc Foust's class.

Returning to the Hum high school, I was dismayed — everyone seemed ancient. So many heads were gray, others white and still others, shiny bald. Discussing it with a few guys, we agreed, looking back, most governesses, housemasters and teachers seemed to be in their mid-forties or even older, though maybe it just seemed so to our youthful eyes.

Years after graduating, I learned why they were older and, most revealing, how exceptionally well educated they were. It's said the reason why the school, wealthy because of Stephen Girard, had such an extraordinary faculty was because it offered, along with the salary, a pension program, unheard of in secondary education, especially during the Great Depression of the 1930s. It made sense that those who moved inside Girard's walls to teach the orphans then would have seemed mature when we sat in their classrooms in the 40's and 50's. And so we attended classes taught by one of our "Docs" — Haskell, Foust, Presson, Wolf, McIlhattan, Dulebon. White and Dunlap. Dr. Horning headed the instrumental music department while Dr. Banks directed vocal music. Most of the elementary school teachers had at least one degree, some had two; many in the Middle School had Master's degrees as did some housemasters from Junior School to Allen Hall. And all top administrators had doctorates such as Dr. Odgers, the president, (former Dean of Women at Penn) or Dr. Cooper, the High School principal and Dr. Walcott, Director of Secondary Education. The Girard staff degrees, from first grade on, came from such schools as Penn, Columbia, Mount Holyoke,

320

Duke, Bates, William & Mary, Temple, Amherst, Ursinus, Gettysburg, Villanova, Bowdoin, Cornell, Harvard, Franklin & Marshall and Princeton. If our overall education was influenced by two universities, they were Columbia and the University of Pennsylvania.

I believe the administrators and teachers really did strive try to educate us. Knowing our backgrounds as fatherless boys with mothers, not well educated — possibly a factory, plant or mill worker like my mother — struggling to support and bring up our siblings. Our teachers felt it imperative that we do our best and "study hard" from first grade to graduation. Most had the passion, sometimes meanly used, to have us learn. They wanted to equip us to be the best educated members of our families, able to rise to better economic levels; in most cases the first to graduate from college. I never thought of any as an encouraging advisor and becoming a teacher's "favorite" brought with it the nickname; "Doc so-and-so's son," an unwanted label. We were supposed to be totally independent and individually responsible which doesn't foster a mentoring climate. We were also verbally harangued about inattention or poor academic results, reminded of all the money spent on us in the form of clothes, food, facilities and educational opportunities, often ending with "this whole class is flunking!" In English class, when you didn't quote Byron correctly, Caswell McGregor summoned up the guilt trip in his Harvard drawl, "Do yuh love yuhr mothah?" implying she sent you here, a heartfelt choice, so you would get a better education, and look how you reward her.

Even in your first years at Girard, in the West End or Junior School, you weren't exactly coddled. To a great extent it depended on your governess. Most were motherly, but determined to keep control and, I believe, tried not to show partiality. Some were strict, others more harsh in their management and punishment. My governess, Miss Saunders, never physically punished anyone, preferring to take away privileges. You quickly learned which governesses would push, slap, or forcefully strike a mischief maker, even if they weren't from her section. Housemasters were all less forgiving, some seeming to search out transgressors so they could physically punish them as an example to the rest of us.

321

As you grew older, fewer staff members showed an interest in you, unless you were breaking the rules or failed to do homework. Increasingly, you knew what was supposed to be done and you alone were accountable for its accomplishment. Nor did I see much mentoring among classmates. It was not a Hummer's habit to ask one of the smart guys in Calculus or Chemistry if they'd go over some problem area with them. Sympathy or pity throughout life for Hummers was rare, probably reflecting the basic tenet of growing up at Girard: the only person you should depend on is yourself.

Our religious education was unusual in that Stephen Girard's will ruled that no clergyman of any faith ever be allowed on the grounds. He required that all instructors should "take pains to instill into the minds of the scholars the purest principles of morality, so that, on their entrance into active life, they may, from inclination and habit, evince benevolence towards their fellow creatures and a love of truth, sobriety, and industry, adopting at the same time such religious tenets as their matured reason may cause them to prefer."

Our exposure, basically Judeo-Christian, did not focus on religious rites; there were no fire and brimstone threats, no Confessions and no Communion. No administrator or chapel speaker ever wore religious garb. Each Sunday morning, every Hummer gathered in the Chapel to sing hymns, say the Lord's Prayer and listen to the Glee Club's anthem. Although the Bible was read, there were no church sermons; prominent educators, judges, lawyers, physicians, scientists and business executives told of individuals, biblical and not, and their situations and actions, inevitably linking the message to moral standards and ethical behavior. Many were interesting and instructive while others were downright dull.

Though ministers, rabbis and priests were not allowed on campus, boys were not denied exposure to them. If a mother requested that her son attend religious services off campus, Girard ordered him to go.

Only when I got to college did I realize what an exceptional education we were exposed to at Girard; whether we took advantage of it is another question.

FIFTY-NINE

May 2, 1952

Dear Mom,

    I'm sorry I haven't written sooner. We've been really busy since our class moved from Bordeaux Hall (and Senior-1) to Allen Hall (and Senior-2) for our last six months. It's odd not sleeping in a dormitory. There are two, four and six man rooms. Am in with five other guys. Our teachers are really piling on the homework, I guess because we have to pass our finals to graduate in June, and that's just seven weeks away. (I did ask about graduation tickets and will let you know.) The class voted to use suede paper on the cover of The Corinthian, our yearbook. Since I'm Class Treasurer, I have to get every classmate (53) to give me their money for that and for the photographer to take their individual pictures. I'm also on the staff of the Corinthian and am Co-Editor-in-Chief of the Girard Magazine, the Hum's creative writing publication, with Vic Tunila, who lives on Meade Street back home. You met him. I'm glad the swimming season is almost over and I told Coach Wolstenholme that I couldn't play baseball this past season. Too much to do. I guess when I get home I can get a job and earn money so I can go to college. I'll get catalogs from Wilkes and Kings Colleges and see if they have advertising courses. Have to go now. Time for dinner. I miss you and Janet and if you don't hear from me much, I'll be trying to make sure I pass everything and graduate. Will let you know about the tickets.

    Love, Nicholas
P.S. Tell Aunt Edith thanks for the money.

SIXTY

Headed for lunch from Allen Hall were Stan Boswell, Henry Gentry, Joe Camperson and Nick. Stan and Henry were in a carefree mood. Beakey Cunningham, the housemaster, saw them when they leaped off the steps and called them tipsy. When the noontime music began from atop Founder's Hall, Henry, always zany, began skipping in time to the music, a brisk version of The Colonel Radetsky March. Stan joined him, entwining arms like the dancing girls at the Troc and setting off catcalls and whistles from those walking behind.

Henry called out, when they stopped prancing, "Got your letter, Stan, to prove you can graduate?"

"Yeah, I'm gonna have it in my pocket in case they don't call my name. I'll run up and wave it in old Doc Odgers' face!"

"What's this letter stuff?" Camperson asked.

"It's from the Board of City Trusts saying we can graduate."

"What?" Joe and Nick said in unison.

"Last semester, me, Stan and Zeke Kalinsky got called up to the office. They noticed that we have birthdays in February and Zeke's is in March."

"So?"

"We were still in S-1, but when we got to S-2, the next semester, we'd turn eighteen before graduation day."

"And, Stan said, according to Girard's will, you can only stay here until you're eighteen, then you're out."

"I never heard of that," Camperson said, "that can't be true."

"Well, it's true," Stan stated emphatically.

"That's why we stopped hopping the wall this semester and we only smoke down at Woarman's."

"Remember, in the old days the Hum sent guys to learn a trade with someone outside the Hum, like Oliver in Dickens. Y'know, indentured orphan stuff. Maybe they didn't even have graduation then 'cus they were signed up to apprentice with a carpenter or surveyor or whoever they were working for. At eighteen, though, they were out for good. Had to leave the Hum and work for the man, probably live with him until their contract was up."

"And the rule must still hold," said Henry, 'cus they told the three of us to write a letter to Philadelphia's Board of City Trusts — they oversee the Hum — and ask for permission to graduate, though we'll be eighteen then."

"What happened?"

"Well, my mother was really upset; but she knew from the past that she signed me over and couldn't do anything about it. Zeke didn't tell his mom. He says she gets sad sometimes when he has to come back after vacations. Says she's sorry she enslaved him, but that's only when she has a couple drinks before dinner. He wishes she'd marry some guy and stop carrying a cross for his dad."

"So we got together and wrote the letters, but we changed them so they wouldn't look exactly alike, and turned them in at the office."

"And?" Henry threw his hands up in relief.

"We got letters back saying they gave us permission to graduate." Stan's grin disappeared fast, "But they turned Zeke down."

"What?" the other two chorused.

"An' I don't know why. But he just got his stuff, said goodbye to a couple guys and left, right in the middle of the semester."

"Maybe his grades were bad. Henry thinks it was because of his record. He got caught a lot 'n he got in trouble not too long ago."

"We'll never know," Camperson said scornfully, "the Hum doesn't tell you anything they don't want to."

"Well, at least you guys'll graduate," Camperson said to which they dramatically joined arms again and began animatedly skipping along to a Sigmund Romberg melody coursing out from Founder's Hall above them.

SIXTY-ONE

Sitting on his bed, Nick looked around the empty six-man room. His roommates, Ernie, Sid, Joe, Jim and Don were gone. They had all shaken hands, then bear-hugged each other, knowing they wouldn't get a chance after the ceremony. Together, the class had gathered at the back of the Chapel for its walk down the main aisle to the traditional Elgar music. The Commencement Service ended, as they had every year, with the graduates in front of the student body, administrators, teachers and guests, singing The Farewell Song. He remembered when he and other newbies were astonished at the first graduation they attended, belittling the Seniors for crying; then, year after year, as they grew older, and moved forward, they began to sense how the Seniors felt and were no longer amused. Now Nick knew. Even tough guys wiped their eyes and only a few weak voices were heard over the organ during the last verse:

"Farewell, farewell, dear temple on the hill,
we'll not forget you 'til our hearts be still."

After the ceremony, having recovered, they joined their families, posed for pictures, and rushed back to Allen Hall for their suitcases and boxes of possessions. Eyes were red, goodbyes were quick. No one said much. With handshakes and sympathetic hugs, everyone of Nick's classmates stopped at the room that morning to say an extra goodbye to Ernie Podagrosi.

Years ago, Ernie was easily recognized as the biggest kid in Junior School. When they became classmates he told Nick how he was picked on by governesses in the West End and housemasters in Junior School as an example to others. It continued, he said, in Good Friends and Lafayette until he finally got to the halls where there were lots of older kids his size. Nick recalled how his name contributed to his unfortunate prominence; passing a childish community's mutual memory test meant being able to call out his full name.

"Hey, it's Ernesto Giovanni Celestino Defrancisco Podagrosi!"

Ernie's mom died of cancer just five weeks before graduation. She had only been to the Hum once, in 1943, when she brought him to Girard. He was allowed to take some final exams early so he could go to her funeral back home. Nick thought it was probably too far for his relatives to come to graduation in Philadelphia for one day. It was nice of Sid Sterling's uncle to offer to drop him off at the train station.

"Nick?" Charlie Mangione stood at the door. "I signed your Corinthian, didn't I?"

"Yeah, Charlie, you did. And I signed yours."

"Well, keep in touch, I put my phone number small above my picture. Call me, and we'll get together." Before Nick could reply, Charlie said, "Gotta run, my stepfather hates it when anyone keeps him waiting." And he was gone.

Charlie, like his roommates, knew Nick wasn't going home. Reaching in his breast pocket, Nick took out some envelopes and set them on the bed beside him. Not realizing it, he sighed.

Last week was so busy with everyone signing everyone's yearbook and trying to say good-byes without seeming dopey to teachers and housemasters. Some members of the incoming graduating class he knew from the Glee Club, the Dramatic Club, the Print Shop and class teams he played against, came up to him and shook his hand. Everyone asked the same question.

"What are you going to do when you get out?" His answer, "I'm not going home. I'm starting to work in some place called Upper Darby," brought "Congratulations," and "Good Luck" from adults; surprised looks and cautious "Great!" from the Hummers.

Putting an envelope in his hand, Aunt Kay from Brooklyn kissed him and said she knew his dad was very proud of him today. After she waved down a cab and went off to the train station, Uncle

327

Ralph said they should get started for home. His mom kissed him, hugged him hard and kissed him again, tears streaking her makeup. She said they were tears of happiness, but he knew they were bittersweet.

Long ago, in Good Friends, when he noticed older kids coming to the Martz Bus station alone, he began saying his goodbyes at home, too. Each vacation since, sitting in the bus watching young mothers trying to hold back tears as they kissed their little Hummers goodbye, Nick was reminded how much his mother must have loved him to give him up and send him so far away. Today was bittersweet, he knew, though she'd never say it; because, after all these years, he still wasn't coming home.

He hugged her one more time, taking in a deep draught of her Evening in Paris perfume. Walking through the gates, he watched as they drove down Girard Avenue, waving goodbye.

"Yo, Nick!" Jock McKnight had called from a car window as it approached the open gates. On his way to his beloved Lewistown, Nick expected. "Good luck staying in the city by yourself. I'll see you next Founder's Day." The people in the car seemed to look at him with big eyes.

◆

Now, returning to the empty room, he opened the envelopes, read the verses and took out the gifts of money. Five-dollars from aunts and uncles, twenty from his mom and twenty-five from Aunt Kay. He sorted them with all the other money he'd tried to save this semester and what he earned last summer helping Mr. Buziak at his grocery store on Meade Street. But paying for his class photo and extra prints for everybody at home and chipping in to buy special suede paper for The Corinthian, and bouquets and taxi fares for the Battalion Prom and the Senior Prom used up most of it. Now he had a hundred and five dollars, more than he'd ever had before, though he'd need to pay the landlady sixty dollars today when he got to her house. At least he'd start earning money next week. He hoped it would be enough to

328

get along. He could get a job on weekends, too. "C'mon, guys, whatever it takes," some of his buddies used to call out whenever some new, wearisome something had to be done. He'd come to feel it was a Hummer's motto.

He wished he'd had some time alone with his mom so he could tell her he wanted to come home now; maybe he would be able to this summer on weekends, and explain, not just in a letter, how he suddenly got this job in Advertising — the one thing he wanted in the world.

"You sure are lucky to have someone call and ask if there were any boys graduating who were interested in advertising," Dr. Zeil, the housemaster, had told him when they met in his Allen Hall office two weeks ago. "So I called Mr. Daffin in the Print Shop and he said he had one boy who was interested." Handing Nick a three by five card, he said, "This has the company name and address on it and the owner's name."

"Yes, sir," Nick replied, not looking down at the card.

"I don't know what the job entails, but I do know he specifically wants a Girard boy. That, and I think you know it, is because of the reputation of the school. We tried to raise all of you to be good workers at whatever you do. Housemasters and governesses have tried to make you accountable for your actions since you were a little guy in Junior School. By now you should know to take your responsibilities seriously. Even people you thought were mean and unfair really wanted you to grow up to be independent, to stand on your own and, we hope, to take the initiative. Employers are happy to learn they don't have to stand over someone all the time."

"I looked up your record before calling the man back. There were some behavior transgressions when you were younger, but that seems to have stopped." He arched an eyebrow, "Or maybe you learned how not to get caught." Nick smiled, but didn't look at Dr. Zeil. "Mr. Daffin said you did well in Printing. Your grades were fairly good and you were involved in quite a few activities, and secretary of

329

the National Honor Society. What I didn't tell the man when I called him back was that you lived in Wilkes-Barre. I figured you knew when you accepted the job you'd have to resolve that."

"I have a place to stay, Doctor Zeil," Nick answered. "Mr. Sweigart announced a while ago about people calling in wondering if anyone wanted to rent a room."

"That," Doctor Zeil said, "is also because Girard's reputation convinces them our boys will be upright."

"I've rented a room and I'll get cereal in the morning and whatever they have for dinner."

"How much?"

"Fifteen dollars a week."

"That's a good deal, don't mess it up. Stay courteous, keep your room neat and clean. Thank them and do whatever extra things you see will be helpful."

Nick hoped it was a good deal. When he described it at the table, Smokey Stover said when his brother Chuck graduated, he got a job in Reading, but it was so far from their house in Chester and he didn't have a car, he had to rent a room. "That old lady was nasty. When she was out back of their row home and little kids went down the alley, if she was watering her flowers, she'd spray the kids passing by. And not for fun either. And she was a lousy cook, too. Chuck bought a little salt shaker he kept in his pocket. And when she or the old man weren't looking, he used it. He said it was worse than Hum food."

"Did your brother ever get out of there?" someone asked.

"When he got a second raise later that year, he bought a used taxi and moved home. Said it was worth getting up at six in the morning to get out of that place. Oh, and the old man had his special chair in the living room, but the TV set was across the way. So, when Chuck went up to his room or came down he had to cross in front of the television, and the old bastard always acted grumpy like it was a big deal. Just before Chuck left, he found out the old man, who pretended like he was a boss at Strawbridge's, always squawking to the old lady about how the managers did things wrong...well it turned out, one of his important jobs was to put stamps in the stamp machines."

The guys hooted at that one and Sterling cried out, "Well, at least she couldn't ruin his Wheaties!"

"Are you kidding? He said she gave their scruffy old dog more milk than she gave him in the morning. And she musta got up real early to put some out for the dog, cus it was always warm. Ugggghhh!"

Nick looked up. Doctor Zeil was waiting for an answer. "I'm sure it will be fine, sir," hoping he sounded appreciative, and that Dr. Zeil knew he was grateful.

Dr. Zeil was everybody's favorite. He was artistic, witty and had a sense of humor that disarmed everyone, even complainers had to laugh. He owned a narrow home on historic Elfreth's Alley, the oldest street in America with people still living on it. And he had each class, a few at a time, visit him there. He was proud of it and so were the guys.

"Do you have a Work Permit? It's needed if you want to work at a full time job and you're under eighteen."

"I do, Dr. Zeil."

"Sorry, I still have one question. How did you get so interested in Advertising?"

"I always liked writing compositions for Dr. Haskell, and I wrote some articles for the News . . . "

"And you were Co-Editor of The Girard Magazine."

Nick paused, thinking back, "I always liked to look at the ads in the magazines at the Library, Life, Look, The Saturday Evening Post. I liked to see how they tried to sell things. And then, when I was in Mariner, I read Your Career in Advertising by Dan River and he said one of the best jobs was to be a copywriter, to come up with ideas about selling the products and writing the words to go with the artist's design, and that good ones were paid lots of money. I really became interested."

"So, you'd like to create advertisements?"

"Yes."

"Well, good luck. Not many Hummers are so sure of what they want to do. That should put you a good jump ahead. Come show me an ad you've created someday." And he patted Nick on the shoulder as he left.

Later that same day, when Nick went to get his mitt from the room for a pickup baseball game, he saw Joe Tobin and Al Toizer.

"Hey, you guys go home on weekends, what's the best way for me to get to Fifty Eight Forty Five Chestnut Street?"

"That's way out in West Philly. Joe should know that," Al said. Joe squinted one eye as he thought about it. "Easiest way would be to take the trolley I take to go home to Overbrook. Get the Fifteen in front of the Hum and stay on it until it gets to Sixtieth Street. That'll take almost an hour. The driver'll call it out. Get off, cross the street cattycorner and get on the Route Forty Six, going South. When it gets to Market Street, you'll know; you can see the Elevated up above. Get off at the next block, that'll be Chestnut, and you only have a block or so to walk. And don't forget to ask for a transfer when you get on the Fifteen."

SIXTY-TWO

It was 4:15 when Nick boarded the Fifteen, got his transfer and started for the back of the trolley. Most people were working at this hour on a Thursday, so the car was almost empty. Sliding onto the wicker seat, his suitcase beside him, he looked across at the Hum. It looked like a photo on a calendar — no one in sight now, the high wrought iron gates still open, the sun shining on Founder's Hall with its tall columns and broad steps and the circle in front of it dark green with grass and rhododendron contrasting with the white trunks of birch trees and the pink circles of fallen Magnolia blooms. It had to be everyone's favorite view of the Hum. The trolley suddenly surged forward. Above the wall Nick could see the High School study hall windows where everyone heard Lenore call up to him. For a second he pictured her standing by the basement door, waving him to come closer. He wondered where she was and sighed with an accepting sadness knowing he'd never see her again. Morosely, he watched the roof of the Chapel and the top floors of Lafayette go by. Leaning close to the window as the trolley picked up speed, he could just make out the black metal fire escape on the side of Good Friends where he almost slipped off that icy night. It seemed like a great adventure now, but he'd still never tell his mom. As the trolley passed the outdoor playground toilet, Nick hoped a pair of hands would suddenly grasp the top of the wall, followed by a leg and then a Hummer, but it didn't happen. How many times had he and his buddies scaled that exact spot; sometimes paying for it, though a paddling didn't seem so bad now.

Making an S-turn around the end of the school, the Fifteen continued out Girard Avenue. There was Gates' candy store; he wondered if the owners were still taking advantage of little Hummers. The Big F's marquee lights were dark, too early for a movie. An old man pushed his way out of the German Bakery's screened door holding a white carton with both hands. It was years since he'd split a bag of broken donuts with guys on the way to the park. The trolley lurched on, clanging angrily at trucks and cars that slowed its progress.

Leaving homes and stores behind and entering the edge of Fairmount Park, it stopped opposite the Zoo. Nick looked up to see the railroad bridge off to the right, high above the streets where he and Ernie and Reds were almost run down by the GG-1 locomotive. The trolley, noisy now with a group of school children recounting the antics on Monkey Island, started into West Philadelphia. The streets were lined with businesses on the ground floors and apartments above. Some stores had signs reminding shoppers: GRADUATION GIFTS and DON'T FORGET YOUR GRADUATE.

As they waited for a big truck that was backing up several times trying to turn a sharp right, a trolley heading East on Girard Avenue stopped next to them. Nick glanced over and saw a girl opposite, expressionless, seeming to contemplate him. Before he thought of how he might respond, the trolley moved forward and she was gone. It wasn't Dana, but it could have been with her dark brown hair and pensive look. He planned on thinking about her when he got settled in the quiet of his room; now she had invaded his mind. He'd gotten a letter from her about a week ago, enthusiastic about his graduation and looking forward to his coming home. She was hoping, at the end of her exams and the start of summer vacation, to get a part-time job at The Boston Store so they could go to Harvey's Lake and Moyer's Grove on weekends. She expected he would have a job, too. She said she wouldn't leave home to go away to college; probably go to Kings or Wilkes in town. He hadn't written back right then, as he should have. He might have blamed it on all the things that were going on as graduation approached, but he couldn't.

He recalled how, in the Junior School, you were told often what you had to do. As you grew older, in Good Friends and Lafayette, you were reminded of it. By the time you entered the halls, Banker and

Merchant, it was rarely stated. You knew, as did every Hummer, that you couldn't escape your responsibilities.

Once, when Nick openly admitted he hadn't spent time on the history assignment, Dr. Wolf didn't respond angrily, as Nick expected. "It's okay with me that you don't know enough about the Monroe Doctrine," shocking everyone with his unconcerned attitude. "Just keep in mind what I call the Girard Doctrine. You've probably heard variations on it." In as grave a voice as the little man could project, he said, "Girardians know what they have to do. Whether you do or don't, you must learn to live with the consequences. And that's not just here, inside these walls, it's for the rest of your life." Nick learned, as now, the often painful results of that simple code. He would write to Dana tonight and mail it in the morning.

How different she was from Lenore. He hadn't noticed Dana last Christmas when she stopped by with some of Janet's friends before they went off shopping. Then he did notice her at Easter. Dark brown hair, a heart shaped face, brown eyes and lips that they say in the movies are "full." She didn't talk continuously like the others, but responded with comments that were clever and humorously sarcastic, like a lot of Hummers. She wasn't as slim as Lenore, but what the guys would call "very built." She never got to see the Hum, or Founder's Hall on Prom Night, although guys would have rushed to sign her up for dances. One summer night before his mother and Janet returned from downtown, he called out to her as she passed by. She sat on the steps with him, asking about school. She didn't laugh as much as she smiled an appreciative smile. When she said she'd stayed too long, he asked her if she'd like to go to a movie sometime. They did, then, often. He felt so comfortable with her and she said she liked being with him. She played cello with the state high school orchestra and, he learned from Janet, was a National Honor Society member her Junior year. Though her parents were Russian Orthodox, they knew he was

Protestant but they welcomed him. Maybe they thought he'd become a big city boy and wouldn't return to Wilkes-Barre.

How ironic that he was, after all, staying in Philadelphia. Summer vacation ended quickly and she promised to write. He taped the photo she sent to the inside his locker door and everyone commented that she was really good looking. Now, everything would end. He would be here, not going home for summers or even sure he'd get home much at Easter or Christmas. He might get the bus home Friday night and come back Sunday afternoon, but he couldn't do it every weekend. His mother would want him to be with the family, seeing everyone and visiting his grandmother in Parsons, Wilkes-Barre's Russian section. Even if he could be at home and go to Wilkes College he'd have to come back to Philadelphia or go to New York to try to work for an advertising agency. Then, when the unbelievable opportunity happened, and he got the job, it decided a lot of things. He thought of calling her on the phone but knew he'd get it all wrong. Tonight he would have to find a way to explain it so he didn't hurt her; he'd tell that he really cared for her and was sorry too, the way things were working out.

He never got a chance to say goodbye to Lenore. Now it's Dana, and he has to say goodbye. He'd never had such a terrible writing assignment at the Hum.

"Fifty Second Street, comin' up!" The driver's voice startled Nick. Riders had lined up by the rear door. As soon as the last one got off, the bell clanked and the trolley moved forward. It wasn't long until he called out, "Sixtieth Street. Sixtieth Street." Then he heard the man announce, "Here comes the Forty Six, folks. Go over to it as soon as you get off. He won't wait long."

Following the group across the street, Nick boarded, gave the driver his transfer and took a seat. Joe Tobin was right, Sixtieth Street was loud and frantic, people jostling each other as they hurried along the crowded sidewalks, the street itself a solid line of cars and trucks as far ahead of the trolley as Nick could see. And stores. A fish store, a flower shop, food markets, a shoe shop, a laundromat, clothing for men, clothing for women, clothing for kids and a Jewish Deli, crowded inside like the one on Ridge Avenue where Art Felberbaum used to buy those fat, sour pickles.

"Market Street. Market Street. Transfer here for the Frankford-Market Street El," the driver called out.

Seeing the erector set steel girders holding up the El tracks and the stairway to the station above, Nick realized there was another way to get to his room. He could have walked down to Broad Street, taken the subway to City Hall and transferred over to the El which had a station at 60th Street.

As the trolley crossed under the Elevated, he noticed two young workers in dirty overalls and mud-caked boots sitting across the aisle, sullenly scrutinizing him and whispering to each other. He looked at them intently until they looked away. Probably wonder why I'm wearing a suit and tie and have a suitcase on my lap. He felt for the little memo pad in his breast pocket. Tonight, in his room, he'd ask to borrow the phone book to study the maps. He'd write out directions and tomorrow, get up early and take the El to 69th Street, where Joe told him Upper Darby began. He'd find Long Lane and the agency office building. Coming back he'd know how long it would take him to get there on Monday morning.

Standing alone in front of the exit door, Nick suddenly felt uneasy. First it surprised him, but then it grew into a frightening presence. He felt dizzy and began to sway. His hand burned when he touched his cheek. His mouth was dry, and he kept taking deep breaths. He shook his head to fight it.

I passed the physical exam last month. I'm never sick. I can't be sick!

A bell jangled wildly as the trolley jolted to a stop, the overhead strap he was holding started swaying him back and forth. Grabbing a

337

railing, he tried to steady himself. Through the door glass a street sign read: CHESTNUT STREET–60ST-100 South. The door was about to open on an unknown world and he couldn't escape it.

There was no Hum for him to go to where he was safe behind its wall. His classmates were all gone. His mom was at home. He was going to be alone with strange people in a strange place. Moving down to the bottom step, Nick closed his eyes and let his suitcase fall against the still-closed folding doors. He saw a child being strangled and reached up to pull his tie loose. Breathing hard, he heard a man say, "Life at Girard can be difficult and it's not always fair. You must learn to depend only on yourself."

Nick wanted to call out to the man, "I have. I have."

As quickly as it came, the surge of fear began to ebb, a sense of relief slowly rising in him. The quiet confidence of which he was so secretly proud returned. Reaching for the suitcase, he faced the door.

He was starting again in a new world, just as he did as a newbie so long ago. Why should he be frightened now? He'd survived life at Girard, resettling with strangers each time he moved from building to building, learning to cope with all kinds of kids and adults, living with the rules, the problems and punishments, fair and unfair. He'd learned to manage loneliness and to appreciate the unspoken brotherhood between Hummers, supportive and loyal, but still independent. And the genuine attempts by the adults to educate him and make him a responsible person.

Life at Girard had taught him the one person he needed to depend on was himself. This time he wasn't starting out as that confused, little newbie. This time he was a Hummer and could depend on himself.

Grabbing up his suitcase when the trolley door opened, Nick stepped out into his new world.

A Timeless Bond

It happened many times over the years; on the boardwalk at Atlantic City, at restaurants from Philadelphia and New York City to San Francisco's Embarcadero and St. Thomas in the Caribbean. For others it may have been anywhere in America, or even abroad. I'd overhear in a passing conversation the word "Girard." When I called out in a just loud enough voice, "Hummer?" he'd turn and his look conveyed in that second an understanding of a life we shared that no wife, child, or longtime friend ever could.

Upon graduation, Girardians are called exHummers, but I don't believe exHummers exist. After growing up in that culture for eight to eleven years, child to youth, you can never be an "ex". You remain a Hummer for life. Even those who hated it and never returned after graduating cannot deny that their lives were indelibly stamped, their actions inevitably forged, by the Girard experience. I wonder what Dickens would have thought of Hummers; poor orphans away from home, crowded with others behind the walls of a rigidly structured world controlled by strangers, with no appeal for injustices or punishment. So many were eventually sent out into the world, a suitcase packed with clothes in one hand, a bag of personal possessions in the other and a few dollars in their pocket.

Dickens would have appreciated the traumatic first days of Hummers. Though most newbies had spent a few days or even longer away from home in the company of relatives or friends, none were prepared for the overwhelming panic that came with their mother's sudden disappearance, leaving them surrounded by hundreds of strange boys who acted as though you didn't exist or silently scrutinized you. With a life so frightening, loneliness easily assaulted you. Days, you were lonesome in the crowd, trailing behind it. Nights were spent trying to ignore the sobbing of others and failing. Sympathy was rare. Those who had lived through it impatiently expected you to get over it. You did, first by learning not to show it, suffering quietly after lights out;

then, over the next few months, loneliness began ebbing away, returning when reading a letter from home.

If growing up at Girard seemed like a 1940's creation by Charles Dickens, I think Sam Clemens would have considered Hummers an urban version of his young heroes. While Huck Finn and Tom Sawyer's escapades took place in a small town and on the Mississippi, young Hummers, when they strode through the open gates on Saturday and Sunday afternoons, were free to search for exciting adventures in the heart of America's third largest city. The streets of Philadelphia were their rivers, streaming past center city skyscrapers and elegant stores, through picturesque and seedy neighborhoods, under elevated trains and down into noisy subway stations. Roaming free, they observed life on the busy rivers and explored the nation's largest city park.

Our experiences growing up at Girard can never be denied or forgotten. The word "Hummer" distills it, linking strangers who shared those extraordinary years and recognize each other as unspoken brothers in a unique society. No one can be an ex-Hummer.

STEPHEN GIRARD
*Mariner, Merchant, Banker
and Philanthropist*

1750—1831

Stephen Girard And His Legacy

Stephen Girard, a patriot and one of America's early heroes, is also one of our country's forgotten giants and philanthropists. Virtually unknown in most American households, he vigorously defended America's rights to navigate without restriction on the high seas, helped the colonists' fight for freedom by sending his ships through the English blockade to bring supplies to America and its allies, and later was the major financier of the War of 1812 for the impoverished young country.

He was an entrepreneur, an innovator, a visionary, a humanitarian and for much of his life, America's wealthiest citizen. And, when he died in 1831, he left the bulk of his fortune to establish Girard College, a school for poor, fatherless boys.

Eldest son of a sea captain, Stephen Girard was born in Bordeaux, France on May 20, 1750. Girard was born sightless in his right eye and, because of his affliction, was cruelly teased by other children.

At that time, Bordeaux was a major port of call on many trade routes throughout the world. Seafaring was a family tradition starting with his grandfather, and Stephen, like his father, Pierre, had his first sea voyage at the age of 13. Though young to be an apprentice officer, or *pilotin*, he was nevertheless ready, having been well schooled by his father. This training continued on one of Pierre's ships where he learned navigational skills and the business of buying and selling cargo.

He was confirmed by the French government as a certified merchant marine captain at age 23. He then borrowed heavily to become part owner of a ship, and set his course between and beyond French ports to the West Indies, Charleston, S.C., and New Orleans. This marked the start of an extraordinary career for the young Frenchman who was destined to become the richest man in a country which did not yet exist. Though he had no formal education, Stephen

Girard had a penchant for self-improvement and the pursuit of knowledge all his life. It was said that the works of Voltaire, Rousseau and other philosophers accompanied him on his voyages.

In June, 1776, he was forced to make port in Philadelphia to avoid the English blockade of New York City. Having arrived on the eve of the American Revolution, Girard seemed to have caught the Spirit of '76, and decided to stay. He perhaps also recognized the new opportunities for maritime trade if America prevailed over the British.

In the spring of 1777, Stephen noticed a young Irish beauty, Mary Lum, as she crossed Vine Street to draw a pail of water. He was attracted to her immediately and after their initial acquaintance, she soon returned his affections and, following a brief courtship, Mary, 18, and Stephen, 27, were married.

The English blockade made it impossible to obtain marine insurance, so Girard set up shop on land by opening a dry goods store on Water Street bordering the Delaware River. Later, just before Philadelphia was captured by the British, he and Mary relocated the successful enterprise to Mount Holly, New Jersey. After General Howe and his Redcoats left Philadelphia, Girard returned, and declared his allegiance by becoming a citizen of the new United States of America. He now turned back to the sea, not as a sailor, but as ship owner. Like George Washington, he called upon a neighbor, Betsy Ross, to request that she make flags for his ships. His fleet sailed the world — from Amsterdam to Lisbon, and Batavia to Canton — carrying grain, wine, tobacco, cloth, cheese, coffee, meats and other staples. For the next 30 years, he would oversee his marine empire until he decided to liquidate it, adding to his already sizeable fortune.

In 1793, Philadelphia, the nation's capitol and largest city, was afflicted with the Yellow Fever plague. Death came to one in every 10 citizens. The Federal Government was suspended, as President George Washington and elected officials fled the city. The mayor's impassioned call for help brought only 10 volunteers, among them the 43 year old Stephen Girard. He took charge of Bush Hill, a converted mansion near Sixteenth and Spring Garden streets, which was being used as the city's hospital for the mortally ill. Dismissing unreliable doctors, he hired new ones and imposed strict hygiene rules. His unselfish example of personally administering to dying patients inspired other to join him. Suspending all business activities, he spent his energies caring for and comforting the dying, fearlessly undertaking a deadly mission in which two of his fellow volunteers would succumb to the plague. His heroic efforts during the Yellow Fever epidemic dramatically revealed Girard's bravery and compassion for others. He and fellow workers won honors and citations for "magnanimity and patriotism," and, among ordinary citizens, Stephen Girard became a household name.

In 1811, 20 years after establishing the First Bank of the United States, the federal government decided to get out of the banking business. Believing the First bank's closure would create a worrisome financial climate throughout the country, Girard, in a daring move, bought the charter and the building located on Third Street, south of Chestnut and employed most of the First Bank's staff. He was able to pay off stockholders, put money in the cash drawers, reopen the bank, and embark on a new career as a banker. Relieved Americans were in awe of this individual who was able to fund a major financial institution with $1,200,000 of his own money.

When America declared war on England for its punishing import restrictions, the young country found itself running out of money. In desperation, it turned to its richest citizen. In the year 1812, at age 62, Girard was well aware he could lose his fortune if England won. But he immediately pledged five million dollars to the war effort and persuaded a friend, David Parish, to borrow from him an additional three million for the cause. Two million more came from John Jacob Astor, the fur magnate, and together, these tycoons, plus other smaller investors provided the needed sixteen million dollars, and saved the young nation from bankruptcy and perhaps losing its hard-won independence. Remembering, years later this critical time when he was Secretary of State, President James Monroe, in 1822, appealed to Girard for a loan of $40,000 to pay his personal debts. Girard granted the loan — a small sum compared to bailing out the U.S. Treasury.

For all his business success, Girard's private life was filled with heartache. Eight years after his marriage, the love of his life was declared incurably insane. With a staff of aides, he was able to care for Mary at home. But five years later, he agreed to move her to Pennsylvania Hospital, the nation's first and only hospital at the time, and of which he was a benefactor. Mary remained there for 25 years until her death in 1815.

Girard's vision for the city led him to invest in valuable tracts in what is now Center City, fashionable Society Hill, and South Philadelphia and in rural areas of north and central Pennsylvania. His holdings included stores, warehouses, piers and a factory. He oversaw work crews to insure his reputation for building fine quality three- and four-story brick homes, and invested additional funds in huge coal and timber tracts.

In 1831, the last year of his life, Girard was busy with a full work schedule, reflecting his credo, "to rest is to rust." One significant transaction was the purchase of a 43-acre tract, Peel Hall Farm, just north of the city; now a short drive from City Hall. In December, he contacted influenza, then pneumonia developed, and on December 26, Stephen Girard died at the age of 81.

Flags were flown at half-mast throughout the city and on ships in port. Newspapers were filled with tributes recounting his many philanthropic endeavors. Nearly 20,000 people lined the streets to witness the funeral procession which was a mile in length. Girard's huge funeral procession was second to only Benjamin Franklin's 1790 funeral procession.

His net worth at his death was about seven and a half million dollars. After providing generous sums to relatives, servants, ship captains and widows of friends, he bequeathed funds for two new public schools, and for building a new street along the Delaware River. But the childless millionaire also left to the City of Philadelphia, two million dollars to build a school for "the education and maintenance of poor, male, white orphans between the ages of six and 10...." He left the remaining millions to operate the school in perpetuity.

On January 1, 1848, Girard College opened with 95 students. The school was called a "college" because the term was commonly used in Bordeaux to designate boys' schools that prepared students for university. Girard's will dictated everything from the 10-foot stone wall surrounding the campus and specifications for all the buildings, except Founder's Hall, to the curriculum to be taught. He prohibited clergy from entering the campus, but he encouraged teaching the ideals of Christianity, and instilling in the scholars, "the purest principles of morality."

After completing their studies, the young orphans were "bound out" as apprentices, living and training with master tradesmen in printing, iron working, tanning, pharmaceuticals, merchandising, and architecture. Most left the school at 15 or 16, and lived with their masters until their indenture was completed. By the 1900s, the college had become a boarding school with student holidays allowing some half-day visitations by mothers, family and friends. In the 1930s a unique double curriculum was instituted. In addition to their academic classes, boys were given introductory courses in carpentry, drafting, electricity, pattern making, printing and office skills, from which they selected one. They then went to the "shop" for half a day and to regular classes the other half. This double curriculum enabled students

346

to get an excellent academic education plus a vocation "to fall back on."

For more than 160 years, the academic and social standards have remained high at Girard, mirroring the educational quality and moral development fostered by dedicated teachers and administrators.

Stephen Girard's Legacy ... over 160 years later

In 1968, after years of litigation, Stephen Girard's will was reinterpreted to admit non-white boys. Then in 1984, girls were permitted to enroll. Children from financially needy families who are academically capable and motivated for Girard's rigorous boarding school education make up the student body, now predominately African American.

Today, Girard College, a co-ed, multi-ethnic, college preparatory boarding school, continues to serve the noble goal envisioned by the quiet, unpretentious philanthropist. It has been over 160 years since Girard's humanitarian vision became a reality. Though the school has changed in many ways, it remains true to his desire to educate the underprivileged, and continues to reflect his credo:

"When I am dead, my actions must speak for me."

Lew Rinko graduated from Girard College in June, 1952 and began his advertising career at a suburban Philadelphia agency. He gained experience working at several agencies while earning a Marketing degree from Temple University. At age 32, he opened Rinko Advertising in Center City Philadelphia. Over the next 35 years he served Cigna, DuPont, Bell Atlantic (Verizon), Kraft, (Glaxo)Smith-Kline and many smaller clients. He also owned and published for twelve years, *The Swarthmorean,* the community newspaper in the college town of Swarthmore, Pennsylvania, where, now retired, he and his wife, Kay, have lived since 1968.

CPSIA information can be obtained at www.ICGtesting.com
Printed in the USA
BVOW032056250213

314168BV00003B/24/P

9 780578 104324